923-

MARK HUSBANDS
AND DANIEL J. TREIER,
EDITORS

THE COMMUNITY
OF THE WORD

TOWARD AN EVANGELICAL
ECCLESIOLOGY

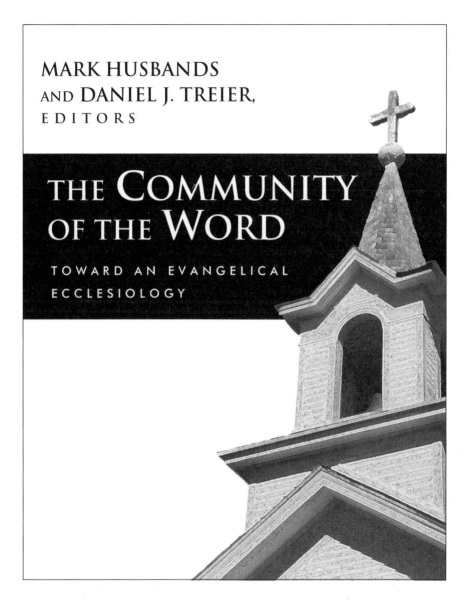

InterVarsity Press
Downers Grove, Illinois

Apollos
Leicester, England

InterVarsity Press, USA
P.O. Box 1400, Downers Grove, IL 60515-1426, USA
World Wide Web: www.ivpress.com
Email: mail@ivpress.com

APOLLOS (an imprint of Inter-Varsity Press, England)
38 De Montfort Street, Leicester LE1 7GP, England
Website: www.ivpbooks.com
Email: ivp@uccf.org.uk

InterVarsity Press®, U.S.A., is the book-publishing division of InterVarsity Christian Fellowship/USA®, a student movement active on campus at hundreds of universities, colleges and schools of nursing in the United States of America, and a member movement of the International Fellowship of Evangelical Students. For information about local and regional activities, write Public Relations Dept., InterVarsity Christian Fellowship/USA, 6400 Schroeder Rd., P.O. Box 7895, Madison, WI 53707-7895, or visit the IVCF website at <www.intervarsity.org>.

Inter-Varsity Press, England, is the publishing division of the Universities and Colleges Christian Fellowship (formerly the Inter-Varsity Fellowship), a student movement linking Christian Unions in universities and colleges throughout Great Britian, and a member movement of the International Fellowship of Evangelical Students. For information about local and national activities write to UCCF, 38 De Montfort Street, Leicester LE1 7GP, email us at email@uccf.org.uk, or visit the UCCF website at www.uccf.org.uk.

Scripture quotations, unless otherwise noted, are from the New Revised Standard Version of the Bible, *copyright 1989 by the Division of Christian Education of the National Council of the Churches of Christ in the USA. Used by permission. All rights reserved.*

Design: Cindy Kiple

Image: Buccina Studios/Getty Images

USA ISBN 0-8308-2797-8
UK ISBN 1-84474-082-X

Printed in the United States of America ∞

Library of Congress Cataloging-in-Publication Data

The community of the Word: toward an evangelical ecclesiology / Mark Husbands and Daniel J. Treier, editors.
    p. cm.
  Includes bibliographical references and index.
  ISBN 0-8308-2797-8 (pbk.: alk. paper)
  1. Church. I. Husbands, Mark, 1961- II. Treier, Daniel J., 1972-
  BV600.3.C66 2005
  262—dc22

                                        2004025504

British Library Cataloguing in Publication Data

A catalogue record for this book is available from the British Library.

P	19	18	17	16	15	14	13	12	11	10	9	8	7	6	5	4	3	2	1
Y	19	18	17	16	15	14	13	12	11	10	09	08	07	06	05				

CONTENTS

INTRODUCTION

MARK HUSBANDS AND DANIEL J. TREIER

The church, therefore, lives in that sphere of reality in which it is proper to acknowledge and testify to reconciliation because we have been reconciled; in which it is fitting to make peace because peace has already been made; in which it is truthful to speak and to welcome strangers, because we ourselves have been spoken to and welcomed by God, and so have become no longer strangers but fellow-citizens.

JOHN WEBSTER, *WORD AND CHURCH*

What does it mean for the church to live in the sphere of forgiveness and reconciliation? Is it the case that the body of Christ is indeed, as John Webster suggests, a place of reconciliation, peace, truthful speech and openness to strangers? The "sphere of reality" of which Webster speaks is, as the contents of this volume seek to capture, a community of the Word. As evangelicals, language of the "community of the Word" strikes us as somewhat foreign: not because we fail to love Holy Scripture or wish to elide the task of bearing witness to the gospel, but because so often we seek to do all of this alone, alienated from the larger body of Christ. The hope of the gospel is that we have indeed been reconciled to God in Christ, and hence, as the community of the Word, are so moved to invite others into fellowship with the risen Lord. During the conference titled "The Community of the Word: Toward an Evangelical Ecclesiology"—held in April 2004 by the Wheaton College Graduate School; the Department of Bible, Theology, Archaeology and World Religions; and Inter-Varsity Press—we began with the preliminary but altogether necessary question of whether an "evangelical" doctrine of the church exists or, for that matter, is even possible. Motivations for pursuing this question were several.

MOTIVATION FOR THE QUEST

First, our sequence of conference themes became theologically instructive. Two years previously, the conference explored contemporary relationships between evangelicals and Roman Catholics. A year later, it was appropriate to explore justification by faith, since that doctrine regarding salvation is often perceived to be the chief cause for division within Western Christianity. Dialogues concerning justification have repeatedly demonstrated, however, that understandings of the gospel imply particular approaches to the nature and practices of the church (as well as vice versa). Ecumenical achievements that move toward consensus or at least coexistence regarding the language of justification do not remove the challenges of disagreement over indulgences, Marian dogma, penance, purgatory or sacramental life—and these have implications, at least indirectly, for the nature of salvation. As a corollary, at the 2003 conference, one presenter emphasized the danger of the Protestant evangelical tendency to consider justification an individual matter to the neglect of the church as that which is, likewise, "simultaneously justified and sinful." This danger is of course real and its recognition helps to place the concern of personal salvation in its proper context.

Second, contemporary evangelicalism frequently fragments over ecclesiological concerns. Again, dialogue about justification by faith was instructive. Despite ecumenical activity and achievement, evangelicals themselves are surfacing deep differences over the nature of salvation and sanctification. Some see the evangelical movement, at least in North America, as deeply indebted to traditional elements of Reformed theology; others seek to encourage the further recovery and influence of its non-Reformed voices, such as Anabaptist, Baptist, Wesleyan/Holiness, Pentecostal and non-denominational traditions.[1] Moreover, fragmentation runs not only between evangelical traditions but often

---

[1]Regarding the gospel in particular, on issues such as atonement or the imputation of Christ's righteousness, see Mark Husbands and Daniel J. Treier, eds., *Justification: What's at Stake in the Current Debates* (Downers Grove, Ill.: InterVarsity Press, 2004), and literature referenced therein. Historiographically, in various works George Marsden has been taken to emphasize evangelicalism's Reformed heritage, whereas Donald Dayton has helped to energize "varieties of American evangelicalism" (including a book by that title). Michael Horton represents a sort of Reformed via media on the historical questions, while appealing for evangelical traditions to be more "traditional" and less concerned about "evangelicalism"; see "The Battles over the Label 'Evangelical,' " *Modern Reformation* (March/April 2001): 15-21. See also the work of D. G. Hart, author of the first chapter in this volume.

across them—regarding the nature and importance of creeds and confessions; the authority of Scripture; approaches to evangelism and mission; and reaching a telling point of conflict with respect to the so-called worship wars, over the issue of church music in particular. Is it likely or even possible to imagine that any common elements of a doctrine of the church could help to keep evangelicals together?

Third, church growth raises both opportunities and obstacles for evangelicalism. If fragmentation has energized quests for evangelical identity, so also should the growth of the church—especially varieties of Pentecostalism—in the global South.[2] Western evangelicals may be growing increasingly cautious about what they seek to export, so as to distinguish better the relationship between gospel and culture(s). Yet the question arises: what have we to offer the rest of the world? In what ways should we respond to the global work of God's Spirit, even in our own culture(s)? Indeed, certain statistics purportedly congratulate North American evangelicalism, at least in comparison to Europe, for faithful propagation of the gospel. Much of this growth accompanies newer forms of church life and appeals to the language of "community." But does the pursuit of growth justify any and all ecclesiological means, notwithstanding their apparent efficiency—or, often, do the means even qualify as "ecclesiological," having resulted from study of what God has revealed the church to be? Such questions may disturb evangelicals; that pressure aside, however, the desire for resolution on these matters assumes a common desire for the mission and witness of the church to flourish in North America and worldwide.

Fourth, evangelical ecclesiology is so frequently charged with being "in crisis" or even "nonexistent," that we could no longer ignore the question of what constitutes an "evangelical ecclesiology." Confirmation of this comes from any number of angles. (1) Others have recently taken up similar concerns.[3] (2) Even on a charitable reading, the dominant resources shaping pastoral ministry and church life among "evangelicals" are significantly nonecclesiological and often, perhaps not surprisingly, nontheological.[4] (3) It is a frequent complaint among evangelical theologians and teachers that solid and accessible monographs

---

[2]On which see the oft-cited Philip Jenkins, *The Next Christendom: The Coming of Global Christianity* (New York: Oxford University Press, 2002); the judicious and extensive work of scholars such as Lamin Sanneh and Andrew Walls deserves a wide and appreciative audience. One such example is the recent volume by Lamin Sanneh, *Whose Religion Is Christianity? The Gospel Beyond the West* (Grand Rapids: Eerdmans, 2003).

[3]John G. Stackhouse Jr., ed., *Evangelical Ecclesiology: Reality or Illusion?* (Grand Rapids: Baker Academic, 2003).

[4]See, e.g., Jonathan Wilson's essay and in particular his reference to what contemporary pastors are reading.

and textbooks on the doctrine of the church are difficult to find. (4) Quite regrettably, it is certainly the case that the wider intellectual influence of evangelical ecclesiology is almost nil, whatever the movement's populist impact. (5) As the history of Wheaton College illustrates, for example, many evangelicals have been confessionally vague or even silent about the church—on occasion such neglect was deliberate; regardless, the ecclesiological vacuum has had severe consequences for subsequent generations of earnest, dutiful and intelligent Christians. (6) Finally, we may mention the comparative irrelevance of North American evangelicals with respect to public theology. Despite evangelical politicians holding influential positions, and the occasional panic that ensues over a possible cultural takeover, evangelical voices (plural!) have alternated between being selectively shrill or conspicuously mute. Indeed, evangelicals cannot simply be characterized in terms of a commitment to a given political ideology, and in one sense this increasing lack of evangelical consensus regarding cultural engagement may be cause for relief, until our common life of public witness might be deemed to have been properly shaped by a genuine hearing of the Word.

Although we tend to *agree* on some issues (say, opposing abortion-on-demand), we seldom achieve accord on how to address them; moreover, we tend to *disagree* not only about many issues but also about their relative importance for Christian witness. When the very existence and wellbeing of the church is a matter of confession, and not simply *adiaphora,* the apparent lack of evangelical agreement on the precise entailments of the ministry of reconciliation is a serious matter indeed. The current global situation makes North American disagreements about the church's place in God's kingdom not merely sad but deeply grave: our differences, frequent accommodation to culture,[5] and attendant weakness, have real consequences affecting the concrete lives of countless brothers and sisters around the world. Furthermore, our blushing disregard for, if not isolation from, a concrete expression of solidarity with them certainly weakens our Christian witness as much as it affects their worldly circumstances.

To chronicle these motivations behind a conference on evangelical ecclesiology is not to be sour but sober, for the gospel offers hope, in the certainty that nothing shall ultimately prevail against God's church (Mt 16:13-20). Evangelical sins against God's ecclesial purposes are met with invitations to repent,

---

[5]The extent and peril of such accommodation is much debated; see, e.g., Alan Wolfe, *The Transformation of American Religion: How We Actually Live Our Faith* (New York: Free Press, 2003), and the many responses to it.

rather than immediate removal of our lampstands (Rev 1–3). And besides, there are signs of life. Many in evangelical churches continue to live saintly, countercultural and sacrificial lives; the gospel continues to crucify and raise many to new life in Christ; a multitude of parachurch efforts bless the church and the world via holistic forms of mission. On the theological scene, evangelicals are beginning to find their voice within the academy, and there continues to emerge a greater appreciation for and openness to a diversity of theological conversations between brothers and sisters around the world. Concerning ecclesiology in particular, we are growing in nuanced and critical appeals to community and in sensitivity to culture(s); moreover, the "missional church" movement with its marked attention to the gathering, upbuilding and sending of the church by the Spirit manifests quite substantial theological maturity. Should its influence continue to increase, this gift holds much promise for evangelical (and some nonevangelical) church life and witness. In short, the relative sobriety of this book should, above all, press us into readiness for action, rather than relinquishing all hope (1 Pet 1:13).

OVERVIEW OF THE QUEST

In order to complement other discussions and to convey a distinct theme, our quest for the possibility of an evangelical ecclesiology unfolds in five steps. Many of the essayists self-identify as "evangelical" or work within evangelical structures and institutions; among these we have sought to represent, within manifest limitations, the variety of ecclesiologies in the movement. Other essayists speak to evangelicalism as friendly outsiders; as confessionally orthodox Protestants, with constructive criticism they invite evangelicals to attach themselves more closely to the church's "great tradition." Of course the relation between this great tradition and "mainline" churches has never been more complex than it is today, and some essayists reflect this complexity in relating both to mainline and evangelical contexts.

The discussion begins with a backward glance in part one, so that we may look at the crisis of evangelical ecclesiology in historical context as much as possible. Part five looks ahead at how evangelical churches ought to engage culture. In between, we explore a theological argument for conceiving of the church as being "the community of the Word" in the hope that such an approach may offer evangelicals a compelling way forward in their growing attention to the nature and identity of the church. Part two explicates this theme dogmatically, first in essays by John Webster and then in an overview of the missional church movement by Darrell L. Guder. Part three addresses the ethical dimension of the church's life, with particular reference to the question of how its speech faithfully attests to the divine Word. Part four connects Word and sacrament, as diverse understandings of sacramental life are offered with a view toward their relative significance regarding the nature of the church itself. The book concludes with Ellen T. Charry's conference sermon delivered in Edman Chapel, Wheaton College, representing a clear exhortation to take the Word into our very being: as we celebrate the Eucharist, we experience concretely and corporately the drama of Christian moral life—an ecclesial and Eucharistic event that is missional, ministering the Word by making communally visible a gracious alternative to a pervasive culture of death.

With this broad outline in view, we now turn to a brief examination of the particular essays.

Part one looks back at the church in "evangelical" theologies. We need to ask why evangelicals have found no ecclesiological consensus regarding the centrality and efficacy of the divine Word. Why have we factored so little into the moral life of our communities in certain ways, and fostered a seemingly anti-sacramental ethos? D. G. Hart (chap. 1, "The Church in Evangelical Theologies, Past and Future") begins provocatively by highlighting the difficulty and subjectivity involved in defining *evangelicalism*. Hart contrasts several prominent forbears of contemporary evangelicals with the nineteenth-century high-church theologian J. W. Nevin. Evangelical heroes such as George Whitefield, Jonathan Edwards, Charles Finney and Charles Hodge illustrate the "proclivity for personal piety over its corporate alternatives, for egalitarian over hierarchical structures, and for divine immediacy over human mediation in the experience and reception of grace" (p. 25). At one level, this historical assertion is not surprising, but by implication, Hart asserts, "For evangelicals to acquire an ecclesiology similar to Nevin's and Calvin's, born-again Protestants may need to abandon those very conceptions that have characterized evangelical Protestantism" (p. 25). No doubt such a claim reflects Hart's own way of contending for his Reformed heritage.[6] Equally, though, Hart's argument should stimulate searching conversation among evangelicals about respecting the particularities of other communions as well.

The following two chapters, also addressing historical dimensions, move deliberately to figures or facets that transcend particular communions, and that tend to have more popular influence. In chapter two, "The Fundamental Dispensation of Evangelical Ecclesiology," Dennis Okholm argues that classic dispensationalism has been one of the decisive factors shaping the prevalence

---

[6]See also his recent *Deconstructing Evangelicalism: Conservative Protestantism in the Age of Billy Graham* (Grand Rapids: Baker Academic, 2004).

of a tellingly low if not putatively absent ecclesiology among evangelicals. Admitting the importance of other factors and the increasing variety within dispensationalism, he insists nonetheless on its cross-evangelical influence: prioritizing God's plan for the nation of Israel places the church in a subordinate position, looking more toward heaven as the locus of God's restoration of humanity, while concentrating upon the ostensible evils of earthly ecclesiastical structures. Contemporary American evangelicals engage the social and political realms in highly selective and idiosyncratic ways that owe much to a version of the gospel in which the church collects saved individuals—a gospel open therefore to pernicious influences of Western culture. Okholm advocates that the church address cultural structures in light of the inaugurated kingdom of God. In chapter three, Jonathan R. Wilson ("Practicing Church: Evangelical Ecclesiologies at the End of Modernity") chronicles popular efforts to support such a mission. He teases out the implicit, and occasionally more explicit, ecclesiologies of Francis Schaeffer, Charles Colson and Ellen Vaughn, Rick Warren, and Brian McLaren. While charitable regarding the intentions and salutary effects of such writings, Wilson criticizes their thin considerations of the church's classic marks—oneness, holiness, catholicity and apostolicity. Constructively, he urges evangelicals to capitalize on their activist tendencies by developing a theological rationale for "improvisational" ecclesiology in order to foster a kind of freedom in witness and mission—freedom that would allow the church to take up its responsibility within but not to its context.

In part two, seeking a deeper theological rationale for an ecclesiology that properly warrants the title "evangelical," John Webster's dogmatic inquiry takes place in two major steps. "The Church and the Perfection of God," chapter four, explores the connection between the gospel and the church with an evangelical concern for their rightful order: "the gospel precedes and the church follows" (p. 76). While no account of the gospel can be complete that neglects the church, Webster is well aware of the need for a bit of "negative theology." The theme of divine perfection, in which God fellowships with us out of the free overflow of his abundant love, aids the church in recovering its fittingly modest and responsible place within the good order of God. Webster thus trims some of the excess from recent "communion" (social Trinitarian) ecclesiologies, before tackling the contemporary emphasis on the church's visibility in chapter five ("The Visible Attests the Invisible"). There he explores the church as the redemptive work of the Holy Spirit, every bit as much as the electing work of the Father and the reconciling work of the Son. The Spirit evokes and sanctifies the very creaturely activities and forms of the church "so that they indicate the presence of God" (p. 102). An evangelical emphasis on the Word of God accords nicely with this understanding of the church's visibility: "the active visibility of the church consists in attestations of the word and work of the God who is its Creator, reconciler and consummator" (p. 104). By viewing the ministry of the church as being that which follows from divine action, Webster is able to express the way in which divine action evokes obedient and modest attention to the church's ministry of Word and sacrament, while safeguarding the constitutive priority of divine perfection. Moreover, such a view certainly provides an impetus for developing consensus among various evangelical constituencies, and for connections between evangelicalism and the wider communions of the church.

The implications of the church being the community to whom the Word is spoken, and the community by whom witness to that Word is borne, are explored by Darrell L. Guder in chapter six ("The Church as Missional Community"). Guder explicates the recent dogmatic trend of viewing the church "missionally"—that is, moving the very notion of mission to the being of the church rather than simply as an adjunct of its ministry and proclamation. This understanding takes account of the fall of Christendom, and the rise of Christian faith in the global South. Yet it bears pointing out that "missional ecclesiology" is not only historically and culturally sensitive, but is also theologically grounded in the reconciliation of God. For mission is not first an activity of the church; it is characteristic of the being and action of God. The church is called, equipped and sent by the triune God as a witness in the ongoing *missio Dei*: "God the Father sending the Son, and God the Father and the Son sending the Spirit was expanded to include yet another 'movement': Father, Son and Holy Spirit sending the church into the world" (p. 124).

Hence our third section of the book examines the content of the church's moral witness and speech. William J. Abraham, in chapter seven ("Inclusivism, Idolatry and the Survival of the [Fittest] Faithful"), suggests the importance of churches pursuing inclusiveness in a fittingly theological and obedient manner. Evangelicals, no doubt, have much to learn here about the need to pursue patterns of speech that befit the welcome and just reach of God's creating and redeeming love. Abraham suggests, however, that without proper theological constraints, "inclusivism" can become a form of idolatry. That problem characterizes some parts of mainline churches, and causes a variety of responses, not least movements for renewal of the sort that have catalyzed evangelicalism. Abraham provides no one-size-fits-all prescription for how evangelicals should relate to mainline communions; indeed, the complexity of that question was evident in many conversations at the conference.

Allen Verhey likewise addresses the church's moral witness to the Word in chapter eight, " 'Able to Instruct One Another': The Church as a Community of Moral Discourse," where he expounds the example of the Christians in Romans 14. To his credit, Verhey does not gloss over the challenges of contemporary culture or of Christian diversity for churches seeking to become communities of faithful discernment. With considerable force, Verhey casts light on the fact that Paul extended a commendation to churches that were still far from perfect, in cultures of complexity rivaling our own.

Part four focuses on the dogmatic theme of the church as the "community of the Word" as it is related to sacramental life and practice. Both the significance and diversity of perspectives pertaining to sacramental theology became clear at the conference. In chapter nine ("Beyond Theocracy and Individualism") Craig A. Carter explores John Howard Yoder's ecclesiology for evangelicalism. From an Anabaptist perspective, what emerges is Yoder's account of church practices as sacraments, "events in which divine and human action coincide" (p. 187). Such a flexible account expands the scope of sacramental life while casting attention upon the distinct sphere of the church's existence over against the world. On this account, the church is clearly an alternative, countercultural community, and egalitarian in the nonviolent practices of the gospel.

Next, two Anglican theologians reflect on the nature of the church as sacramental. Gary D. Badcock, in chapter ten ("The Church as 'Sacrament' "), considers the context of this theological move, arising as it did in contemporary Roman Catholic ecclesiology. According to Badcock, the New Testament concept of *mysterion* suggests that Christ's work is completed in the gathering of the church. In this connection we may consider the significance of the church as the "body of Christ," a statement that is a fitting metaphor rather than being a literal claim about the identity of the church as the present incarnation of God. Of course such Christology and corresponding ecclesiology have implications for how we approach the Eucharist. While challenging evangelicals to take sacramental life much more seriously, Badcock qualifies the charges of anti-institutionalism and individualism that are frequently made against us. He suggests that evangelicals should maintain an emphasis on personal relationship with God, yet construe it pneumatologically, thereby opening up to the ecclesial context and aim of such relationship—a life with God that cannot be had apart from Eucharistic feeding on Christ together.

Ellen T. Charry agrees with Badcock's emphasis to a significant degree (chap. 11, "Sacramental Ecclesiology"). She perceives evangelicalism to be deeply indebted to the radical Reformation in its similarly persistent opposition to what it perceives to be the trappings of medieval ecclesiastical abuses.

By way of critique, Charry urges evangelicals to devote their energy to "focusing on the failures of our own time instead" (p. 202). In concert with a number of scholars in this volume, she locates the church and sacraments dogmatically under the third article of the creed, and thus is able to critique contemporary tendencies to relate the meaning and identity of the church to various institutions or entities with which we are culturally familiar. Precisely this dogmatic *mislocation* of the church is responsible for many of the problems mentioned at the beginning of our introduction. Charry connects "the sacramental principle" to the incarnation of Christ in a manner that accords dignity to the material world. Symbols are thereby powerful learning practices for humans as embodied, communal selves. She widens the sacramental sphere to include an array of symbolic practices, such as footwashing and rites of healing, all of which can contribute, Charry argues, to the formation of the countercultural people of God.

Culture is therefore our fifth focus, looking ahead to a future for evangelical ecclesiology by way of missional engagement. In chapter twelve ("The Church as Social Theory"), James K. A. Smith provides, in the subtitle's words, "A Reformed Engagement with Radical Orthodoxy." He unfolds the radically orthodox vision of the church as itself embodying proper social theory—the creational vocation of human community. The modern state offers an alternative understanding of community that reinforces atomism and individualism instead of bringing about the redemption of humanity. The biblical narrative centered in Jesus Christ and the Spirit's renewing presence distinguish the church as a *polis* that transforms the means and object of creaturely desire. Given the power of transnational, globalized markets, Smith argues, the state is increasingly marginal, with present-day capitalism representing a new empire opposed to the gospel: this empire is complete with its own practices, modes of discipline, and even liturgies. On the basis of a Reformed perspective that emphasizes *structures* (orders) of creation, Smith contends that Radical Orthodoxy's assumption of competition between church and state would need to be reworked. Discussing this dilemma briefly, Smith hints at the possibility of revising both perspectives—the perspective of Reformed Orthodoxy on the one hand, and Radical Orthodoxy on the other—by considering Augustine afresh.

Willie James Jennings (chap. 13) also addresses cultural engagement in terms of the desire of the church. A sometimes-overlooked aspect of ecclesial mission is the question of the brokenness of male-female relationships since the Fall. Contemporary preoccupation with technologies oriented to sight sets this question in astonishingly provocative relief. Desire is not sinful per se, but after the Fall it is now distorted such that "male and female" seems not to identify humanity but to occasion power struggles and the fragmentation of both selves and creaturely relationships in view of "idealized beautiful women." Jennings advocates a Protestant recovery of Jesus as the "holy icon" who rightly orders human desire with a view to making all creatures new. We should open ourselves, it is argued, to God's working through image and art, even using these (as do the Eastern Orthodox) to "guide desire and strengthen devotion" (p. 249). In communion with God, we must also desire, in fitting ways, communion with each other—especially as male and female.

Yet another cultural vision for evangelical churches comes in chapter fourteen from William A. Dyrness ("Spaces for an Evangelical Ecclesiology"). By way of the concept of space, Dyrness likewise attends to social structures and to aesthetic "form." He notes that evangelical ecclesiologies have tended to treat the church *functionally*—in terms of mission or evangelism, or *spirituality,* etc.—with virtually no attention to its actual, concrete place in the world. This unbalanced emphasis grew, Dyrness suggests, out of fearing superstition (as in Calvin's keeping the church doors locked when meetings were not being held) while focusing upon direct, unmediated, personal knowledge of God (as in pietism, revivalism and Puritanism). In an effort to provide a corrective, Dyrness explores the social, historical and symbolic spaces of the church. He aims not only to address the postmodern penchant for the aesthetic manifest in, for example, the emerging church movement but also to focus attention on the plurality of places around the world in which the gospel is taking root.

Even Ellen T. Charry's sermon, which closes our volume, takes contemporary culture(s) very seriously. Evangelicals have advocated this for quite some time now, but arguably have done so very selectively—witness our North American complacency under the influence of global capitalism, the inroads of disordered desire, and our ignorance of God's designs for material space. Evangelical Christians and churches alike seem to make visible only select aspects of the gospel, thereby failing to pay full attention to the promise of being one, holy, catholic and apostolic body.

This volume represents a significant theological claim: a properly evangelical commitment to the task of seeking to live out the gospel requires a life of joyful and obedient participation in the church as the "community of the Word." By giving such prominence to the church as the concrete sphere of divine reconciliation—that sphere within which God has brought peace, truthful speech and a generous embrace of strangers—we have sought to provide impetus for the expression of a properly evangelical doctrine of the church. We fully recognize that not every evangelical ecclesiology is represented in this book. Moreover, we concede that evangelicals will sustain deep and ongoing ecclesiological disagreements—not least over (1) the meaning and implications of the marks one, holy and catholic, for denominational participation and congregational interaction; as well as (2) the nature and importance of the sacraments. Surely some criticisms of evangelical ecclesiology stem from dislike or disdain, rooted in a false depiction of the church as institution. By way of contrast, when the church is regarded and inhabited as a community of the Word, living in constant submission to and reliance upon the God of the gospel, there is ample reason for hope. We believe that evangelicals from diverse traditions can maintain their Christ-centeredness, celebrate the variety of the Spirit's ministry, and emphasize personal conversion, while being a genuine community of the Word. The priority that evangelicals rightly accord to the gospel need not exclude the church. In point of fact, evangelicals cannot fail to emphasize their essential participation in the life, ministry and witness of the church, and therefore seek its well-being, without either misunderstanding or neglecting elements of the gospel.

It may yet be possible for evangelicals to offer a distinctive version of ecumenism to the wider Christian world, but only if we recover a deep and lasting commitment to the value and distinct witness of our own churches as well— for they are an essential part of the good news, by which God disciplines and nurtures robust visions of Christian life. It is, after all, in and through the ministry of the church that the triune God sanctifies our worship and witness. Thus we hope that this book will help readers attend to the historical particularities of North American evangelicalism; to the dogmatic possibilities of an evangelical ecclesiology for mission and moral life; to the question of sacramental participation as somehow ingredient to the church's very existence; and to a corresponding engagement with culture(s) in a way that is both mature and responsible—making visible a communal witness to God's living, eloquent Word in the power of the Spirit.

We hope too that this brief introduction and the essays themselves convey a sense of the stimulating conference we enjoyed in April 2004. The volume as a whole should be evidence enough of the varied yet mutually beneficial conversation that we were privileged to share. For all of this, we thank our participants for their spirit of warm Christian fellowship.

Beyond the speakers, we owe acknowledgment and heartfelt gratitude to others whose gracious support, assistance and encouragement made the Thirteenth Annual Wheaton Theology Conference possible—for particular assistance we thank Ann Gerber, Chris Bernard, Amanda Holm, Sarah Kerr, Travis McMaken and James Taylor. Fellow theologians at Wheaton continue to provide wise counsel and ongoing support in many ways. Furthermore, the conference and work of scholarship represented by this volume would simply not happen without the financial assistance of InterVarsity Press and, in particular, the friendly advice of Bob Fryling, publisher, and Gary Deddo, associate editor for academic books. Finally, we express our thanks to the dean of humanities and theological studies, Jill Peláez Baumgaertner, and the chair of the Department of Bible, Theology, Archaeology and World Religions, Richard Schultz, for their ongoing care and attention to fostering theological scholarship at Wheaton College.

PART ONE

THE CHURCH IN "EVANGELICAL" THEOLOGIES

Looking Back

1

The Church in Evangelical Theologies, Past and Future

D. G. Hart

Evangelical ecclesiology, like beauty, is in the eye of the beholder—where some see biblical insight or faithful witness, others discern great confusion leavened with good, maybe even godly, intention. For this reason, the many-splendored character of evangelical ecclesiology requires some sort of map or travel guide to figure out the best route for a propitious journey. Theology is generally a better source for agenda setting than history. But the limitations of this writer as well as the wishes of book editors require a historical approach in the reflections that follow. A good historical place to begin consideration of "the church question" among evangelicals is with John Williamson Nevin, arguably the foremost high-church Protestant that nineteenth-century America produced. The point of starting with Nevin is not to cite him as an expression of evangelical ecclesiology. Definitions of evangelicalism are sufficiently murky—and I hope growing even murkier—to render the label *evangelical* almost as subjective as beauty. Instead, Nevin is a useful historical point of departure because he defined what was at stake in the doctrine of the church with incomparable insight.

One of the more poignant pieces that Nevin wrote over the course of his long life was an autobiographical essay from 1870. Composed when he was sixty-seven, Nevin's essay reflected on his upbringing among Pennsylvania's Scotch-Irish Presbyterians; his early education at Union College and Princeton Seminary; his brief tenure as professor at Princeton before teaching at Western Seminary in Pittsburgh; and the factors that led him to join the German Reformed Church and teach at its seminary in Mercersburg where he, along with Philip Schaff, developed a theology of the same name. The particularly stirring episode from Nevin's early life comes from his days as an undergraduate at Union College. He had as a boy at Middle Spring Presbyterian Church been reared "according to the Presbyterian faith as it then stood." For Nevin this meant a form of piety that was covenantal and churchly, begun in baptism, and sustained by catechesis in the broadest sense to include family instruction and public worship, with the end of such nurture being communion in the Lord's Supper. As Nevin summarized it, "In one word, all proceeded on the theory of sacramental, educational religion, . . . holding the Church in her visible character to be the medium of salvation for her baptized children."[1]

This system of churchly devotion received a significant challenge when Nevin went off to Union College in New York. There he encountered a rival piety in which the individual and the pursuit of conversion and holiness had made the church virtually superfluous. According to Nevin, the revivalist-driven faith of New England Puritanism "brought to pass, what amounted for me, to a complete breaking up of all my previous Christian life." He explained:

> I had come to college, a boy of strongly pious dispositions and exemplary religious habits, never doubting but that I was in some way a Christian, though it had not come with me yet (unfortunately) to what is called a public profession of religion. But now one of the first lessons inculcated on me indirectly by this unchurchly system, was that all this must pass for nothing, and that I must learn to look upon myself as an outcast from the family and kingdom of God.[2]

So Nevin submitted to the "mechanical counsel" and "anxious meetings" and experienced a conversion that was "very morbid rather and weak." In retrospect, he asked, "Alas, where was mother, the Church, at the very time I most needed her fostering arms? Where was she with her true sacramental sympathy and care?"[3]

As moving as Nevin's plaintive recount of his conversion may be, the point in citing his own experience is to establish a historical benchmark by which to evaluate evangelical ecclesiology. This Mercersberg theologian's conception may have been flawed, and certainly many of Nevin's contemporaries argued as much, but he was at the heart of nineteenth-century debates over the church question. In those debates Nevin articulated a doctrine of the church that at times he argued was rooted in an older Protestant outlook from the sixteenth

---

[1]John Williamson Nevin, *My Own Life: The Early Years* (1870; reprint, Lancaster, Penn.: Historical Society of the Evangelical and Reformed Church, 1964), pp. 2-3.
[2]Ibid., pp. 8-9.
[3]Ibid., pp. 9-10.

century. Conversely, he spotted among his Protestant contemporaries, many of whom we would regard as evangelical, an ecclesiology that was as novel as it was modern. The fundamental difference between the old Protestants like Calvin and Luther and the new ones like Edwards and Hodge was whether the church was a subjective, invisible quality shared by the truly converted or an objective medium of grace outside of which there was no ordinary possibility of salvation. For Nevin, Calvin had it right when he described the church as a mother from whom "there is no other entrance into life, save as she may conceive us in her womb, give us birth, nourish us from her breasts, and embrace us in her loving care to the end."[4]

Of course, Nevin's delineation of the issue will strike some as inherently prejudicial to evangelicals since born-again Protestants by definition trust the inner workings of the Spirit more than the external operations of the Christian ministry. Still, as biased as Nevin's understanding may be, it is nevertheless useful for gaining some perspective on evangelical conceptions of the church. For when judged by a sacramental and covenantal ecclesiology evangelicalism's remarkable genius or supreme defect—depending on your perspective—is more readily discernible. Without such a standard the task of describing evangelical ecclesiology resembles the problem the king's men confronted in the fallen Humpty Dumpty—can evangelicalism's many idiosyncrasies be cobbled together again into a coherent ecclesiology? What follows is a brief summary of teaching on the church, both explicit and implicit, by prominent evangelical theologians and interdenominational organizations. In sum, this overview reveals the evangelical proclivity for personal piety over its corporate alternatives, for egalitarian over hierarchical structures, and for divine immediacy over human mediation in the experience and reception of grace. Although such contrasts will likely create few surprises, what may startle is the implication that for evangelicals to acquire an ecclesiology similar to Nevin's and Calvin's, born-again Protestants may need to abandon those very conceptions that have characterized evangelical Protestantism—or, that evangelicalism is a novelty, not conservative.

THE OXYMORONIC CHURCH

Bruce Hindmarsh, church historian at Regent College, could not have said it better than, when giving a similar talk on the history of evangelicalism for a comparable conference on evangelicals and the church, he asserted that the phrase *evangelical ecclesiology* "is an oxymoron, like 'an honest thief' or 'airline

---

[4]John Calvin *Institutes of the Christian Religion* 4.1.4.

food.' "[5] His account of evangelical ambivalence about ecclesiastical structures stresses political and social circumstances in the early modern West more than religious sources, but Hindmarsh does highlight important early precedents for later evangelical practices. Among Pietists and some Puritans in the seventeenth century emerged the building blocks of an evangelical approach to the church. Some English Protestants, for instance, began to require for admission to membership a personal testimony of grace. In Germany, through the work of Philip Jakob Spener, another hallmark of evangelicalism arose, this time the small group. The hope of Pietists who followed Spener was to renew the established churches through small bands of believers, colleges of piety, where members pursued godliness in a more direct and intimate setting than the formality of the Lutheran ministry. Closely related was the work of Count Nikolaus von Zinzendorf, the leader of the Moravians. Zinzendorf, like Spener, recognized the importance of small groups though the Moravians possessed a communitarian ideal that Pietists seldom exhibited. At the same time, Zinzendorf regarded the local gatherings of Moravians as a means for reviving all the established churches, Reformed, Lutheran and even Roman Catholic. In effect, the religious experience of the small group and the fellowship nurtured in that setting transcended the ecclesiastical orders that western Christianity had inherited either from Rome, Wittenberg, Geneva or Canterbury.

Hindmarsh sees these preliminary evangelical stirrings culminating in the ecclesiology of the legendary revivalist, George Whitefield. Three distinct ideas about the church characterize Whitefield's understanding, according to Hindmarsh. The first is that evangelical religion, with its stress upon the individual and small group, made superfluous a particular "visible form or organization of the church."[6] Here Hindmarsh quotes a letter from Whitefield, an Anglican, to Phillip Doddridge, a Nonconformist, on the issue of church order. According to Whitefield, the differences between the Church of England and Protestant dissent were secondary to the main concern, which should be "to be assured that we are called and taught of GOD, for none but such are fit to minister in holy things."[7] As Hindmarsh puts it, Whitefield discerned the key ingredient to the secondary status of the church: "one could regard church order as essential, as the Protestant Orthodox did, or one could regard regeneration by the Holy Spirit as essential, as evangelicals did, but one could not do

---

[5]Bruce Hindmarsh, "Is Evangelical Ecclesiology an Oxymoron? A Historical Perspective," in *Evangelical Ecclesiology: Reality or Illusion?* ed. John G. Stackhouse Jr. (Grand Rapids: Baker Academic, 2003), p. 15.
[6]Ibid., p. 32.
[7]Ibid.

both." Of course the question, as some of those Protestant Orthodox would put it, is whether the Spirit operates so freely from the ministry of the church, thus suggesting that this either-or proposition did not cover all possibilities. Still, following the lead of certain Puritans, Pietists and Moravians, Whitefield reduced questions of church order to the status of *adiaphora*, choosing instead to look to the invisible church extending to evangelicals both inside the churches, whether established or dissenting, and especially to those local gatherings of sincere believers' fellowship and holiness.

From this followed Whitefield's second important notion about the church, namely that the true church is not limited to correct forms. Typical of this outlook was an expression of solidarity that the evangelist communicated to a Presbyterian minister through correspondence:

> What a divine sympathy and attraction is there between all those who by one spirit are made members of that mystical body, whereof JESUS CHRIST is the head! . . . Blessed be God that his love is so far shed abroad in our hearts, as to cause us to love one another, though we a little differ as to externals: For my part, I hate to mention them. My one sole question is, Are you a christian? . . . If so, you are my brother, my sister, and mother. . . . Yet a little while, and we shall sit down together in the kingdom of our Father.[8]

As Hindmarsh rightly observes, the evangelical indifference to forms and church structures transformed the question about the character of the true church into one about the nature of the true Christian. In effect, Whitefield discarded the marks of the church for the marks of the Christian. To be sure, this move was partly the result of deep ambivalence about the ecclesiastical establishments and the degree to which national and cultural functions swallowed up their spiritual tasks. Even so, not to be missed was a fundamental reconception of the way of becoming a Christian. It was not simply that the churches were ineffective but that the work of the Spirit was sovereign in regenerating and sanctifying believers, so sovereign that to suggest the church was necessary for genuine faith was to imply that divine agency was dependent upon human activity. To countenance that kind of dependence, no matter how corrupt the church, was tantamount to affirming that men and women could thwart the powerful work of the Spirit.

The third characteristic of Whitefield's understanding of the church, one less intentional, was a tendency toward separatism. As much as the evangelist promoted the ideal of universal brotherhood through the bonds of Christ, thus

---

[8]John Gillies, ed., *The Works of . . . The Revd. George Whitefield* (London: n.p., 1777), 1:126, quoted in Hindmarsh, "Is Evangelical Ecclesiology an Oxymoron?" p. 33.

seeking to avoid the competition and division that insistence upon correct church order generated, Whitefield could not prevent divisions within the evangelical movement. In some cases he even precipitated them. As Hindmarsh well notes, Whitefield and the Wesleys divided in 1739 over the Calvinistic doctrine of free grace, and one year later the issue of quietism separated the Moravians from the Wesleys and Whitefield. Consequently, despite the pious desire to avoid the forms and structures that so often divided Protestants, forms and structures inevitably arose among evangelicals. And the characteristic that has marked American evangelicalism according to many scholars, namely, the formation of ministerial fiefdoms organized around the ministry and personality of one person, was also true of eighteenth-century transatlantic evangelicalism. Without the order of a church to absorb and channel religious devotion, an informal episcopacy developed with Whitefield the bishop of his own followers, and John Wesley and Zinzendorf following suit. As Hindmarsh well summarizes, "If one rejects visible order, one will sooner or later simply fill the vacuum with another form of visible organization."[9] The question that evangelicals have rarely asked in response to that reality is whether church order possesses a normative character that parachurch ministries lack.

Evidence of the failure to think through the formal and structural aspects of the Christian faith is not difficult to find. The examples chosen here come from the writings of Jonathan Edwards, Charles Finney, Charles Hodge and E. J. Carnell. But, before proceeding to these representative evangelical treatments of the church, the point should be underscored that one searches in vain for a textbook of evangelical ecclesiology. The reason stems directly from the revivalistic and pietistic impulses that informed Whitefield's understanding of the Christian ministry in relation to genuine faith and real assurance of salvation. Because of the shift from marks of the true church to characteristics of true spirituality, evangelicals, no matter their ecclesiastical affiliation, write little about the church as a mediator of grace and ordinance of divine mercy. Instead, to the degree that they write about church ordinances or the Christian ministry they do so invariably in connection with the individual believer's faith and holiness. Unless the church contributes tangibly to the individual's conversion and sanctification, it rarely emerges in evangelical writing as an object of sustained attention. Just as important is the flipside to that assertion. Because the formal or institutional church often functions as a barrier to genuine spirituality, evangelicals have been prone to disregard it as essential to

---

[9]Hindmarsh, "Is Evangelical Ecclesiology an Oxymoron?" p. 34.

the Christian walk. At best, the church is a site for the inspiration and fellowship of those really saved, at worst a scheme of forms and offices that prevent free and open communion between God and his people.

Jonathan Edwards was one of the rare evangelical worthies who made his mark not as an evangelist or parachurch leader but as a regular, settled pastor. As a minister in Massachusetts' Standing Order he was, consequently, more aware of the obligations of church order and more thoughtful about their limitations than other evangelical theologians. As David Hall argues in his introduction to Edwards's *Ecclesiastial Writings*, the Northampton pastor until 1743 held together two incongruous features of his Calvinist heritage on the church, first the idea that the church was a comprehensive body that included both the regenerate and the unregenerate, and second the notion that the church should be a gathered communion of visible saints.[10] One aspect worth highlighting even in this preliminary description is Edwards's understanding of the church, along with the New England Puritan tradition, on the basis of membership rather than the Christian ministry. Even before Edwards began to raise the bar for church membership in Northampton his thought about the church revolved around those characteristics of the saints rather than the church's formal mediation of grace. As such, in his Miscellany on Church Order (462), written in 1730, Edwards addresses exclusively the standards of membership. He begins by asserting that "The method in all congregations of Christians ought to be this: none should be admitted to any church privilege, to have their children baptized, or to be looked upon as of the visible Church of Christ, but those that come to the Lord's Supper."[11] Of course, because of the later controversy in Northampton over Edwards's restricting the Supper to those church members who could render an adequate narrative of their conversion, this statement about church membership in 1730 has significance beyond its simple assertion of one set of privileges for all within the church. Still, the entry is revealing in that Edwards pays no attention to the qualifications for and duties of the ministry, or the nature and function of the sacraments in a three-page treatment of "Church Order." Where he does comment on the formal aspects of the church, such as an early Miscellany on ministers, his thoughts are almost perfunctory: "Although ministers are not properly governors but only leaders . . . yet for the same reason as they may teach and instruct their flocks, they

---

[10]"Editor's Introduction," in Jonathan Edwards, *The Works of Jonathan Edwards, 12: Ecclesiastical Writings*, ed. David D. Hall (New Haven: Yale University Press, 1994), p. 50.

[11]Jonathan Edwards, *The Works of Jonathan Edwards, 13: The "Miscellanies,"* ed. Thomas A. Schafer (New Haven: Yale University Press, 1994), p. 503.

may instruct the people who it is amongst them that doth those laws and who not; this is part of their business and teaching. For the same reason, 'tis their business to instruct who are worthy of the name of Christians among them and who not, and the people are as much obliged to believe these instructions as they are the rest, and no more."[12] Such sentiments may have reflected an admirable lack of interest by Edwards in his own status as a minister. Just as likely, however, they reveal that an identification of true religion with personal experience inevitably leads to a low view or even disregard of the nature and functions of the Christian ministry as constitutive of the church.

According to David Hall, Edwards changed his mind about the comprehensive or covenantal nature of the church as a gathering of saints and hypocrites during the early 1740s. Hall argues that the position that pushed Edwards in the direction of a pure church comprised exclusively of true believers was his construction of genuine piety in the book, *Religious Affections* (1746). In Hall's opinion the chief point of this book is that distinguishing the godly from the profane is a judgment possible to Christians. Consequently, *Religious Affections* is bound up with delineating signs of grace and sanctification in believers' lives that demonstrate genuine faith. Holy affections, according to Edwards's logic, "have a governing power in the course of a man's life,"[13] thus establishing the principle that the external and internal, practice and grace, are one. Of course, an implicit point in Edwards's search for true Christianity was the blemish that hypocrites foisted on the church. He was in *Religious Affections* not simply trying to defend the revivals from their religious despisers but also attempting to establish more generally a base line for discerning true faith, whether in the lives of saints awakened through revival or in those quickened in less dramatic ways.

Edwards's interest in signs of genuine religion did not simply change his understanding of the church as the pure assembly of saints, but it also discounted the role of corporate church life as evidence of true faith. Here his comments on Northampton converts from the 1730s are instructive. One woman in particular drew Edwards's attention in a letter from 1735. This woman was "modest," "bashful" and "pious," not necessarily the sort of attributes we would ascribe to an unregenerate person. Yet, having witnessed the effects of conversion on other town folk and requested from God a "more clear manifestation of himself," she received that for which she asked and experienced "a sense of [God's] glory and love" that lasted intermittently for

---

[12]Ibid., pp. 188-89.
[13]Quoted in "Editor's Introduction," *Works of Jonathan Edwards, 12*, p. 57.

days until one afternoon she began to sink under this sense. When neighbors discovered her, they feared she would die because of the intensity of her experience. Edwards himself visited her and heard her speak "in a manner that can't be described" of "the sense she had of the glory of God, and particularly of such and such perfections, and her own unworthiness, her longing to lie in the dust, sometimes her longing to be with Christ, and crying out of the excellency of Christ, and the wonderfulness of his dying love."[14] What is striking about this woman is that she was devout, a regular participant in public worship, someone who attended faithfully the means of the Christian ministry. Yet for Edwards these displays of Christian observance were insufficient for demonstrating true faith because they were also practices that hypocrites could perform. As such, another criterion was necessary, one that penetrated to the heart. In so striving for a gauge to heart religion, the church for Edwards became superfluous. If this sounds too strong, remember that in all of Edwards's published works in the Yale series only one is devoted to ecclesiastical writings and that volume contains his reflections on the controversy over higher standards for admission to the Lord's Supper, thoughts that concern not what the church ministers in the sacrament but what qualifications believers need to manifest for participation.

A similar fixation on the personal qualities of believers, as opposed to their relying upon the ministry of the church, shows up in the writings of the nineteenth century's great evangelist, Charles Grandison Finney. The search for references to the church in the revivalist's writings is indeed a frustrating one. In Finney's lectures on systematic theology, for instance, his preoccupation is with the *ordo salutis*, that is, the experience of salvation in the individual believer. As such, questions about revelation, God, the Trinity, anthropology— the classic topics of dogmatics—are absent, including the church. Instead, Finney treats extensively the nature of the moral law, human ability and responsibility, love, sin, the atonement, regeneration, justification and sanctification, a topic meriting six chapters out of thirty-eight thus establishing the evangelist's perfectionist reputation. In such a sequence the one place where Finney could well have discussed the importance of the church in the life of the believer was in chapters devoted to "evidences of regeneration." But here the discussion turns out to be almost exclusively personal and psychological. Both saints and sinners, he explained, desire their own happiness and that of

---

[14]Jonathan Edwards, "Benjamin Colman's Abridgement, November 1736," in *The Works of Jonathan Edwards, 4: The Great Awakening,* ed. C. C. Goen (New Haven: Yale University Press, 1972), pp. 105-6.

others, seek the vindication of righteousness, know the difference between what is right and wrong, abhor sin, delight in justice and truth, pursue business affairs honorably, and display selflessness. But these were merely external similarities in which divergent motives produced outward conformity. Conversely, saints and sinners differed in their hearts, the former pursuing "disinterested benevolence," reason, reform of society, self-denial and holiness, in contrast to the latter's selfishness, prejudice, self-righteousness and self-gratification. Nowhere does Finney comment on church membership or attendance as evidence of regeneration. For him the processes of salvation are so individual that corporate responsibilities and benefits remain invisible. Here the language of Finney's own Westminster Shorter Catechism might have appealed to his pronounced sense of moral duty when the Westminster Divines described faith, repentance and the "diligent use of the outward means whereby Christ communicates the benefits of redemption" as the three responses necessary to "escape the wrath and curse of God." But not even stakes that high could prompt Finney to incorporate church membership and the Christian ministry in his dissection of genuine Christian experience.[15]

A similar attitude toward matters ecclesial emerges from Finney's *Lectures to Professing Christians* (1836/1837). Here, however, when he refers to church activities or services he does so in disparaging terms, thus raising the perennial revivalist fear about the church, namely that it promotes nominal faith. In this series of discussions Finney nuanced his distinction between saints and sinners to include three groups among professing Christians: true saints, "legal" believers and those motivated by public opinion. The middle category, that of legal Christian, is revealing of Finney's regard for the church and its practices. These believers who in Finney's terms "are actuated by self-love or by selfishness" make religion a "subordinate concern" by limiting Christian activity to formal or public exercises. "They consider religion," he declared, "as something that ought to come in by and by, as something that ought to come in and find a place among other things, as a sort of Sabbath-day business, or something to be confined to the closet and the hour of family prayer and the Sabbath, and not as the grand business of life." In effect, these legal Christians "make a distinction between religious duty and business, and consider them as entirely separate concerns."[16] These same Christians, Finney argued, when

---

[15]J. H. Fairchild, ed., *Finney's Systematic Theology* (abridged; Minneapolis: Bethany Fellowship, 1976).

[16]Charles G. Finney, *Lectures to Professing Christians* (1837; reprint, New York: Garland Publishing, 1985), p. 68.

calling a minister look for someone to feed and save them, not a man to preach for the conversion of sinners.[17] As church members, these legal Christians are ashamed to go forward to the anxious seat, justifying such reluctance with the idea that believers ought not be "enthusiastic" but should seek instead a "more sober and consistent way in religion."[18] Finney does concede that true conversion will yield a love of meetings for worship where the true saint delights in prayer and praise, "in hearing the word of God, and in communion with God and his saints." But the false saint only attends religious meetings "because he thinks [it] a good place to prop up his hope."[19] The clear impression Finney leaves is that where the Christian ministry involves more than the conversion of the lost it embodies selfishness and hence false religion. Such an outlook obviously has little room for those means of grace such as word and sacrament that Protestants historically believed were ordained to build up believers in faith and hope. For Finney such edification manifests a concern for self that conflicts with evangelism.

The propensity of Edwards and Finney to stress the personal experience of faith over an ecclesial Christian identity might be understandable in the context of their active promotion of revivals, but the case of Charles Hodge, remembered more as Presbyterian than evangelist, is harder to explain and so all the more revealing of evangelicalism's subjective and individualistic conception of the church. The theologian who arguably embodied the Princeton Theology more than any other member of the seminary's storied faculty, Hodge was a Calvinistic stalwart, defending the Reformed tradition against all critics. In the new egalitarian and democratic setting of the American republic, Calvinism stressed divine sovereignty in almost monarchical terms and human inability in a manner that contradicted the nation's "can-do" spirit. Hodge's defense of Reformed Christianity was impressive for its erudition and chutzpah. Still, he generated his own set of critics within Reformed circles thanks to a conception of the church that frustrated high-church types like Nevin, a student and colleague of Hodge's at Princeton, and divine-right Presbyterians like James Henley Thornwell. The source of his critics' frustration was Hodge's idea of the church that was closer to evangelists like Edwards and Finney than to Presbyterians and Reformed like Calvin and Knox.

Hodge's ecclesiology is useful to the purposes of this paper for two reasons. First, he was writing at a time when theologians like Nevin and those at the

---

[17]Ibid., p. 71.
[18]Ibid., p. 125.
[19]Ibid., p. 162.

forefront of the Oxford movement were attempting to rescue the church from neglect by revivalist-friendly Protestants. Second, unlike Edwards or Finney whose doctrine of the church is more implicit than explicit, Hodge deliberatively and self-consciously articulated an ecclesiology that he believed was faithful to the Bible, and to his theological tradition of Reformed Christianity, and that he believed withstood the dangers of both high- and low-church tendencies in nineteenth-century America.

Two essays are particularly instructive for understanding Hodge's ecclesiology. The first was published in 1846 in response to the Anglican High churchman, Henry Edward Manning. Here Hodge reduced the various Christian notions of the church to three, the evangelical, the Ritualist and the Rationalist. He believed that one's ecclesiology flowed directly from one's account of salvation (i.e., theology). So intent on defending the Reformed doctrine of salvation and the importance of the imputed righteousness of Christ, Hodge believed the evangelical theory of the church began and concluded with the status of the individual Christian believer. "The fundament principle" of evangelical ecclesiology, he wrote, was that "true believers" are the elect or called-out ones. As such, if the body of Christ consists of those with true faith, who have received the promise of the Spirit and exhibit the Spirit's presence with appropriate spiritual fruit, then the church is its members.[20] In fact, the "only essential mark" of the church for Hodge was "the profession of true religion."[21] These professors as "visible beings" gave the church its visibility, not ordinances or sacraments. The invisible character of the church stemmed from the difference between its real and nominal members. Consequently, Hodge did almost everything in his power to avoid the Ritualist error of defining the church by its organization, officers, or word and sacrament. For him the Christian ministry was tantamount to creating a barrier between believers and the God who sovereignly and mysteriously saves.

When Hodge turned to developments in his own communion, specifically the attempts of some Old School Presbyterians to assert the divine right of Presbyterian polity, his personal and individualistic notion produced a feeble defense of Presbyterianism. Here a second essay, written after the General Assembly of 1860 where Hodge and Thornwell matched wits over the rights and prerogatives of church courts, is instructive. The latter had argued that the Bible taught and so required a Presbyterian form of church government, and that

---

[20]Charles Hodge, "Theories of the Church," in *Discussions in Church Polity* (New York: Charles Scribner's Sons, 1878), pp. 40-41.
[21]Ibid., p. 54.

because of Presbyterianism's divine provenance his denomination could not treat procedural matters as ones of convenience or efficiency. Hodge, however, saw no such blueprint for Presbyterian order in Scripture and insisted that the Bible only required a generic set of principles. "What we hold," he wrote, "is, that the leading principles thus laid down in Scripture regarding the organization and action of the Church, are the parity of the clergy, the right of the people, and the unity of the church."[22] For some of the divine-right Presbyterian party, Hodge's ecclesiology made Presbyterianism merely a preference, easily exchanged with a Baptist or Congregationalist model. But for Hodge this was the genius of American Presbyterianism since it maintained that the New Testament taught a form of government but allowed "wide" discretion "in matters of detail, which no man or set of men, which neither civil magistrats nor ecclesiastical rulers, can take from us."[23]

Hodge's argument clearly frustrated staunch Old Schoolers but it should not have surprised them since his modest ecclesiology stemmed directly from his evangelical theory of church. For the Princetonian the most important feature of the church was true faith. He even referred to this as the essential mark of the church. From that starting point Hodge would have had to perform backflips to arrive at Thornwell's divine-right position, so important was personal as opposed to corporate religion to the Princeton professor. Yet this evangelical, revivalist emphasis on the true faith of the individual caused such a die-hard defender of the Westminster Confession to miss important sections in the chapter on the church. Hodge's evangelical theory could find support from the first paragraph of chapter twenty-five which states that the "catholic or universal church, which is invisible, consists of the whole number of the elect" [25.1], though interestingly what for Hodge was visible for the Westminster Divines was invisible. But the chapter goes on in paragraph two to give support to higher-church types who were quarreling with Hodge to recognize that the organization and activities of the church and its officers were not indifferent or supplemental to real faith but essential to Christianity. Here the confession teaches that the *visible* church "is the kingdom of the Lord Jesus Christ, the house and family of God, out of which there is no ordinary possibility of salvation" [25.2]. In paragraph three the Divines added that to this visible church Christ gave "the ministry, oracles, and ordinances of God, for the gathering and perfecting of the saints, in this life, to the end of the world" [25.3].

---

[22]Charles Hodge, "Presbyterianism," in *Discussions in Church Polity* (New York: Charles Scribner's Sons, 1878), p. 122.
[23]Ibid., p. 131.

To say that the marks of the church could be discerned from its ministry was not as farfetched as Hodge insisted. But his commitment to the genuine experience of individual believers prompted this sturdy Presbyterian to neglect significant sections from his own theological tradition.

One last example to round out this survey of evangelical reflection on the church comes from the twentieth century in the work of another Presbyterian, Edmund P. Clowney, who wrote the volume on the church in the InterVarsity Press series Contours of Christian Theology. The book is a marvel at least from the perspective that the author found a way to articulate his Presbyterian convictions in a sufficiently generic manner to satisfy the demands of an evangelical publisher. Evidence of Clowney's Presbyterian heritage comes in his discussion of the marks of the church, a chapter that excels in contrast to Edwards, Finney and even the Presbyterian Hodge because of its insistence upon preaching, the sacraments and discipline as signs of a true church. Clowney here echoes an older Protestant perspective on the objective character of the church through the Christian ministry. His positive evaluation of the external and corporate nature of the church leads to a nuanced but critical distinction between the church and parachurch. Parachurch agencies, Clowney writes, lack "some of the marks of the church" and so need denominations because they do not "provide the ordered structure of office, worship, sacrament and discipline that a denominational church offers."[24] For Clowney, then, the church is more than simply a fellowship of real believers. It has a formal structure that is evident even apart from an individual's or group's faith.

Yet Clowney's account of what these marks do moves his otherwise improved estimate back toward the low-church outlook of mainstream evangelicalism. For instance, in his chapter on the nurture provided by the church, a topic that could easily elicit references to the church as mother, Clowney backpedals, offering instead a discussion of the Trinity's work of nurture and the aims of nurture in the Christian life. He rounds out the chapter with reflection on the nurture provided to Christian children in the home and schools. But he neglects the Christian ministry and the means of grace. For whatever reason he fails to attribute nurturing efficacy to the marks of the church he elaborated earlier in the book. Instead, his conception of nurture possesses the telltale mark of evangelical ecclesiology, namely, an emphasis on the immediate work of God on the soul and a resistance to mediation in the divine work of salvation. Part of the reason for Clowney's reluctance to go all the way with his understanding of the church's marks may be a fear of

---

[24]Edmund P. Clowney, *The Church* (Downers Grove, Ill.: InterVarsity Press, 1995), p. 107.

clericalism. In another chapter, this time on the church's structure, Clowney discusses the offices of ministry in a way that flattens most distinctions between ministers and members. In a statement that would have perplexed if not astounded Nevin and Calvin, Clowney asserts, "The general and special offices share all the goals and means of ministry."[25] A further casualty in Clowney's handling of pastoral office is silence about the sacraments. His discussion of the ministry of the Word centers on preaching or evangelism but includes practically no recognition that restricting the administration of the Lord's Supper and baptism to clergy might yield a higher and more sacramental view of the church as a means of salvation. Consequently, despite an initially promising discussion of the marks of the church, Clowney falls back to the default position of evangelical pastors and theologians before him: the action in the church is not with those who perform certain holy activities but with all of God's people who have been saved not by mediation but by the direct and powerful work of God.

THE LOGIC OF PIETISM

What then accounts for evangelicalism's congenital avoidance of a sacramental or mediatorial understanding of the church? One answer could be as Nevin's critics had it: Protestantism in its very nature demands repudiation of a high view of the church and its ministry as the means by which salvation proceeds. But as Nevin attempted to show—and at times did so successfully— the sixteenth-century reformers, and the creeds and confessions the Protestant churches produced, all manifested a high view of the church. This was particularly evident in the one great concern of Nevin's career, namely, the Lord's Supper. Whereas for paleo-Protestants like the Lutherans, Reformed and Anglicans, something actually happened in the administration of the sacrament (though real presence never achieved a uniform meaning), for neo-Protestants like the evangelicals the Supper was largely symbolic or testimonial. As such the issue that Nevin raised is very much pertinent to assessing evangelical ecclesiology: does the church communicate or mediate grace through Word and sacrament? Settling questions about the historic Protestants is beyond the scope of this paper. But this all too brief survey of American theologians gives a fairly reliable indication that evangelicals are decidedly hesitant to answer that question in the affirmative, because of a prior conviction about the necessity of conversion and true faith for membership in the church. So the question to follow is why evangelicals look at the church from the bottom-side up, that

---

[25]Ibid., p. 208.

is, from the perspective of admission and membership, rather than from the top-side down—from the perspective of the church's mission and its means for accomplishing this work.

In the essay already mentioned, Bruce Hindmarsh explains the peculiar character of evangelical ecclesiology as a function of momentous social and political changes in the seventeenth century. On the one side were the religious wars both on the Continent and in England which indicated the real liabilities of an ecclesiastical order enforced by the magistrate. According to Hindmarsh, in the light of these new political realities, "It would be more possible now to conceive of the church as being among all the visible churches and to realize this ideal in public contexts and new forms alongside the formal, institutional church."[26] At the same time important developments in travel and communication prompted a larger "traffic of ideas, people, and goods in the North Atlantic, and evangelicals were at the forefront of the flux and excitement this created."[27] In effect, evangelicalism grew out of the fertile soil of modernity where "traditional ties to the family and the land, the squire and the parson, were broken, and religion increasingly operated in a world in which people understood themselves as mobile, free moral agents."[28] Such social and political forces, Hindmarsh argues, gave shape to the new forms of ministry evangelicals would use while also creating the sort of dislocated people to whom evangelicals would minister. As important as these points are especially for considering the structural arrangements that inform Christian ministry and association, modernity is not a sufficient ground for personal, experiential, unmediated devotion. In the religious free market of modern society, highchurch communions are in no more of a disadvantage to compete for souls than low-church congregations. The rational autonomous self can just as freely choose to commune with Christ at the 11:00 Anglo-Catholic service as he or she can at the megachurch's Saturday night seeker service. Thanks to modernity the high churches lost the backing of the state. But statistics indicate churches like Rome still holding their own in the apparently low-church environment of markets and nation-states.

In his twenty-fifth anniversary history of the National Association of Evangelicals, Bruce Shelley offered an explanation for evangelical ecclesiology that looks less to external than to internal factors. In a surprisingly frank conclusion to a book intended for inspiration, the Conservative Baptist church histo-

---

[26]Hindmarsh, p. 23.
[27]Ibid., p. 28.
[28]Ibid., p. 29.

rian faulted evangelicals for neglecting the church. "It should be a source of deep concern to evangelicals," he wrote, "that, while professing faith in an infallible Bible, they have produced so few worthy books on the Biblical doctrine of the church."[29] Here he proposed several questions about terms familiar in discussions of the church but as vague as they were common. What was the correct basis for church union? What did "visible," "invisible" and "pure" mean in understanding the church?[30] Shelley believed evangelicals possessed little insight into the nature of the church because they had "traditionally stressed those doctrines which bear directly upon the experience of the new birth." He added, "By rejecting the sacramental view of salvation, they have found it natural to neglect the doctrine of the church."[31]

Shelley's reflections on evangelicalism in the mid-1960s help to explain why the phrase *evangelical ecclesiology* inevitably invites chuckles. Evangelical piety is inherently suspicious of the church as a medium of salvation. On the positive side, evangelical forms of devotion have so stressed the direct work of the Holy Spirit in the life of the believer that Christians' embodied existence seldom becomes a factor in understanding the process of salvation. After all, Christians are not simply souls but ensouled bodies, in which case religious means that affect or go through the physical senses may be as important for spiritual life as the necessary work of the Holy Spirit. That is certainly the import of passages such as Romans 10 where the apostle Paul writes about the necessity of preaching and hearing the Word for true belief, or even Christ's commission to his disciples at the end of Matthew where he regards teaching and baptizing as means of discipling the nations. As some Christian traditions have it, such a conception of the Christian ministry does not diminish the necessity of the Spirit's regenerating power. Neither does the necessity of the Holy Spirit make unnecessary the work of pastors who preach and administer the sacraments. Instead of the either-or approach that evangelicals have taken, churchly Christianity has insisted on both means of grace and the work of the Spirit.

The other factor in evangelical piety that undercuts the church and the Christian ministry is a fear of hypocrisy and nominal Christianity. Pietists and revivalists both recognized correctly that forms of churchly Christian devotion, such as attending worship and participating in the means of grace, can be faked. So in order to correct for the abuse that comes with going through the motions, evangelicals concocted various other measures of genuine Christian-

---

[29]Bruce Shelley, *Evangelicalism in America* (Grand Rapids: Eerdmans, 1967), p. 124.
[30]Ibid., p. 127.
[31]Ibid., p. 124.

ity, from religious affections and personal testimonies to speaking in tongues. The problem here, though, is that not even these spiritual displays guarantee real faith; people can fake religious enthusiasm, though perhaps with greater effort, as much as eating a small piece of bread and drinking a sip of wine or grape juice. Still, this problem has not stopped evangelicals from seeking visible signs that indicate spiritual authenticity. Nor have evangelicals found forms of devotion that open up the hidden recesses of the human heart. Meanwhile, the quest for religious certainty has for almost three centuries taken evangelicals down a path which, at its outset, veered sharply from the churchly and sacramental forms that characterized Christianity prior to 1700. For evangelicals to find their way back will take a considerable hike.

But when they get back to the Canterbury or Wittenberg or Geneva trail, will they still be evangelicals? That is a question likely to haunt discussions of evangelical ecclesiology because, at least as I have argued, evangelicalism with its stress on the personal and subjective is inherently antagonistic to the corporate and formal ways of churchly Christianity (whether Protestant or Roman Catholic). Perhaps other contributors to this volume will render this construction of evangelical ecclesiology a caricature. But to do so, defenders of evangelical ecclesiology will need to provide a rationale for the church that moves beyond the Christian ministry as a spiritual vitamin that supplements a healthy personal religious diet to an older rendering like Calvin's which regarded the church as the very sustenance of Christian life, apart from which believers have no hope of salvation.

2

THE FUNDAMENTAL DISPENSATION OF EVANGELICAL ECCLESIOLOGY

DENNIS L. OKHOLM

This chapter really began with my early catechesis in dispensationalism. The most formative years of my Christian youth were spent in a Conservative Baptist Association church pastored by a very capable graduate of Bob Jones University and Dallas Theological Seminary, a summer youth intern attending Dallas, and a subsequent youth pastor educated at Multonomah School of the Bible. We had regular visits by the likes of Earl Radmacher from Western Conservative Baptist Seminary who lectured glazed-eyed laity about Greek verb tenses and Pauline sentence constructions to convince us that the "sign gifts" I had witnessed in my earlier Pentecostal days were no longer operative; we lowered the ceiling fans so things wouldn't get out of hand with subversive charismatics and came close to making a policy prohibiting speaking in tongues on our church campus. The journey continued with an early to mid-70s education at Wheaton College and Trinity Evangelical Divinity School, the former taught by professors who signed a confessional statement which committed them to a premillennial eschatology that included the "imminent" return of Christ (essentially dispensationalism[1]) and the latter being supported

---

[1]On the use of *imminent* Craig Blaising makes this observation: "In the Bible and prophecy conferences of the late nineteenth century, the imminent return of Christ meant belief in premillennialism. . . . That coming could take place literally at any moment. Consequently, when dispensationalists spoke of imminency, they spoke primarily of the pretribulational rapture. By the insistence of Arno Gaebelein, C. I. Scofield and others at the turn of the century, imminency came to be defined exclusively by the doctrine of the pretribulational Rapture." *Nearness* came to be seen as the posttribulational stand according to dispensationalists such as John Walvoord (Craig A. Blaising and Darrell L. Bock, *Progressive Dispensationalism* [Wheaton, Ill.: Victor, 1993], pp. 20-21). It *is* difficult to see how one could seriously insist that Christ's return will be "imminent," yet hold to a posttribulational view, unless it is not possible to know whether we are in "the tribulation."

by the dispensationalist Evangelical Free Church of America. It would be years later while at Princeton that I would find myself home at last with Reformed theology in a mainline church. Among other discoveries, I had found a church with the more robust ecclesiology for which I had searched and a healthier polity rooted in connectionalism and an ecumenical spirit.

Reflecting on my own journey led to a hunch: Is it the case that fundamentalist dispensationalism has been, in part, responsible for the absence of a robust evangelical ecclesiology outside of mainline circles?

If this is the case, perhaps it is corroborated by other related features of non-mainline evangelical churches and schools. For example, the kingdom of God was the primary focus of Jesus' earthly ministry and teaching, yet it is rarely mentioned in evangelical pulpits. In fact, my evangelically reared students find it surprising that Jesus talked primarily about the kingdom and virtually not at all about "soul winning." My evangelical students and fellow evangelical parishioners speak of law in the Old Testament and grace in the New Testament as different ways of salvation. Many evangelicals still separate social justice from evangelism or argue that social issues, such as racism, are simply "matters of the heart," ignoring their systemic dimensions. Evangelicals think of salvation as "going to heaven," but rarely if ever talk of salvation as involving a redeemed creation and the "new earth." My evangelical students believe that the church is dispensable in the Christian life and that the important thing is one's individual relation to Christ, with or without the church.

My hunch is that the dispensational heritage in the fundamentalist past of much of nonmainline evangelicalism is largely to blame for these phenomena. If it is in the past, haven't we gotten well past this influence? Are we not beating a dead horse? Actually, the horse is not even lame, let alone dead. Timothy Weber estimates that dispensationalists "make up about one-third of America's forty or fifty million evangelical Christians."[2] So Craig Blaising does not exaggerate when he writes:

> Dispensationalism may not be a household term, but it designates one of the most widespread and influential traditions in evangelical theology today. If you are an evangelical Christian, it is most likely that you know of some who call themselves dispensationalists. And it is just as likely that you have certain beliefs and interpretations of Scripture that have been shaped in some way by dispensationalism.
>
> From its introduction in the Bible conferences to the present day, dispensation-

---

[2]Timothy P. Weber, *On the Road to Armageddon: How Evangelicals Became Israel's Best Friend* (Grand Rapids: Baker Academic, 2004), p. 9.

alism has expanded to become one of the most common expressions of evangelical Christianity.[3]

Blaising, along with Darrell Bock, Robert Saucy and others, represents "progressive dispensationalism," which, to the chagrin of what he calls "classical" dispensationalists (they prefer to be called "traditional") has moved in many respects closer to the amillennial position.[4] Yet the classical position of folks like Charles Ryrie, John Walvoord, Earl Radmacher and others still holds sway.[5] In 1992 Stanley Grenz noted that while progressive dispensationalism is prevalent in academia, it has yet to filter through the church; "consequently, the older 'classic' dispensationalism remains a potent force in evangelicalism."[6] A decade later it still remains potent, particularly through the popularizers, especially Tim LaHaye's Left Behind series, the *first* volume of which still ranked 502 on Amazon's chart during the week in 2004 when the *twelfth* and last book was released.[7] The LaHaye-Jenkins books have become the most popular adult fiction series in the United States; the books have sold more than fifty million copies, not to mention the twenty-six-book series for kids with sales exceeding ten million copies (another catechism!).[8] Timothy Weber calls the series "the most effective disseminator of dispensationalist ideas ever," eclipsing the bestselling nonfiction book of the 1970s—Hal Lindsey's *The Late Great Planet Earth*, which itself was translated into fifty languages and sold over thirty-five million copies.[9] In other words, the effects of classical dispensationalism are very much alive among evangelicals.

If Karl Barth was right in thinking that the only excuse for a theologian was to be a servant and critic of the preacher,[10] then the present task is precisely one in which an evangelical theologian should be engaged. Hopefully

---

[3]Blaising and Bock, *Progressive Dispensationalism*, pp. 9, 13.
[4]See Wesley R. Willis and John R. Master, gen. eds.; Charles C. Ryrie, consulting ed., *Issues in Dispensationalism* (Chicago: Moody, 1994), pp. 20-26.
[5]Blaising and Bock put Walvoord and Ryrie in what they call the "Revised" camp (which is of late 1950s to late 1970s vintage); see ibid., p. 7.
[6]Stanley Grenz, *The Millennial Maze* (Downers Grove, Ill.: InterVarsity Press, 1992), p. 94.
[7]It seems to me that this makes laughable Craig Blaising's comment that "some more classical dispensationalists can be found even today" (*Progressive Dispensationalism*, p. 56).
[8]See "The *Left Behind* Series: Is This Christianity?" in *The Week*, April 16, 2004, p. 19. The "good news" is, as the story reports, "when Jesus vanquishes the Antichrist and his human allies at Armageddon, he'll establish a 1000-year reign in which 'cell phones still work,' 'sleep is not needed,' and 'all the world's mountains have been flattened into one terrestrial plain.' "
[9]Weber, *Armageddon*, pp. 15, 191, 194.
[10]William E. Hordern, *A Layman's Guide to Protestant Theology*, 2nd ed. (New York: Macmillan, 1968), p. 131.

we will understand better how the evangelical church ended up with a less than robust understanding of the church, and perhaps we can offer hope that a wider sense of the church and its mission is on the other side of enlightened self-knowledge.

THE RELATION BETWEEN ECCLESIOLOGY AND ESCHATOLOGY

One analyst of dispensationalism has made this poignant assertion: "It would be illogical . . . for one to accept the doctrine of the pretribulation rapture without also accepting the dispensational concept of the church, which has arisen out of its basic principle of interpretation."[11] In this vein, my contention is this: The logic of dispensational eschatology has left us with a church that is somewhat dispensable, detached and withdrawn, separatistic and composed of "saved" individuals.

Such a connection should not surprise us if we understand that ecclesiology cannot be severed from eschatology, because eschatology entails a view of history. One's ecclesiology is embedded in one's understanding of the Christian story. Richard Beaton has put it well:

> Essential to the New Testament metaphor of people of God is an eschatological framework that places the present in the context of the past and the future. As opposed to postmodernity, which rejects any sense of memory and historical continuity, the concept of the people of God can be understood only in light of the past (both Israel's history and the work God accomplished through Christ) and the future (the final consummation of the ages and eternal life). . . . Thus, this people is shaped by the narrative past of the people of God, the present experience of the Spirit, and the future expectations of God's redemptive purposes for creation.[12]

This is precisely the point: many evangelicals have been shaped by a narrative that is dispensational, yet which operates largely at a subconscious level. For many evangelicals, our conception of Christianity and the church has been largely formed by an interpretation of Scripture and of history the source of which most are unaware. George Marsden is right:

> Most people do not think that they think about history [just as, I might add, most people do not think that they think about eschatology], and thus they are seldom aware of the degree to which their perceptions—and hence their practical ac-

---

[11]Clarence Bass, *Backgrounds to Dispensationalism* (Grand Rapids: Baker, 1977), p. 19.

[12]Richard Beaton, "Reimagining the Church," in *Evangelical Ecclesiology*, ed. John Stackhouse (Grand Rapids: Baker, 2003), p. 221. Given this comment, it is strange that in the entire edited volume in which Beaton's essay is found eschatology comes up only once in passing!

tions—are shaped by historical theories. . . . The stance of being at war with modernity has been shaped typically in American evangelicalism by millennial views of history. . . . Moreover, the dispensational view of the millennium that won the day in most of fundamentalism and Pentecostalism posited a more definite view of historical interpretation. . . . God is entirely in control of history, and we can do little more than believe, preach the gospel, shun evil, and wait for God to act.[13]

Several qualifications and clarifications are in order at this point. First, the definition of *evangelicalism* is murkier than it used to be. Accordingly, except when context indicates otherwise, in this paper the term refers to those who by self-definition or with good reason can be linked by heritage or influence to dispensational fundamentalist roots.

Second, not all that is wrong with evangelical ecclesiology can be attributed to classical dispensationalism. Just as George Marsden critiqued the reductionistic mistake of Ernst Sandeen's historical analysis of fundamentalism, so we would do well to remember that cultural factors have been significant in shaping the American evangelical church, as well as other factors in its own past, such as the history of revivalism.

Third, while there are certain features common to classical dispensationalism, not even in its traditional form was dispensationalism monolithic. There were disagreements at points. My purpose is not to join the fray, though it will become obvious that I appreciate the infighting that has resulted in significant reconsiderations of some of dispensationalism's key features.

Fourth, it is not my intention to debate interpretations of Scripture, particularly since hermeneutical principles are presupposed by various sides in eschatological debates to the point that the discussion may be almost incommensurable. Adopting an eschatology for most people probably has less to do with biblical interpretation than it does with a whole host of influences. I want only to show (however loosely) in what unhappy ways evangelical ecclesiology has been affected by, and continues to be affected by, dispensational eschatology.

THE UNHAPPY ECCLESIOLOGY OF CLASSIC DISPENSATIONALISM

A very brief primer on the essence of dispensationalism. Though many are familiar with the history and details of dispensationalism, a very brief primer will help to orient us before looking at the features of classic dispensationalism that, in

---

[13]George Marsden, "Evangelicals, History, and Modernity," in *Evangelicalism and Modern America*, ed. George Marsden (Grand Rapids: Eerdmans, 1984), p. 96.

my judgment, have adversely affected the evangelical church and its mission.[14]

In the late 1820s a Brit named John Nelson Darby defected from the Anglican Church to join a sectarian group known as the "Brethren," disavowing all church order and outward forms of religion.[15] A few years later a split among the sectarian ranks led Darby to found the "Plymouth Brethren." Central to his teachings was the notion that a "literal" reading of the Bible uncovered seven periods or "dispensations" from creation to the coming millennial reign of Christ. A dispensation refers to God's *oikonomia*—God's administration of earthly affairs. In each dispensation God reveals new requirements to test humans, humans fail to obey, and God judges before a new dispensation begins. Thus, "the continuous relation of God to man, from Adam to the present, [changes] with each dispensation."[16] The seven dispensations are the ages of innocence, conscience, human government, promise, law, grace or church,[17] and kingdom. Jesus Christ offered to Israel the promises of the kingdom that were progressively revealed in the Davidic covenant, but since Israel rejected Jesus as its Messiah, the world entered into a new dispensation at Pentecost— that of grace during which the church spreads God's message of salvation to any who acknowledge Jesus Christ as Savior. This sixth dispensation precedes the return of Christ when he will rapture the church out of this world and take it to its reward in heaven before his thousand years of theocratic reign on earth

---

[14]See Weber, *Armageddon*, chap. 1; Randall Balmer, *Mine Eyes Have Seen the Glory*, 3rd ed. (New York: Oxford University Press, 2000); Grenz, *Millennial Maze*; George Marsden, "From Fundamentalism to Evangelicalism," in *The Evangelicals: What They Believe, Who They Are, Where They Are Changing*, ed. John Woodbridge and David Wells (Nashville: Abingdon, 1975); George Marsden, "Evangelicals, History, and Modernity"; Blaising and Bock, *Progressive Dispensationalism*; Willis and Masters, *Issues*.

[15]In a recent book edited by Stephen Hunt, *Christian Millennialism: From the Early Church to Waco* (Bloomington: Indiana University Press, 2001), Mark Patterson and Andrew Walker argue that the earliest and clearest articulation of dispensationalism was by the Albury Circle that organized around the London preacher Edward Irving in the 1820s and their publication *The Morning Watch*. Darby was important in popularizing dispensationalism, especially in North America, but the former worked out its key tenets. Still, Weber argues that Darby's teaching of a pretribulation rapture made his version of futurist premillennialism unique (see *Armageddon*, p. 24).

[16]Lewis Sperry Chafer, *Major Bible Themes* (Chicago: Moody Press, 1944), p. 98. Also see *The New Scofield Reference Bible*, comments on Genesis 1:28, where Scofield defines a dispensation as "a period of time during which man is tested in respect of obedience to some *specific* revelation of the will of God." Cf. *Rightly Dividing the Word of Truth* (Findlay, Ohio: Dunham, 1957), p. 18: "These periods are marked off in Scripture by some change in God's method of dealing with mankind, in respect to two questions: of sin, and of man's responsibility. Each of the dispensations may be regarded as a new test of the natural man, and each ends in judgment—marking his utter failure in every dispensation."

[17]It is "church" in *The New Scofield Reference Bible*, but Ryrie kept "grace"—the older denotation.

predicted in Revelation 20, the kingdom that commences after seven years of tribulation—the seventieth week of those predicted in the book of Daniel (hence the designation pretribulational premillennialism, referring to the timing of the church's rapture).[18]

In nineteenth-century America this view found fertile soil, which Darby discovered when he came to the United States in 1862. While New England Puritans had been premillennial in their theology, most precursors to evangelicalism in pre-Civil War America were postmillennial, believing that Christ was establishing his kingdom on earth *now* and would therefore return for his church *after* the millennium. But the war and reconstruction, industrialization, urbanization and immigration in the latter half of the nineteenth century, along with German higher criticism and Darwinian evolutionary theory (calling into question a literal understanding of the biblical text), was the fertile seedbed in which dispensationalism would firmly take root in American fundamentalism.

The teaching spread through leaders such as Dwight Moody, Reuben Torrey, A. J. Gordon, James Gray and A. C. Dixon. Institutions such as Moody Bible Institute and the Bible Institute of Los Angeles (or Biola, as it is known today) made dispensationalism part of their doctrinal foundation.[19] At the beginning of the twentieth century, a Congregational minister from Dallas, Cyrus Ingerson Scofield, established a Bible correspondence course, the Scofield School of the Bible in New York City, and Philadelphia College of the Bible. His reference Bible was published by Oxford University Press in 1809, a Bible that many American Protestants read from the bottom up. It was eventually superseded by the study Bible of Charles Ryrie, a former member of Dallas Theological Seminary.

Lewis Sperry Chafer, a graduate of Oberlin College and an evangelist who had met Scofield at the Moody Bible Conference center in Northfield, Massachusetts, succeeded Scofield as pastor of the First Congregational Church in Dallas in 1923. He responded to what the World's Christian Fundamentals Association called "one of the greatest needs of the hour," namely, "the establishment of a great evangelical premillennial seminary." So on October 1, 1924, thirteen students gathered for classes at the Evangelical Theological College, later to be named Dallas Theological Seminary, with Chafer as its first president.

---

[18]For a late twentieth-century representative account of the seventieth-week events, see Weber, *Armageddon*, pp. 150-52.

[19]"Almost without exception, the scores of Bible institutes that were founded between 1880 and 1940 taught dispensationalism" (Weber, *Armageddon*, p. 35).

Today, Blaising at Southwestern Baptist Theological Seminary, Bock at Dallas and Saucy at Biola advocate "progressive dispensationalism," which reduces the dispensations to as few as two—dispensations which fall under the rubric of God's program of establishing divine rule over the earth.[20] In fact, the dispensations are not seen merely as different arrangements between God and humans, but as

> successive arrangements in the progressive revelation and accomplishment of redemption. . . . to a future culmination in which God will *both* politically administer Israel and Gentile nations *and* indwell all of them equally . . . by the Holy Spirit. Consequently, the dispensations *progress* by revealing different aspects of the final unified redemption.[21]

Ryrie, however, thinks these progressives have compromised the sine qua non of dispensationalism: the *clear* distinction between Israel and the church, the replacement of a consistent use of literal interpretation with a "complementary" hermeneutic, and substitution of God's doxological purpose with Christocentricity.[22]

With this brief introduction, we turn to the unfortunate implications for evangelical ecclesiology that are entailed in the logic of classical fundamentalist dispensationalism. Specifically, whether intended or not, the nonmainline evangelical church becomes largely dispensable, somewhat Gnostic or docetic, separatistic, and advocates a soteriology that is somewhat escapist, individualistic and reductionistic. In addition, law is pitted against grace, and there is almost a doctrinaire Zionism.

The dispensable church. As we have seen, traditional dispensationalists taught that the Davidic covenantal dispensation came to an end when the Jews rejected Jesus as their Messiah. Between that Israelite kingdom of the Old Testament and the millennial kingdom predicted in Revelation, we now live in an interlude—the "church age." The Davidic covenant is postponed until Christ's return; the prophetic clock is temporarily on hold; God has pushed the "pause button." When God's program with the church is completed, then the focus

---

[20]See Blaising and Bock, *Dispensationalism, Israel and the Church: The Search for Definition* (Grand Rapids: Zondervan, 1992).

[21]Blaising and Bock, *Progressive Dispensationalism*, p. 48.

[22]Ryrie, in Willis and Master, p. 21. But see Grenz's criticism in *Millennial Maze*, p. 118: "even progressive thinkers are willing to speak of Israel and the church as 'distinguishable covenant participants' who 'comprise differing peoples.' From the perspective of nondispensationalists, this distinction only serves to continue the dispensationalist denial that the church is the climax of the divine program inaugurated in the Old Testament. And this is the basic objection critics lodge against dispensationalism in any form."

will shift back to Israel and the promises made to her, Daniel's prophetic clock will start ticking again commencing the seventieth week, Israel will accept her true Messiah and will enter the millennial era of peace and righteousness.[23] The church is not a completion of what God began with ancient Israel, but is either a separate phase (as in classical dispensationalism) or an inauguration phase (as in progressive dispensationalism).

What lies behind this understanding of the church's role in biblical history is dispensationalism's dichotomy between Israel and the church. This is what has been entailed in "rightly dividing the Word of truth." And it is the basis for the traditional dispensationalist concept of the church as *parenthetical* to God's evolving purposes in the history of earthly redemption.[24]

Chafer went farther. While Harry Ironside had called the church a "parenthesis" in God's total redemptive scheme, Chafer made it clearer that "the church has no connection with God's previous acts in history and a subordinate role":

> The new, hitherto unrevealed purpose of God in the outcalling of a heavenly people from Jews and Gentiles is so divergent with respect to the divine purpose toward Israel, which purpose preceded it and will yet follow it, that the term *parenthetical*, commonly employed to describe the new age-purpose, is inaccurate. A parenthetical portion sustains some direct or indirect relation to that which goes before or that which follows after: but the present age-purpose is not thus related and therefore is more properly termed an *intercalation*. The appropriateness of this word will be seen in the fact that as an interpolation is formed by inserting a word or phrase into a context, so an intercalation is formed by introducing a day or period of time into a calendar.[25]

As Scofield made clear, the church is born in Acts 2 and has its earthly career terminated in 1 Thessalonians 4.[26] Though the role of the church's relation to the millennium is not always crystal clear in dispensationalism, the church is raptured out before the tribulation because it is not part of the kingdom whose restoration is initiated through the remnant that survives the tribulation.

It is precisely the parenthetical status of the church in God's program with

---

[23]See Grenz, *Millennial Maze*, p. 97.

[24]See Bass, *Backgrounds*, pp. 23, 26.

[25]Chafer, *Systematic Theology*, 4:41. Perhaps C. H. Mackintosh, a faithful interpreter of Darby, put it most succinctly in a citation that Weber uses to illustrate dispensationalism's characterization of the church as a parenthesis, occupying a "prophetic time warp": "The Christian must never lose sight of the fact that he belongs to heaven" (Weber, *Armageddon*, p. 23).

[26]From *Scofield's Bible Correspondence Course*, 19th ed. (Chicago: Moody Press, n.d.) pp. 23-25, as cited in Bass, *Backgrounds*, p. 28. He also cites the Chafer quote above.

Israel that Ryrie believes is compromised by progressive upstarts who are dangerously teetering toward amillennialism. Saucy, for one, makes Ryrie ponder whether or not the "Jewishness" of the millennium will be deemphasized.[27]

The point here is that, though it was not intended, the church almost becomes God's consolation prize—a parenthetical entity whose job is the restraint of evil, self-edification and evangelism until God takes her out of the picture and picks up where he left off with Israel. Stan Grenz puts the criticism sharply:

> These viewpoints, even in their less radical expressions, run the risk of a crucial theological danger, namely, the reduction of the centrality of the church. Although important distinctions do exist between Israel and the church, the New Testament clearly teaches that the church is neither a secondary nor a preliminary program, but the crowning product of all God's activity in history. Other dispensationalists such as Charles Ryrie indicate that the goal of history is not the church, but the millennium. During that era God will fulfill the divine promises to national Israel. Ryrie's view begs the critics to ask how the church fits into the anticipated Jewish millennium. To the extent that dispensationalism in any form subordinates the church to Israel (albeit perhaps not overtly or consciously) it risks becoming a Judaizing tendency in the church.[28]

In fact, Grenz goes on to suggest that despite even the attempts of progressives, it "simply may not be possible to construct a separate theological understanding for Israel that does not detract from the primacy of the church in the program of God for the salvation of the world."[29] In what follows, Grenz echoes Clarence Bass's criticism that not only does it detract from the glory of the church that stems from the crucified and resurrected Christ when the church is excluded from God's redemptive plan begun in Israel and completed in the millennial literal fulfillment of the Abrahamic and Davidic covenants, but, more significantly, the "emphasis upon the national restoration of Israel is, at the same time, a de-emphasis upon the triumph of the cross, by which believers are made members of the body of Christ, the church."[30]

While progressive dispensationalists do not make the radical distinction, Darby and others distinguished the "kingdom of God" (which has to do with God's universal sovereign reign in the hearts of humans) from the "kingdom of heaven" (God's earthly rule which God promised to Israel and to whom he

---

[27]See Ryrie in Willis and Master, pp. 22-26.
[28]Grenz, *Millennial Maze*, p. 123.
[29]Ibid., p. 124.
[30]Bass, *Backgrounds*, p. 33.

will again offer it at his second advent). This latter kingdom is distinctly Jewish; the promised land will be occupied, the throne of David will again be established, the temple will be restored, and sacrifices will again be reinstituted. That is, the kingdom is a restoration of Israel, not the consummation of the church. While the gospel Jesus preached was of the kingdom, the gospel of grace was preached when the church was instituted as it was revealed to Paul.[31] As one somewhat unsympathetic critic of traditional dispensationalism put it:

> The blessed hope of the church has been Christ's returning for the *church*, to establish His reign through the *church*, so that every tongue should confess His preeminence in the *church*. The blessed hope for the dispensationalists, seemingly, is that Christ will rapture the parenthetical church so that He may reign through *Israel*, not the church.[32]

Is it any wonder that the central motif of Jesus' preaching of the kingdom is not heard from evangelical pulpits? And is it any wonder that one of the proudest declarations of evangelicals plastered on the bumpers of their automobiles is a warning that the car will be "unmanned" when the rapture occurs? The "blessed hope" of the church is its raptured going, not some anticipated kingdom.

The heavenly church. Given what we have pointed out about the church's parenthetical role, it is not much of a leap to see that for classic dispensationalism the church's hope is realized more in heaven than on earth. Darby was very clear about this:

> It is this conviction, that the Church is properly heavenly, in its calling and relationship with Christ, forming no part of the course of events of the earth, which makes the rapture so simple and clear; and on the other hand, it shows how the denial of its rapture brings down the Church to an earthly position, and destroys its whole spiritual character and position.[33]

The union of Christ and his church is heavenly. The church will reign with Christ as joint-heirs of all the inheritance in heaven. The earthly church's pur-

---

[31]Ibid., pp. 29-31. See Bass's citation on p. 36 of J. Dwight Pentecost from his book *Judgments*, p. 49: "The Gospel of the Kingdom is not being preached now; for after the final rejection of the Kingship of Christ by the Jews at the stoning of Stephen, God called another man, Paul, and revealed to him the Gospel of Grace. When God will have completed the body of Christ, and will have taken them to be with Himself at the rapture . . . then . . . the gospel of the kingdom will be preached in all the world."

[32]Ibid., p. 45.

[33]Quoted from *The Rapture of the Saints*, Collected Writings, 4:237, in ibid., p. 39.

pose is to manifest God's activity of love and holiness through the power of the Holy Spirit. When this testimony is completed, it will be given its heavenly character in the glory of Christ.[34] In fact, the individual believer is not baptized into a church here on earth, but into a heavenly relation with Christ.

The most devastating result of this heavenly emphasis is to follow, but it should be pointed out that the constant refrain that the church is in the world but not of the world encourages a gnosticizing, docetic mentality. The visible earthly manifestation of the church as the body *through* which Christ accomplishes his work is deemphasized. Dispensationalism tended to leave the evangelical church detached, withdrawn and introverted, waiting to be raptured from the world with its evils. In fact, ironically, after the fundamentalists lost the battle by the mid-1920s to reclaim the major denominations, they were emboldened by their dispensational eschatology that assured them they possessed the only true understanding of what would unfold in the world's future (including the eventual demise of heretical mainliners). So they took a sectarian posture, seeking recruits one-by-one while they—the insiders—awaited vindication at the rapture. (The popular movie *A Thief in the Night* portrayed this attitude, as does the Left Behind series.) Grenz notes that this posture actually risks capitulation to the secular mindset dispensationalists sought to avoid:

> All too often the practical outworking of the expectation of a pretribulational rapture degenerates into a flight from the world, rather than engagement with the task of finding solutions to the deep problems that confront humankind. . . .
>
> Suspicion of involvement with the task of seeking solutions to the world's problems and the expectation of being caught away from the time of trial—these two attitudes so readily connected with dispensationalism—fit well with the escapist mentality of contemporary Western society. The similarity is evident in the proliferation of Hollywood superhero fantasy productions, which reveal an uncanny resemblance to the pop end-times scenario: A violent redeemer figure from the realm beyond the earth in the nick of time rescues the innocent humans from wicked, demonic adversaries.[35]

Fortunately this escapist mentality has been changing in many evangelical churches, but more on that later.

The separatist church. One of the reasons for Darby's insistence on the heavenly character of the church may have been his conviction that Christendom was apostate, that the modern-day church lies in ruins, and that any attempt to restore the ruined church would be a sinful act and doomed to failure. The

---

[34]Ibid., pp. 117-19.
[35]Grenz, *Millennial Maze*, pp. 120-21.

spirit of separation and exclusivism characterizes the traditional dispensational church. It has led one critic to ask very pointed questions about this emphasis and to bemoan the "devastating effects of this spirit upon the total body of Christ":

> It is appropriate to remark . . . that Darby's doctrine of the church is most important today for its practical effects, rather than for its theological arguments. If one believes that virtually all of Christendom is apostate, and that the unity of the church is maintained by separation from evil, then one will separate himself from that apostate Christendom. This is what the Darbyites did, and this is what the dispensationalists still do.
>
> The separatist spirit and exclusivist attitude toward truth is one of the tragic aspects of the development of Darby's doctrine of the church. Is it too severe to say that the spirit of the movement is as important as its eschatological chronology? Is it too general a conclusion to say that the doctrines of dispensationalists have existed conjointly with the spirit of independency in church groups? Whatever evaluation history may make of this movement, it will attest that dispensationalism is rooted in Darby's concept of the church—a concept that sharply distinguishes the church from Israel, assigns an exclusivist role to the church in an apostate Christendom, gives the church a heavenly title and futuristic character, grants each local church independency because each comprises the body of Christ, and maintains unity through separation from evil.[36]

This spirit has made evangelicals suspicious of organized, institutional churches. True, some churches *did* abandon central doctrines of the Christian faith, but the divisive spirit of the dispensationalists often demanded more than even these criteria to be the true church.[37] Indeed, ecumenism is not even a consideration.

The church of saved individuals. With the notion that Jesus could return at any moment while the world got worse and worse, dispensational fundamentalists and their evangelical heirs could decode world history with their literal interpretation of biblical prophecy and watch the world self-destruct. Combined with their belief in the imminent rapture of the church, these dispensationalists, with some exceptions, were relieved of the obligation to engage in social and political restructuring. Political activism is not the job of the church. Engagement with the world is selective, "focused on individualistic, moralistic, and short-term goals."[38]

---

[36]Bass, *Backgrounds*, p. 127; also see pp. 46-47, 99.

[37]See ibid., p. 145.

[38]Grenz, *Millennial Maze*, p. 119. "Classical dispensationalists tend to be, in the words of Assemblies of God minister Dwight Wilson, 'pessimistic, fatalistic, nonpolitical, and nonactivist.' "

In fact, it is interesting to observe that a former dispensational Wheaton theologian, Henry Thiessen (whose *Lectures in Systematic Theology* was in use for some time at the college) and Robert Saucy (in *God's Program for the Church*)[39] switch from the collective reference to the church to the personal reference to the individual Christian when they move from more "spiritual" descriptions of the church's life to its social responsibilities in the world. This may explain why the evangelical understanding of its relation to the world often resembles a Lutheran "two kingdoms" theory rather than Niebuhr's "Christ transforming culture." And this is reinforced by dispensationalism's notion that the church's pretribulational role is to be a restrainer of evil (à la 2 Thess 2:6-8), since once the church is raptured out of the world the full force of evil will be felt during the tribulation.[40]

One anomaly to this attitude that God is in control of history such that all we can do is preach the gospel, shun evil and wait for God to act, is the white evangelical view that the United States is God's chosen nation. According to George Marsden, both the dispensationalist retreat from ameliorating social ills and the Puritan notion of God's covenanted people play seemingly bipolar roles in evangelical attitudes toward the culture, such that the Pat Robertsons and the Jerry Falwells can engage in culture-building, even with their pessimistic interpretation of this pre-tribulational world.[41] Timothy Weber attributes this to a "logic of their own": dispensationalists can give up on the world and engage it simultaneously. Not only does this have to do with the politics of Israel's future, but also with stemming the tide of moral decline in the United States, "giving the devil all the trouble we can till Jesus comes" so that America might "endure until the Lord comes to evacuate his people."[42]

I recently found one amusing example of this *combination* of a pessimistic dispensational understanding of history and a "Christian America" when I was culling through books sent to me for evaluation. Self-published with the clever title *The Second Coming of Babylon*, the author set out a dispensational scenario that supported a literal reading of the Bible's reference to the present-

---

[39]Henry C. Thiessen, *Introductory Lectures in Systematic Theology* (Grand Rapids: Eerdmans, 1949) and Saucy, *God's Program for the Church*, p. 94.

[40]Grenz, *Millennial Maze*, p. 107.

[41]See Marsden, "Evangelicals, History, and Modernity," p. 96. Actually, Weber identifies Robertson as one who "more or less followed the dispensationalist scenario"; he is premillennial, but seems to lean toward a posttribulational view. In any case, Weber concludes that Robertson is "much more interested in stopping the forces of one-worldism than in explaining or proving the elaborate dispensationalisst system." See Weber, *Armageddon*, pp. 192, 205-7.

[42]Weber, *Armageddon*, pp. 46, 199-203.

day resurgence of ancient Babylon in the coming tribulation. The author was perceptive: he anticipated the American reader's query how a city in Iraq could become the economic center of the world when Wall Street currently holds that position. His answer: the rapture! There are so many Christians in the United States that when the rapture occurs it will leave mortgages unpaid, service industries underpopulated, and so forth. The United States economy will collapse. Into the vacuum will sweep the restored ancient city of Babylon. Indeed, dispensationalism is alive and well in the United States.

Of course, this reticence of church engagement in political and social realms is exacerbated by the dispensationalist emphasis on personal salvation. Progressive dispensationalist Craig Blaising explains it well:

> The heavenly nature of the church's salvation was interpreted by classical dispensationalists in an individualistic manner. Political and social issues were *earthly* matters which did not concern the church. The church was a spiritual unity found in Christ. This unity manifested itself not only in the oneness of Christ but in the oneness of personal salvation—the individual nature of salvation. Issues in the church were individual, private, spiritual matters, not social, political, earthly matters. . . . The heavenly, individualistic, and spiritual nature of the church could not be more distinct from the earthly, social, and political nature of Israel and the Gentile nations.[43]

It is true that the 1970s *Body Life* phenomenon initiated by Ray Stedman and Gene Getz's focus on "one another" verses in the Bible modified the highly privatized view of classical dispensationalism.[44] But even this was not turned outward to address systemic issues in the political and economic realms.

At this point, Lesslie Newbigin astutely observes that the problem with such a purely individualistic conception is that it

> robs human history as a whole of its meaning. According to this view, the signif-

---

[43]Blaising and Bock, *Progressive Dispensationalism*, pp. 26-27. Blaising includes what he calls "revised dispensationalists" in this description as well. This reductionistic understanding of salvation may help explain John Walvoord's harangue against the soteriological emphasis of progressives when he writes, "The Scriptures, of course, do not support the idea that God's only purpose in the world is to save the elect. The Bible reveals that He is manifesting His glory, His perfections, both in the natural world and in the plan of salvation. . . . The whole theory that all kingdoms should be reduced to the soteriological equivalent is not what the Bible teaches in its doctrine of the various kingdoms." Walvoord believes that this, along with the concept that all the kingdoms are phases of one kingdom, "eliminates" any real physical, political kingdom of David if his kingdom is viewed as exclusively soteric. (See Willis and Master, *Issues*, p. 85. It seems that Walvoord's idea of what is salvific does not include the physical realities of God's creation.)

[44]Blaising and Bock, *Progressive Dispensationalism*, pp. 33-35.

icance of life in this world is exhaustively defined as the training of individual souls for heaven. Thus there can be no connected purpose running through history as a whole, but only a series of disconnected purposes for each individual life. History, on this view, would have no goal, no *telos*.[45]

It will be important for the final section of this paper to note that progressive dispensationalists are significantly moving away from this exclusively reductionistic, individualistic understanding of salvation. In fact, in his explanation of the progressive's insistence that the church is an inaugurated form of the future kingdom of God and, as such, is a manifestation of the eschatological kingdom, Blaising writes:

> The church is a manifestation of the eschatological kingdom because it is an assembly of people whom the Messiah, acting with royal authority, has put into relation with one another, bound by the inaugurated blessings of peace, righteousness, and justice through the Holy Spirit. . . . This requires recognizing that the church is a society. Its structural relationships can be analyzed sociologically. The plural, communal nature of the church constitutes the church's social reality. The issue here is that Christ intends to redeem humankind *socially* as well as individually. *The social redemption of humanity begins in the church*.[46]

Blaising goes on to suggest that structural sin in society can be addressed first by attending to social reform within the church; then "the external social work would be based in a call to Christ *in whom* individual and social conversion go hand in hand."[47]

TWO RELATED LEFTOVERS: THE LAW-GRACE DISTINCTION AND ZIONISM

Somewhat related to the issue of evangelical ecclesiology, and bearing on the recommendation of a seamless biblical story in what follows, one feature of dispensationalism that has leaked into the mindset of parishioners in many evangelical churches is a belief that people were saved in the Old Testament on the basis of works or law-keeping, while those in the New Testament are saved by grace. Not only does concern to "rightly divide the Word of Truth" rip apart Law and Gospel, but also it would probably rankle the likes of the apostle Paul. Worse, it may likely account for a degree of Marcionism with respect to the Old Testament. At the least it reinforces the contrasts between Is-

---

[45]Lesslie Newbigin, *Signs Amid the Rubble: The Purposes of God in Human History*, ed. Geoffrey Wainwright (Grand Rapids: Eerdmans, 2003), p. 24.
[46]Ibid., p. 287.
[47]Ibid., p. 288.

rael and the church, the church and the kingdom, the gospel of the kingdom and the gospel of grace, and so on.

The comments of classic dispensationalists in this regard are striking. Scofield wrote:

> Grace . . . is, therefore, constantly set in contrast to law, under which God demands righteousness from man, as under grace he gives righteousness to man. Law is connected with Moses and works; grace with Christ and faith.[48]
>
> These contrasting principles [law and grace] characterize the two most important dispensations—the Jewish and Christian. The key word to all inspired writings from Ex XX:1 to Mal IV:6 is law. The key word to all the inspired writings from the narrative of the crucifixion in the Gospels to the end of Revelation is grace. . . . It is . . . of the most vital moment to observe that Scripture never, in *any* dispensation, *mingles* these two principles. . . . Everywhere the Scriptures present law and grace in sharply contrasted spheres.[49]

It sounds as if there are two principles of salvation at work, yet dispensationalists deny this. The denial is easily lost on readers of Chafer when he writes, "with the call of Abraham and the giving of the Law . . . there are two, widely different, standardized, divine provisions whereby man, who is utterly fallen, might come into the favor of God."[50]

If this easily fosters a bifurcation of the Testaments and tends toward a kind of Marcionism, it does not foster any anti-Semitism among the dispensational crowd. In fact, they are to be faulted for going too far in the opposite direction. The stark separation of Israel and the church, along with the central role given to the Abrahamic and Davidic covenants and the millennial earthly reign of Israel has often led to *carte blanche* support for any policy enacted in favor of the modern nation state of Israel—even by the admission of dispensationalists' internal criticism.[51] Zionism and classic dispensationalism are bedfellows, and support for the movement persists to the present time in the pro-Israeli political activities of Jerry Falwell, Pat Robertson and other dispensationalists.[52] Timothy Weber carefully documents the pro-Israel dispensational network that repeatedly demonstrates the close connection between belief in biblical prophecy and certain political commitments to Israel. He reports that over one-third of Americans who support Israel do so because they believe the Jews

---

[48]*The New Scofield Bible*, p. 1115 n. 1-2.

[49]*Scofield Bible Correspondence Course*, pp. 27-28; quoted in Bass, *Backgrounds*, p. 34.

[50]From an article titled "Dispensationalism," in *Bibliotheca Sacra* 93, no. 4 (1986): 410, quoted in Bass, *Backgrounds*, p. 35.

[51]See Blaising in Blaising and Bock, *Progressive Dispensationalism*, p. 296.

[52]Ibid., p. 21. On qualifications of Robertson's inclusion at this point, see note 41.

must possess their own land before Jesus can return, and this belief is the "center of the dispensational system."[53]

Our Palestinian houseguest, who was a Wheaton graduate student, found it very difficult to understand the extreme pro-Israeli sentiments that came from two reporters in Jerusalem every Friday over the airwaves of WMBI. The dispensationalists' preference for modern Israel, even to the exclusion of their own Palestinian Christian brothers and sisters, gravely endangers the integrity of evangelical ecclesiology. Referring to an even wider systemic problem within dispensational theology, Blaising penitently admits, "By thinking of the church as a different people group, a race of humanity different from Jews and Gentiles, some earlier dispensationalists have not been as sensitive as they should have been to actually existing ethnic and cultural differences within the body of Christ today."[54]

THE RECOVERY OF A MORE ROBUST EVANGELICAL ECCLESIOLOGY

Can those of us who have been cultivated in the heritage of dispensational fundamentalism recover a more robust evangelical ecclesiology that is not dispensable and escapist, detached and docetic, separatistic and individualistic? Can we recover an ecclesiology that does not tear asunder church and the kingdom of God, law and grace, Old Testament and New Testament, the salvation of the individual and the redemption of the cosmos with its social, political and economic dimensions?

As we have mentioned, to some extent this is already taking place among progressive dispensationalists.[55] If the mindset of the populist evangelical church is any indication, it will take more time for these ideas to filter down.

Perhaps it is more promising to listen to and learn from those voices who are sympathetic to an evangelical brand of Christianity but who align themselves with the wider Christian community, particularly those in the Reformation traditions. Indeed, in the Reformation itself, with which most evangelicals want to identify, we find ample precedent to address dispensationalism's re-

[53]See Weber, *Armageddon*, pp. 11-13 and 220-34. In the final chapter of his book Weber develops an earlier point—namely, that dispensationalists' activities "run the risk of turning their predictions into self-fulfilling prophecies."
[54]Ibid., pp. 50-51.
[55]In Donald Bloesch, *The Holy Spirit: Works and Gifts* (Downers Grove, Ill.: InterVarsity Press, 2000), Bloesch notes that the Brethren movement is a cross between Reformed Pietism and dispensationalism, and the Calvinistic base helps it assimilate into the wider evangelical family (see p. 371 n. 70). This may make the way smoother for progressive dispensationalists.

striction of the church and resist its separation from the total redemptive plan begun in Adam. One need look no further than Heinrich Bullinger's treatise *Die Alt Glaub*, which was typical of the Protestant apologetic—namely, that the faith we hold today is none other than that held by our first parents in the Garden of Eden when they heard the *protoevangelion* of Genesis 3:15. In fact, I had to go no farther than the Episcopal church I attended on Holy Saturday as the deacon read,

> This is the night, when you brought our fathers, the children of Israel, out of bondage in Egypt, and led them through the Red Sea on dry land.
>
>   This is the night, when Christ broke the bonds of death and hell, and rose victorious from the grave.

It was all part of a seamless history of God's redemptive acts. Indeed, the entire Holy Saturday vigil, a practice begun well before the Reformation, has always rehearsed the saving acts of God and his repeated covenantal promises that lead up to the grand announcement, "He is risen!" That is, God has kept his promise and it has become a reality in the resurrection of the One who *is* Israel—Jesus Christ. Such a seamless and integrated salvation history is more faithful to the Christian tradition, let alone to the Lutheran, Reformed and Anglican heritages with which evangelical colleges like Wheaton and Biola and evangelical churches self-consciously seek to align themselves.

Not only will we recover a healthy ecclesiology by locating the church inextricably in the lineage of the covenanting God's faithfulness to his people throughout the biblical story, but we will also need to understand the visible church on the next street corner as a manifestation of the mystical body of Christ throughout all the ages. The nature of the church is not just a federation of local assemblies—an image perpetuated by classic dispensationalism in assertions such as a statement that the one church is "composed of the communities of Christ's people."[56] How can "ambassadors of reconciliation" preach the reconciliation of all things in Christ while they themselves cannot be reconciled to each other? How can we sing without hypocrisy "The Church's One Foundation," affirming that we are in "mystic sweet communion with those whose rest is won" when evangelicals typically retreat to their "holy huddle"? Clarence Bass puts the issue succinctly and poignantly:

> Is not the true church wider in scope than the separatist movements of twentieth-century evangelicalism have been willing to admit? Is not the *unity* of the larger fellowship in Christ more inclusive than the restricted corners of isolationism

---

[56]See ibid., p. 172.

into which some segments of evangelicalism have withdrawn themselves? Is not the fellowship which can be shared in a mutual understanding about the nature and redemptive mission of Christ more important than a restrictive fellowship that centers in a narrowly defined eschatological doctrine?

The world awaits Christ's community, the church. It awaits with its frustrations, fears, complexities, and doubts. The church exists to stand in prophetic judgment against the injustice, disharmony, arrogance, greed, pride, unbrotherliness, and sin of the world. Any theological system which causes a part of the church to withdraw from the larger fellowship in Christ and, by isolationism and separatism, to default its role, is wrong.[57]

In this spirit, it is encouraging to hear progressive dispensationalists speak of the church as the focal point of God's activity in this era of the inaugurated kingdom—as "the showcase of God's present reign through Messiah Jesus, who inaugurates the fulfillment of God's promises."[58] Craig Blaising argues that the church can speak to national justice and peace from the "base" of the future eschatological kingdom. In dispensational language, Blaising recognizes the tension between what is and what will be, and in that sense the activity of the church as a "test community" for social and political righteousness becomes an evangelistic activity:

> Progressive dispensationalism would see Christ's major activity in the world today as the formation of a remnant of people from all the nations who are His own to manifest in an inaugural way the righteousness that He will give to all peoples in that future kingdom. They are an evangelistic community, testifying to the salvific power of Jesus, which is being revealed personally and communally (socially) in the church.[59]

These are encouraging words as they move dispensationalists in the direction of an ecclesiology that overcomes past shortcomings. Indeed, they come closer to a conception of the church's relation to the coming kingdom of God that was articulated by Jacques Ellul in his insightful book *The Presence of the Kingdom*. Ellul insisted that the church must live in expectation of the coming kingdom of God and that world events only acquire their value in the light of that coming kingdom. But instead of waiting for the imminent end to come, Ellul seemed to think of the imminence of the kingdom as the church's role of bringing this coming event into the life of the present world by its actions and

---

[57]Bass, *Backgrounds*, pp. 153-54.

[58]Darrell Bock, "The Reign of the Lord Christ," in *Dispensationalism, Israel and the Church*, ed. Craig Blaising and Darrell Bock (Grand Rapids: Zondervan, 1992), p. 65, quoted in Grenz, *Millennial Maze*, p. 96.

[59]Blaising, *Progressive Dispensationalism*, p. 292.

words. Every Christian who has received the Holy Spirit is a prophet, and since the prophets of Israel always had a political part to play, in its prophetic role the Christian church performs a revolutionary mission in politics by already making actual and present the coming kingdom. Powerfully, Ellul writes:

> This, then, is the revolutionary situation: to be revolutionary is to judge the world by its present state, by actual facts, in the name of a truth which does not yet exist (but which is coming)—and it is to do so because we believe this truth to be more genuine and more real than the reality which surrounds us. Consequently it means bringing the future into the present as an explosive force. It means believing that future events are more important and more true than present events; it means understanding the present in the light of the future, dominating it by the future, in the same way as the historian dominates the past. Henceforth the revolutionary act forms part of history: it is going to create history, by inflecting it toward this future . . . the incursion of this event [of the coming kingdom] into the present is the only force capable of throwing off the dead weight of social and political institutions which are gradually crushing the life out of our present civilization. . . . To abandon this position would mean ceasing to believe that we have been saved, for we are saved by hope, through faith (Rom 8:24), and hope is precisely this eschatological force in the present world.[60]

In a similar vein, Lesslie Newbigin argues that because in Christ the powers of the new age are at work and the domain of heaven has touched that of earth, those who accept Christ come within the sphere of the operations of kingdom powers that are exercised in the world through Jesus. The new age is not simply a distant future reality; it is already here proleptically:

> The oft repeated phrase in the Christian life that the Kingdom of God is already proleptically at work means just this: the prolepsis is not a metaphysical marvel like some recent so-called experiments with time. It is the self-communication of God's will, grasped by faith here and now, which enables us already to live in the light of its final goal.[61]

But as he warns elsewhere, this only works if the end is *really* coming, for what the church now experiences eschatologically is the "shadow of the eschaton cast backwards across time," and, if the eschaton is nonexistent, then the shadow must disappear.[62] It is precisely because future kingdom realities

---

[60]Jacques Ellul, *The Presence of the Kingdom*, 2nd ed. (Colorado Springs: Helmers & Howard, 1989), pp. 38-39.
[61]Newbigin, *Signs*, p. 38; cf. p. 27.
[62]Ibid., p. 34.

are more real than the present fallen cosmos that the church's life in the eschaton's shadow makes it the locus of eschatological realities. This is no excuse for triumphalism nor for a postmillennial posture, for death separates the church's present efforts from the consummation of the kingdom. But even our efforts to overcome that which militates against God's kingdom will not be found in vain (1 Cor 15:58).[63]

The church's agenda then *is* eschatological. The future consummation of the kingdom is the reign of God in *all* affairs of his creation—a future that not only sustains the church in its present existence and activity, but makes its task necessary. If the kingdom comes where God's will is done, as Jesus taught his disciples to pray, then the church must become the present locus of eschatological realities—the portal, if you will, which becomes not merely a preview of a coming attraction, but a means through which the kingdom actually permeates the world.

Here there is no distinction between evangelism and social ministry (though William Abraham is right when he insists that the latter must never be separated from the former[64]). It is all the reclamation of enemy-occupied territory, overcoming the consequences of the Fall, fulfilling the promise of Genesis 3:15, and as church participating in the firstfruits of the redemption of the entire creation, as Paul loudly affirms in Romans 8:18-31.

The church is not some parenthetical or dispensable afterthought, then, in God's salvation history; it is the recipient of the ministry of servant Israel through whom came the Word of God into the world.[65] It was God's intention from the beginning as the fulfillment of the promises made to Eve, Noah, Abraham, David, Ezekiel, Jeremiah, Isaiah and others. It is a "kingdom of priests, God's holy nation" (cf. Ex 19:5-6 and 1 Pet 2:9-10).

---

[63]See ibid., pp. 47, 49-50.

[64]See *The Logic of Evangelism* (Grand Rapids: Eerdmans, 1989).

[65]See Bloesch, *The Holy Spirit*, p. 174, where he reminds us that in this sense dispensationalism has a ring of truth about it, reminding us that God has not abandoned his people Israel and history will not be complete until she fulfills her role in the body of Christ, and insisting that biblical revelation unfolds a drama that will eventually see God's promises fulfilled on earth as well as in heaven. We want to avoid supersessionism; see Gerald McDermott, "The Land: Evangelicals and Israel" in *Books and Culture*, March/April 2003, pp. 8-9, 40-42.

3

PRACTICING CHURCH
Evangelical Ecclesiologies at the End of Modernity

JONATHAN R. WILSON

The natural place to turn for evangelical ecclesiology at a theology conference is to evangelical theologians or to those nonevangelical theologians to whom evangelicals often look. So we might explore the work of Carl Henry, Donald Bloesch, Stanley Grenz or Veli-Matti Kärkkäinen. Or we might examine Karl Barth, Wolfhart Pannenberg, Jürgen Moltmann, T. F. Torrance, George Lindbeck or Ephraim Radner. Any one of these projects would be worthwhile and fruitful. But none would get us close to "evangelical ecclesiology."

In an article published in *Christian Century*, Jackson Carroll reports that a survey of the reading habits of evangelical clergy reveals that no theologian is among their favorite authors, no theology is among their most recently read books, and no theological journal is among their frequent reading.[1] To explore evangelical ecclesiology, we must turn to more popular authors, who tend to be other pastors and practitioners of church leadership, not theologians located in the academy, not even the evangelical academy.

Of course, *evangelical* is an equivocal term. It may be used as John Webster uses it:

> The word evangelical is not used here as a term of discrimination (over against, for example, catholic), but in a more primary sense. An evangelical theology is one which is evoked, governed and judged by the gospel. In this sense, evangelical is simply equivalent to Christian; all Christian theology, whatever its tradition, is properly speaking evangelical in that it is determined by and responsible to the good news of Jesus Christ.[2]

---

[1] Jackson W. Carroll, "Pastors' Picks: What Clergy Are Reading," *The Christian Century* (August 23, 2003). Available online: <http://www.pulpitandpew.duke.edu/pastorspicks.html>.

[2] John Webster, *Word and Church: Essays in Christian Dogmatics* (Edinburgh: T & T Clark, 2001), p. 191.

This is an entirely defensible and even commendable use of *evangelical* that I also endorse. However, *evangelical* may also be used to refer to an evangelical subculture, that much studied group whose identity is still essentially contested. This latter use of *evangelical* is the one governing my investigation of evangelical ecclesiologies, though at the conclusion of this essay I will make some suggestions about "evangelical" ecclesiology in the former sense.

To explore evangelical ecclesiology at the end of modernity, I will explore the ecclesiology implicit and explicit in four popular authors whose evangelical identity is unquestioned: Francis Schaeffer, Charles Colson, Rick Warren and Brian McLaren. The works of these authors span four decades and ministries that represent different institutional settings. I will begin with a survey that seeks as far as possible to be descriptive of these works. Then I will propose some identity markers for evangelical ecclesiology and advocate a normative understanding of evangelical ecclesiology as missional and improvisational.

FRANCIS SCHAEFFER

For many in my generation, the work of Francis Schaeffer was our passage into a larger intellectual world. In many of his writings, Schaeffer placed the church front and center.[3] In these works Schaeffer develops an explicit ecclesiology, though not in the standard form of systematic theology.

In *The Church at the End of the 20th Century,* Schaeffer begins with a cultural analysis that condenses the argument of his earlier books, *Escape from Reason* and *The God Who Is There.* As Schaeffer himself notes, this repetition reflects his commitment to rooting the church in a particular time and place (p. 5). This cultural critique then becomes the basis for an ecclesiology that recognizes the existence of "co-belligerents" with the church in the course of history, the centrality of truth in preaching and in practice, the necessity of "the orthodoxy of community," and the New Testament teaching on "form and freedom" of the church (p. 59).

In his sensitivity to the cultural situation, Schaeffer recognizes that the church's voice on injustice or politics may blend with others. In these cases, Schaeffer wants the church to be clear that these other voices are not allies but co-belligerents. He is, of course, famously concerned for "true truth" in the

---

[3]I will refer parenthetically to the following books by Francis A. Schaeffer: *The Church at the End of the 20th Century* (Downers Grove, Ill.: InterVarsity Press, 1970); idem, *The Church Before the Watching World: A Practical Ecclesiology* (Downers Grove, Ill.: InterVarsity Press, 1971); idem, *True Spirituality* (Wheaton, Ill.: Tyndale House, 1971).

context of late modernity and the subjectivism that he perceived there. But that concern for truth is not limited to propositions for Schaeffer; it extends as well to practice. This theme was perhaps Schaeffer's most significant contribution as he pushed the evangelical church beyond its comfortable practices into a hospitable and compassionate Christianity that welcomed "others"—racial minorities, drug users, dropouts and misfits.[4]

Schaeffer wrestled with two tensions in his work. One was the balance of form and freedom, in which he sought to establish the authoritative guidance of the New Testament teaching alongside the transformations necessary to fulfill the mission of the church as he saw it in a particular cultural moment. The other, more difficult, tension was the challenge of balancing the call to visible purity with the "mark of the Christian"—love.[5] In the midst of our remembering, critically and appreciatively, Schaeffer's "propositional apologetics" we must also remember that he calls "observable love" the "final apologetic": "The world . . . should be able to observe that we do love each other. Our love must have a form that the world may observe; it must be seeable" (*The Mark of the Christian*, p. 34).

Although my purpose here is not to evaluate, even briefly, Schaeffer's ministry, his achievements in evangelical ecclesiology can only be understood well against the backdrop of his own militantly separatist and fundamentalist heritage. Under the pressure of a missionary situation and in faithfulness to the gospel, Schaeffer develops an ecclesiology that goes beyond his own heritage. In Schaeffer's work we find someone who engages the world as the place of mission, not as something to be repelled or walled off. Of course, he is not the first or only evangelical to do this, but his writings develop and popularize an evangelical engagement with culture out of concern for the church's mission.[6] Second, in a missionary situation, Schaeffer engages issues about the oneness, holiness, catholicity and apostolicity of the church that were seldom problems for the fundamentalist tradition in which he had been rooted. This wrestling gave rise to some unresolved tensions in Schaeffer's ecclesiology that continue in some evangelical ecclesiologies today, but drop away from others.

---

[4]See *Church at the End of the 20th Century*, pp. 105-12; *True Spirituality*, pp. 168-71.

[5]*The Mark of the Christian* (Downers Grove, Ill.: InterVarsity Press, 1970) was first included in *The Church at the End of the 20th Century*, and then published in the same year as a separate work.

[6]Carl Henry and others had already initiated this movement of serious cultural engagement. Schaeffer does so as an evangelist and popularizer rooted in the church not the academy.

CHARLES COLSON

Twenty-two years after Schaeffer's *The Church at the End of the 20th Century*, Charles Colson and Ellen Vaughn published *The Body: Being Light in Darkness*.[7] Colson and Vaughn retrieve much that is characteristic of Schaeffer's earlier work.[8] They begin with cultural analysis to root their ecclesiology in a particular time and place. They have the same concern for co-belligerents, truth and community that characterized Schaeffer's work.[9] But in the midst of this retrieval, they also extend their ecclesiology into three additional areas.

First, they make significantly more use of church history than does Schaeffer. True, Schaeffer provided a historical narrative, but it was done primarily to show the course of culture as it rebelled against God. In *Being the Body*, the authors interweave exemplary stories from the history of the church to display the roots of our life and to guide our present and future life. The message of these examples is that we have much to learn from past centuries.

Second, the authors broaden the identity of the church they address and learn from. The global vision of the church that they display contributes wonderfully to enlarging the world of North American Christians.[10] But they also enlarge the boundaries of evangelical Christianity beyond Schaeffer to include Catholic Christianity. And in these examples, they are not merely recognizing co-belligerents but allies with whom we are to practice visible unity in action.[11]

The third change that Colson and Vaughn reflect in their work is a thicker account of the call to justice. This concern for justice is present in Schaeffer's

---

[7]Charles W. Colson with Ellen Santilli Vaughn, *The Body: Being Light in the Darkness* (Dallas: Word, 1992). An updated, post-9/11 version of the book has been issued as *Being the Body* (Dallas: W Publishing, 2003). This new edition responds to 9/11 and diagnoses the early response from the church in the U.S. as moving toward Christian faithfulness, then changing direction. It uses this turn of events to call once more for greater faithfulness in the church.

[8]This relationship between Colson's work and Schaeffer's could be pursued at many levels. For its clearest expression, compare Charles Colson and Nancy Pearcey, *How Now Shall We Live?* (Wheaton, Ill.: Tyndale, 1999), which is dedicated to Francis Schaeffer, with Schaeffer's own *How Shall We Then Live?* (Westchester, Ill.: Crossway, 1983).

[9]Although it is not central to my concern in this chapter, I must register my opposition to the use of "worldview language" by many evangelicals, including Schaeffer, Colson and Vaughn. This language is pervasive and formative. I may identify my opposition cryptically by noting that the church does not proclaim or live by a "worldview." We proclaim news of God's work of redemption centered in Jesus Christ and continuing throughout history. Christianity is not a set of ideas; it is the power of God in Christ to redeem the world. And we live in this redemption by the power and guidance of the Holy Spirit. My late professor of theology, Klaus Bockmuehl, first taught me that worldview language "will not do."

[10]I regret that the limitation of my own knowledge prevents me from incorporating insights from the church in the Southern hemisphere. I am committed to correcting that in the future.

[11]Charles Colson is, of course, one of the architects of *Evangelicals and Catholics Together*.

work, but in a thinner, nascent way. Colson and Vaughn develop it in detail and make it much more central to their account of "being light in darkness."[12]

Finally, we should note that the authors begin with the overarching concern that the church lives *coram Deo*. As they move into their exposition they assert that "what the church needs most desperately is holy fear. The passion to please God more than the culture and the community in which we spend these few, short years."[13] And they note early on the discomfort that they may cause as a result of their broad commitment to "one holy catholic and apostolic church."[14]

In *Being the Body*, the authors, perhaps consciously, follow the outline of the creed. In part one, "What Is the Church?" they exposit the oneness of the church. In part two, "The Church Against the World," the themes are really drawn from the church's holiness and catholicity (though less from the latter). Finally, in part three, "The Church in the World," the apostolicity of the church guides the equipping of the saints for ministry and mission.

RICK WARREN

Third, the purpose-driven phenomenon is well known in North American Christianity and beyond. *The Purpose-Driven Life* has sold over fifteen million copies; its success has picked up Warren's earlier book, *The Purpose-Driven Church*, and given it greater influence than it had on its initial release.[15]

In *The Purpose-Driven Church*, we move into a world very different from that of Schaeffer, Colson and Vaughn. Their ecclesiology is close to the surface of their work and the attentive reader can discern the guidance that they are drawing from Christian tradition. But it is difficult to discern any ecclesiology that guides Warren's book. This absence, or perhaps less tendentiously, this silence, implies a number of things.

Before turning to the implications of that silence, a brief digression is warranted, because the very character of Warren's book affects its impression. Warren's work is very simply written and organized. The chapters consist

---

[12]"Being light in darkness" is given even more prominence in the revised edition by the rearrangement of some chapters so that the book concludes with "Lighting the Night" and "Go Light Your Candle." This rearrangement reflects the authors' response after 9/11, but it does seem to lose some of the firm foundation of the previous edition, which concluded with "The Fear of the Lord is the Beginning" and "Coram Deo."
[13]Colson and Vaughn, *Being the Body*, p. 28.
[14]Ibid., p. 14.
[15]Rick Warren, *The Purpose-Driven Life* (Grand Rapids: Zondervan, 2002); idem, *The Purpose-Driven Church: Growth Without Compromising Your Message & Mission* (Grand Rapids: Zondervan, 1995).

mostly of bold headings and italicized statements that are also typically numbered. Text that follows these headings is repetitive; sidebars and boxes highlight portions of the text. This style carries over into content. The book consists of a compilation of Scripture verses, slogans and good advice. None of this is bad in itself, but it does beg the question of ecclesiology.

As I noted, Warren's ecclesiology may only be discerned, if at all, almost entirely in the silences. So with some caution, I will argue that Warren's work reflects the following characteristics.

First, the absence of any critical examination of culture implies that the relationship between the church and culture is unproblematic. The book does argue for cultural sensitivity, but only as a means of communicating the message to a target audience. Culture is not an impediment to faithful discipleship except insofar as we fail to understand the culture and thus fail to communicate and persuade. In short, Warren's ecclesiology is silent on "the world" as a theological challenge.

Second, the reader looks in vain for evidence in this book of the oneness, holiness and catholicity of the church. In this respect, Warren's ecclesiology shows no concern for the particularities of time and place as a theological problem. Even the theme of apostolicity, which a sympathetic reader might discern in the commitment to Scripture and discipleship, loses its significance when it is detached from any particularities, when it lacks content. There is a cultural and historical naiveté running throughout the book. This naiveté allows the author to make many assertions of the following nature: "we should never criticize any method that God is blessing,"[16] as if "God's blessing" is itself an unproblematic term.

Finally, the silences in Warren's work leave untouched the individualism of North American culture. Yes, *The Purpose-Driven Life* begins by asserting that "it's not about you." But the message of the book is that it is about you and your fulfillment. The ecclesiology implied in this book is fully expressed in the earlier book, where the church is instrumental to the fulfillment of individuals. Warren himself supports this conclusion, perhaps inadvertently, when he asserts in other writings and in interviews that his proposal is an "Intel chip" that can be inserted into many different settings.

I have written the foregoing lines knowing the sales figures for Warren's books, his widespread impact on pastors, and the testimony of many to fulfilling lives as a result of his books and seminars. But I am troubled by his unproblematic approach to our cultural and ecclesiological situation. Perhaps the

---

[16]Warren, *Purpose-Driven Life*, p. 156.

popularity of his books indicates a movement of the Spirit. But it may also be a reflection of how well his work reflects back to our culture its aspirations and "values." I pray it is the former; I fear it is the latter.

BRIAN McLAREN

In Brian McLaren's work we encounter an innovative format and creative thinking that nevertheless stand in continuity with the works we have already examined. Two of McLaren's books, *A New Kind of Christian* and *The Story We Find Ourselves In*, are fictional tales that present his vision for Christianity and the church.[17] Our focus here will be on his more expositional ecclesiology, *The Church on the Other Side*.[18] McLaren's format is similar to Warren's, with its bold text, italics and constant numbering, but its ecclesiology is significantly closer to Schaeffer, Colson and Vaughn.[19]

McLaren is sensitive to the cultural context for communicating faith but also recognizes, to a degree, the "world" as opposition to the church and gospel. For example, in an early chapter of *The Church on the Other Side*, McLaren tells us that his first writing of the chapter "implied that God, like any good modern, is interested only in individuals" (p. 34). He calls us to enlarge our vision of reality beyond the individual. In this, he perceives the cultural challenge of modernity. He then spends much of the book identifying the "postmodern matrix" of culture in which we are increasingly moving. At this point, the critical edge he exhibits toward modernity dulls quite a bit as he turns his attention to the postmodern. His approach to postmodernity begins to resemble Warren's approach to modernity: just as modernity is unproblematic for Warren, postmodernity appears to be unproblematic for McLaren.

Moving on from cultural context, McLaren exhibits an ecclesiology con-

---

[17]Brian D. McLaren, *A New Kind of Christian: A Tale of Two Friends on a Spiritual Journey* (San Francisco: Jossey-Bass, 2001); idem, *The Story We Find Ourselves In: Further Adventures of a New Kind of Christian* (San Francisco: Jossey-Bass, 2003).

[18]Brian D. McLaren, *The Church on the Other Side: Doing Ministry in the Postmodern Matrix* (Grand Rapids: Zondervan, 2000). This is a revised and expanded edition of *Reinventing Your Church*.

[19]While McLaren's ecclesiology is similar to those of Schaeffer, Colson and Vaughn, his estimate of our cultural situation differs. Where the others draw significantly on modernity for their understanding of truth and still have a lingering dependence on the Constantinian arrangement of church and culture, McLaren draws on postmodernity. For the conversation between McLaren and Colson, see <www.emergentvillage.com>. For my own evaluation of these complicated matters see Jonathan R. Wilson, *Gospel Virtues* (Downers Grove, Ill.: InterVarsity Press, 1998) for a running critique of modernity and postmodernity, and *Living Faithfully in a Fragmented World* (Harrisburg, Penn.: Trinity Press International, 1997), for an account of church-world relations.

cerned with oneness in his call to "trade-up" from traditions to tradition. He also displays great concern for the apostolicity of the church in vigorous advocacy of its mission. However, the pursuit of apostolic mission threatens to overwhelm any consideration of apostolic faithfulness. That is, where Francis Schaeffer wrestled with "form and freedom" in relation to the teaching of the New Testament, McLaren displays no such anxiety. His eighth strategy advises, "Abandon structures as they are outgrown" by "adopt[ing] a new paradigm for church structure that allows for routine reengineering based on changes in size, constituency, resources, and strategy."[20] This advice is unaccompanied by any cautions, warnings or limitations drawn from apostolic tradition.

Similarly, the ecclesiology conveyed by holiness and catholicity is muted at best in McLaren's work. There is little to nothing about the church set apart or called out as a people by God. McLaren pursues a vigorous critique of the relationship between modernity and Christianity, but even here the problem with modernity seems to be less that modernity is an expression of the "world" and more that it is passé so, thus, any ministry that presumes the culture of modernity will be outdated. Yet even more significant than the absence of the "set apartness" of the church is the absence of its set apartness *to God*. In contrast to Colson and Vaughn, who begin and end their ecclesiology with the fear of the Lord, McLaren's ecclesiology seems driven by the fear of irrelevance. Now, if the church has been called out by God to live for the sake of the world, then irrelevance is a form of unfaithfulness. But fear of irrelevance is not the foundation of ecclesiology; the fear of the Lord is.

EVANGELICAL ECCLESIOLOGY: IMPROVISATIONAL OR INSTRUMENTAL?

The preceding expositions do not form an unbroken record of family descent or a coherent narrative of continuity and development. What the preceding provides is some basis for a thesis about evangelical ecclesiology that may be able to guide us into the future.

Both the best and worst of evangelical ecclesiology are rooted in the passionate evangelical commitment to mission. This engenders flexibility that contributes significantly to the accusation that evangelicals do not have an ecclesiology. We do—but our ecclesiology is so flexible that it is difficult at times to identify an effective one.

Of course, there are times—too many of them—when ecclesiology has been

---

[20]McLaren, *Church on the Other Side*, p. 95.

entirely abandoned in favor of a mission. By this I mean that no critical reflection is taking place on the mission and its attainment. As a result, the life of the church has no implicit or explicit roots in the work of the triune God. At this point the church easily and inevitably becomes instrumental to something other than that mission given by God. Examples from history are many; examples closer to our time, likewise numerous, are also more controversial.

What we evangelicals (as a subculture) need is an evangelical ecclesiology, as an account of the church that holds us accountable to the gospel. Called into being by the good news of Jesus Christ and empowered for witness to that gospel, the evangelical church needs to maintain a *missional* ecclesiology with its commitment to mission, and concomitant flexibility while also remaining faithful to our commission. The best way to describe this and equip ourselves for faithful flexibility is to add to our missional ecclesiology an *improvisational* dimension.[21] When evangelical ecclesiology is improvisational it enables the church to fulfill its mission in changing circumstances.[22] It is wrong to think of faithful and unfaithful improvisation or successful and unsuccessful improvisation. Faithful and successful improvisation is, simply, improvisation.

The strength of evangelicalism is its willingness to adapt its practices to the demands of Christian mission. The weakness is its willingness to neglect our identity within the people of God. An improvisational ecclesiology recognizes the demands of adaptation and faithfulness, committing us to both. We must learn properly to confess in word and deed that the church is one, holy, catholic and apostolic. But what those marks mean in particular times and places requires discernment under the guidance of the Spirit.

If an attempt at improvisation is unfaithful or unsuccessful, it does not attain the status of "improvisation." Rather it becomes *instrumental*. When evan-

---

[21]The argument of this essay had begun to form when I read the following statement that brought my thoughts into sharp focus and encouraged me: "Many Protestant evangelicals are convinced that structures of institutional unity must remain open to improvisation." See Carl E. Braaten and Robert W. Jenson, eds., *In One Body through the Cross*, The Princeton Proposal for Christian Unity, A Call to the Churches from an Ecumenical Study Group (Grand Rapids: Eerdmans, 2003), p. 17. After completing this essay I discovered the use of similar terms in a different context but applied to the church in Mary McClintock Fulkerson, " 'They Will Know We are Christians by Our Regulated Improvisation': Ecclesial Hybridity and the Unity of the Church," in *The Blackwell Companion to Postmodern Theology*, ed. Graham Ward (Oxford: Blackwell, 2001), pp. 265-79.

[22]I cannot develop an argument here for improvisational ecclesiology. If I were to do so, I imagine two lines of argument. One would depend upon a proper understanding of the kingdom-church-world relations that I describe in part three of *God So Loved the World* (Baker, 2001). The other would recount the improvisations of Israel as the people of God in the Old Testament and, since the coming of Jesus, in the continuing history of the Jews.

gelical ecclesiology is instrumental then it fails to enable the church to fulfill its mission in changing circumstances. Such instrumental failure may take place by resisting change and clinging to past forms or it may take place by embracing change that disconnects the church from its life source.

In this light, our preceding exposition gives us examples of improvisational and instrumental ecclesiologies. In my judgment, the ecclesiologies of Francis Schaeffer, Charles Colson and Ellen Vaughn are examples of improvisational ecclesiology. The ecclesiology of Rick Warren is instrumental. And the ecclesiology of Brian McLaren is a still-developing attempt at improvisation. In the last case, I would hope to see further work along the way. To continue with imagery drawn from jazz, McLaren's session in the studio has developed some promising possibilities, but more rehearsal is needed. McLaren's ecclesiology is a work in progress. In a word, it is . . . well, emerging.

With these admittedly strong and unargued claims before us, we are ready to take one more step—to ask, what contributes to ecclesiological improvisation? Just as jazz requires certain skills, training and gifts, so also does, may I say it, church jazz. In this case, improvisational ecclesiology depends on some tacit dimensions that are difficult to identify and are acquired through apprenticeship and practice combined with spiritual gifts. But in addition to these intangibles, there are some clearly identifiable characteristics.

Ecclesiological improvisation is most clearly enabled by submission to the greater reality of the kingdom of God. All of our improvisers acknowledge this, though some aspects of the kingdom are muted in McLaren's work. This submission to the kingdom is taught by the tradition through the language of "one, holy, catholic and apostolic." These characteristics, rightly understood, relate the church rightly to its mission in the world and enable improvisation. Learning the language and practices of unity, holiness, catholicity and apostolicity, gives us the skills and practices to adapt creatively, respond imaginatively and perform faithfully in the midst of the changing cultures of particular times and places.

PART TWO

LOCATING THE CHURCH DOGMATICALLY

4

The Church and the Perfection of God

JOHN WEBSTER

The task of evangelical ecclesiology is to describe the relation between the gospel and the church. It is charged to investigate the sense in which the existence of a new human social order is a necessary implicate of the gospel of Jesus Christ—to ask whether the life of the Christian community is internal to the logic of the gospel or simply accessory and accidental. Are gospel and church extrinsically or internally related? The answer to those questions which I want to explore in these next two chapters can be described summarily in the following way.

I

The matter of the gospel is the free majesty of the triune God's grace in his works of creation, reconciliation and completion. Out of the plenitude and limitless perfection of his own self-originating life as Father, Son and Spirit, God determines to be God with his creatures. This directedness of God to creatures—what we call "grace"—has its eternal origin in the purpose of the Father. The Father wills that—ex nihilo—there should come into being a creaturely counterpart to the fellowship of love which is the inner life of the Holy Trinity. This purpose is put into effect by God the Son. For the Son is both the one "through whom all things were created," and the one through whom God reconciles all things to himself (Col 1:16). He is both maker and remaker of creatures, calling them into being and calling them back into being when they have fallen into estrangement from the one through whom and for whom they are made. And the divine purpose is perfected in the Spirit. The Spirit completes creatures by sustaining them in life, directing their course so that they attain their end, which is fellowship with the Father, through the Son and in the Spirit. Fellowship with God is thus the mystery of which the gospel is the open manifestation (Col 1:26).

Yet this manifestation does not simply take the form of an announcement. As manifestation it is limitlessly potent and creative; it generates an assembly, a social space (we might even say: a polity and a culture). In that space, the converting power of the gospel of reconciliation becomes visible in creaturely relations and actions. That visible form, as we shall come to see, is not a straightforward natural quantity, but is possessed of a special kind of visibility, created by Christ and Spirit and so perceptible only at their behest. Yet there is a form of creaturely assembly to which the gospel necessarily gives rise, and that form is the communion of saints.

The Christian faith is thus ecclesial because it is evangelical. But it is no less true that it is *only* because the Christian faith is evangelical that it is ecclesial; that is to say, its ecclesial character derives solely from and is wholly dependent upon the gospel's manifestation of God's sovereign purpose for his creatures. The church is because God is and acts *thus*. It is, consequently, an especial concern for evangelical ecclesiology to demonstrate not only that the church is a necessary implicate of the gospel but also that gospel and church exist in a strict and irreversible order, one in which the gospel precedes and the church follows. Much of the particular character of evangelical ecclesiology turns upon articulating in the right way the relation-in-distinction between the gospel and the church—"relation," because the gospel concerns fellowship between God and creatures; "distinction," because that fellowship, even in its mutuality, is always a miracle of unilateral grace. It is this particular modality of the encounter between God and creatures—what Christoph Schwöbel calls a "fundamental asymmetry"[1] between divine and human being and action—which I suggest is to characterize both the church's constitution and its continuing existence.

Evangelical ecclesiology is concerned to lay bare both the necessary character of the church and its necessarily derivative character. Two consequences follow. (1) An account of the gospel to which ecclesiology is purely extrinsic is thereby shown to be inadequate. Much modern Protestant theology and church life has been vitiated by the dualist assumption that the church's social form is simple externality and so indifferent, merely the apparatus for the proclamation of the Word or the occasion for faith conceived as internal spiri-

---

[1]Christoph Schwöbel, "The Creature of the Word: Recovering the Ecclesiology of the Reformers," in *On Being the Church: Essays on the Christian Community*, ed. Colin E. Gunton and Daniel W. Hardy (Edinburgh: T & T Clark, 1989), p. 120.

tual event.[2] Among some strands of evangelical Protestantism, assimilation of the voluntarism and individualism of modern political and philosophical culture has had especially corrosive effects, not only inhibiting a sense of the full ecclesial scope of the gospel but also obscuring much that should have been learned from the magisterial Reformers and their high Protestant heirs. "So powerful is participation in the church," wrote Calvin, "that it keeps us in the society of God."[3] (2) Ecclesiology may not become "first theology"; that is, the ecclesiological minimalism of much modern Protestantism cannot be corrected by an inflation of ecclesiology so that it becomes the doctrinal *substratum* of all Christian teaching. In mainstream Protestant theology of the last couple of decades, this inflation has been rapid and highly successful: among those drawing inspiration from theological "postliberalism";[4] among Lutherans who have unearthed a Catholic Luther and a catholic Lutheranism;[5] or among those who describe the church through the language of "practice."[6] The attempted reintegration of theology and the life of the church which stimulates such proposals is, of course, of capital importance; but, as we shall see, the underlying ecclesiology is commonly set out in such a way that it threatens to distort the asymmetry of gospel and church. Annexing much of its basic conceptuality from nontheological theory, it is often underdetermined by exegetical or dogmatic description, so that what is produced can appear more of an exercise in ecclesiality than an ecclesiology. A consequence (or perhaps a

---

[2]For an account of contemporary German Protestantism along these lines, see Christoph Schwöbel, "Kirche als Communio," in *Gott in Beziehung: Studien zur Dogmatik* (Tübingen: Mohr, 2002), pp. 379-435.

[3]John Calvin *Institutes of the Christian Religion* 4.1.3.

[4]A sort of ecclesiology is primary in much "Yale school" theology, though often in somewhat secularized, social scientific or ethnographic versions: see, for example, George A. Lindbeck, *The Nature of Doctrine* (London: SPCK, 1984); idem, "The Church," in *The Church in a Postliberal Age*, ed. James J. Buckley (Grand Rapids: Eerdmans, 2003), pp. 145-65; Hans W. Frei, *Types of Christian Theology* (New Haven: Yale University Press, 1992).

[5]Paradigmatically, Robert Jenson: see *Systematic Theology* (Oxford: Oxford University Press, 1999), 2:167-305; "The Church as Communio," in *The Catholicity of the Reformation*, ed. Carl Braaten and Robert Jenson (Grand Rapids: Eerdmans, 1996), pp. 1-12; "The Church and the Sacraments," in *The Cambridge Companion to Christian Doctrine*, ed. Colin E. Gunton (Cambridge: Cambridge University Press, 1997), pp. 207-25. On the larger context, see the important essay of David S. Yeago, "The Church as Polity? The Lutheran Context of Robert W. Jenson's Ecclesiology," in *Trinity, Time and Church: A Response to the Theology of Robert W. Jenson*, ed. Colin E. Gunton (Grand Rapids: Eerdmans, 2000), pp. 201-37.

[6]Notably Reinhard Hütter, *Suffering Divine Things: Theology as Church Practice* (Grand Rapids: Eerdmans, 2000); Miroslav Volf and Dorothy C. Bass, eds., *Practicing Theology: Beliefs and Practices in Christian Life* (Grand Rapids: Eerdmans, 2001); James Buckley and David Yeago, eds., *Knowing the Triune God: The Work of the Spirit in the Practices of the Church* (Grand Rapids: Eerdmans, 2001).

cause) is a rather immanentist account of the church which lacks strong interest in deploying direct language about God, since the church is the historical medium of divine action. A further consequence is heavy investment in the church as visible human communion. The derivation of the church from the gospel is, accordingly, rather remotely conceived; at best it forms a background affirmation, but one which exercises little critical or corrective force upon the way in which church practice is conceived. In short: Schleiermacher, not Barth.

The required alternative to this ecclesiological hypertrophy is not the atrophied evangelical ecclesiologies which have (not without justice) been the object of Catholic critique. The task is not that of putting the church in its place so much as recognizing the place which is proper to the doctrine of the church in an orderly unfolding of the mighty works of God. What follows is a preliminary sketch of such an account, focused on two related themes: (1) the relation of the church to the divine perfection, in which it is shown that the church is the communion of saints, the assembly of those whom God has consecrated for fellowship with himself through his works of election, reconciliation and consummation; (2) the relation of the visible life and activity of the church as human society and its invisible being as creature of Word and Spirit. As often in evangelical theology, genuine attentiveness to gospel verities entails recognizing distinctions—between God and humankind, between Christ and the church, between the works of the Holy Spirit and the testimonies of the sanctified. Such distinctions are not to the taste of most modern ecclesiology, and sometimes maligned. But they cannot simply be cast aside as the sour fruit of what Lubac called a "separated theology" of nature versus supernature;[7] some deeper account of them is surely needed. Such an account would, I think, show that—made well, under the discipline of the gospel—these distinctions can reflect the proper order of Creator and creatures, restored in Christ and consecrated to blessedness by the Spirit, and gathered now into the communion of saints as they hasten to the courts of God's glory.

II

A doctrine of the church is only as good as the doctrine of God which underlies it. This principle—which is simply the affirmation of the primacy of the doctrine of the Trinity for all Christian teaching—means that good dogmatic order requires that no moves be made in ecclesiology which do not cohere with the

---

[7]Henri de Lubac, *Catholicism: A Study of Dogma in Relation to the Corporate Destiny of Mankind* (London: Burns, Oates and Washbourne, 1950), p. 166.

church's confession of the triune God and of the character of his acts. In terms of the task of constructing a theology of the church, therefore, this means that in its ecclesiology Christian theology must be especially vigilant to ensure two things: (1) that the full scope of the Christian confession of God is operative, and not merely a selection of those divine attributes or acts which coordinate with a certain ecclesiological proposal; (2) that the norm of ecclesiology is the particular character of God as it is made known in revelation, rather than some common term in ecclesiology and theology proper (such as the term *relation,* which is almost ubiquitous in contemporary discussion). Theology must pause before beginning its ecclesiology to ensure a proper demarcation of duties between the doctrine of God and the doctrine of the church; impatience at this point will return to haunt us (as indeed it already has).

It is for this reason that I propose to start from a conception of God's perfection. The prevailing voices in ecclesiology would bid us begin elsewhere, most often in a doctrine of the economic Trinity; that they are mistaken in doing so, and that adoption of this starting-point can lead to misconstrual of the relation-in-distinction between the gospel and the church will, I hope, become evident as the argument proceeds.

What is meant by God's perfection? As I am using it in this context, God's perfection refers to God's metaphysical rather than his moral greatness. God's perfection is not only God's maximal moral goodness; it is the repleteness of his life, the fullness or completeness of his being, the entirety with which he is himself. As the perfect one, God is utterly realized, lacks nothing, and is devoid of no element of his own blessedness. From all eternity he is wholly and unceasingly fulfilled. Conceived in this way, God's perfection stands in close proximity to other divine attributes: for example, to his infinity, that is, the unrestricted character of his being and of his presence to creatures; or to his sovereignty, which is the entire effectiveness of God's righteous rule over all things. Perfection is, however, a more comprehensive concept, indicating the full majesty in which God is who he is.

The perfection of God is not primarily a formal but a material concept; it speaks to us of his life and activity. The perfection of God's *life* is the fullness of unity and relation—that is, of love—which God immanently is as Father, Son and Spirit. In that perfect circle of the unbegotten Father, the Son who is eternally begotten, and the Spirit who proceeds, God is unoriginate and therefore supremely alive with his own life. He does not receive his life at the hand of any other, and no other can modify or extend his life, for he *is* incomparably alive. The perfection of God's *acts* is the pure completeness of the divine work. Like God's life, God's acts are self-derived and therefore self-directed and self-fulfilling. There is no hiatus or insecure pause between God's purpose and its accomplishment in his work, no point at which God must call upon the assistance of other agents to bring his work to its completion. In his freedom, God may choose to consecrate other agents for his service. Yet such consecration does not indicate some lack in God, but rather the mercy with which, in his fullness, he elects to dignify creatures by electing them for his service. And God's work is wholly spontaneous and wholly effective, setting aide all resistance and reaching its end with effortless potency.

Though this conception of God's perfection may initially appear rather remote from the doctrine of the church, the ecclesiological implications are ready to hand. God's perfection is the repleteness of his life and act. But within that life and act there is a movement or turning *ad extra*, in which out of his own perfection God wills and establishes creatures. How are we to conceive the relation between God's perfection and the creaturely realm? More particularly, is God's perfection an *inclusive* or an *exclusive* perfection? To speak of inclusive perfection would be to say that the fullness of God includes as an integral element of itself some reality other than God—that, because creatures are in some way called to participate in God's life, his life is co-constituted by their participation. To speak, on the other hand, of exclusive perfection would be to say that the fullness of God is *a se* and *in se*. God's relations to that which is other than himself are real; but they are the expression of God's freedom, not of a lack, and in those relations creatures do not participate in God but are elected for fellowship and therefore summoned into God's presence. To put the question in terms of ecclesiology, is the church, as the assembly of creatures in relation to God, intrinsic to God's perfection, or externally related to God's perfect being and work? Does God's perfect being include the being of the church?

III

In order to open up these ecclesiological dimensions, we may begin by considering what has been the most important trajectory on the theology of the church over the last forty years, namely "communion ecclesiology."[8] The use

---

[8] The literature is vast, multilingual, and spans the fields of biblical and historical theology, dogmatics and ecumenics. Following J. A. Möhler's 1825 *Unity in the Church* (ET Washington, D.C.: Catholic University of America Press, 1996), the foundational modern text is Lubac's *Catholicism*—surely one of the enduring ecclesiological essays of its century. The most searching Roman Catholic account is J.-M. R. Tillard, *Church of Churches: An Ecclesiology of Communion* (Collegeville, Minn.: Liturgical Press, 1992); the most uncompromising account from a Protestant theologian is to be found in the second volume of Robert Jenson,

of the language of *koinonia* to speak of the nature of the church, its relation to God, and its place in the mystery of salvation is now pervasive. The theology of *koinonia* is generally judged to have proved itself potent in interconfessional dialogue—Anglican enthusiasm has been a decisive factor—especially because of its apparent capacity to provide a comprehensive account of the nature of the church on the basis of which particular confessional divisions (about Eucharist, ministerial order or justification, for example) can be reconceived. Moreover, its rooting of ecclesiology in a theology of revelation and salvation has offered to a range of Christian traditions the resources to develop a richer ecclesiology untrammeled by inherited inhibitions. For Roman Catholics, it has offered a context in which juridical concepts of the church can be related to the life of the church as saving mystery; for many Anglicans, it has enabled a fresh articulation of the theology of the historic episcopate as "sign" of unity; for a significant body of Lutherans, it has made possible a move away from the externalism of inherited Lutheran doctrines of the church and a reintegration of the theology of the church and the theology of salvation.

Communion ecclesiology is not so much a consistent set of doctrines as a diverse collection of approaches to topics in ecclesiology, sacramental theology and ecumenics, all bearing some strong family resemblances. For our present purposes, two aspects of communion ecclesiology call for attention: its dogmatic arrangement and its metaphysical substructure. Both turn on a key question: what is the relation of the church as creaturely communion to the perfection of the divine communion of Father, Son and Spirit?

In terms of the dogmatics of communion, we may begin from a summary statement of communion ecclesiology from one of its finest expositions, Jean-Marie Tillard's *Eglise d'Eglises:*

> *Communion* with God (himself Trinitarian *communion*) in the benefits of Salvation acquired by Christ (whose incarnation is a realistic *communion* between God and

---

Systematic Theology. The influence of J. Zizioulas, *Being as Communion: Studies in Personhood and the Church* (New York: St Vladimir's Press, 1985) is pervasive. The ecclesiology of Vatican II, *Lumen Gentium* is of central significance; on this, see Walter Kasper, "The Church as Communion: Reflections on the Guiding Ecclesiological Idea of the Second Vatican Council," in *Theology and Church* (New York: Crossroad, 1989), pp. 148-65. On ecumenical materials, see the reports by S. Wood, "Ecclesial Koinonia in Ecumenical Dialogues," *One in Christ* 30 (1994): 124-45; H. Schülte, *Die Kirche im ökumenischen Verständnis* (Paderborn: Bonifacius, 1991); G. R. Evans, *The Church and the Churches: Toward an Ecumenical Ecclesiology* (Cambridge: Cambridge University Press, 1994), pp. 291-314, and especially Nicholas Sagovsky, *Ecumenism, Christian Origins and the Practice of Communion* (Cambridge: Cambridge University Press, 2000). More generally, see Jérome Hamer, *The Church Is a Communion* (New York: Sheed and Ward, 1964); Dennis M. Doyle, *Communion Ecclesiology: Vision and Versions* (Maryknoll, N.Y.: Orbis, 2000); Christoph Schwöbel, "Kirche als Communio."

humanity) and given by his Spirit, the fraternal *communion* of the baptised (recreating the connective tissue of torn apart humanity), all of it made possible by *communion* in the once-and-for-all (irreversible) Event Jesus Christ which *communion* in the apostolic witness guarantees throughout the centuries and which the Eucharist celebrates (sacrament of *communion*). There is the Church in its substance.[9]

From that, three interlocking doctrines can be teased apart. First, the doctrine of God. The Christian doctrine of God is the doctrine of the Trinity, conceived as a *koinonia* of divine persons. God's unity is thus not undifferentiated homogeneity but the rich life of communion between Father, Son and Spirit, a communion which is mutual and open.[10]

Second, the doctrine of salvation. Made in the image of God, the end of the creature is to participate in communion with God and all other creatures. Sin is a turn against this creaturely finality, a breach of communion with God and therefore with others (the language of sin as individuality is pervasive). The end of salvation is the reintegration of human persons in communion, both with God and with others. And this end is not attained simply in an extrinsic or declaratory fashion—as it were by a divine announcement of the end of hostilities—but intrinsically: by the incarnational union of God and humanity in Jesus Christ. The Word's assumption of humanity is thus not merely a device to secure a divine sin-bearer, but the resumption of communion between God and creatures.

Third, the doctrine of the church. The incarnational communion is savingly extended in the church, for the church is intrinsic to the Christological mystery of the union between God and humanity. Christology and ecclesiology are mutually implicating. That is, the church is not simply an external assembly around the saving action of God, or an arena in which the benefits of salvation are distributed: rather, as communion it is ingredient within the mystery of salvation. In the church's communion, salvation is not so much confessed as bodied forth; the church *is* saved humankind, the social reality of salvation. Consequently, as the gathering of the new humanity into communion with God in Christ, the church is essentially visible as a form of common life and a part of the world's historical and material economy.

> [I]t is precisely as a polity—a people joined in a common life animated by the
> expectation of God's kingdom—that the church is the body of Christ, and vice-

---

[9]J.-M. R. Tillard, *Church of Churches*, p. 319.

[10]This teaching is often derived from a reading of Cappadocian Trinitarian theology, which is taken to be paradigmatic for a theology in which God's being *is* his Trinitarian communion; for some doubts on the viability of this reading of the relevant patristic texts, see A. de Halleux, "Personalisme ou Essentialisme Trinitaire chez les Pères Cappadociens?" in *Patrologie et Oecumenisme* (Leuven: Peeters, 1990), pp. 215-68.

versa. An immediate implication of this is that it is precisely as a public phenomenon—an 'outward', 'bodily', and 'visible' community—that the church is an eschatological reality, participating in the newness of the resurrection; likewise, insofar as the church bears eschatological predicates, it is precisely as a public phenomenon, as a polity, that it does so.[11]

In Eucharistic theology, this means that the Eucharist cannot be thought of as a retrospective memorial of an absent event, or an illustration of an inner spiritual transaction; rather, it *is* communion: participation in Christ, salvation present and operative and not simply indicated. In terms of the order of the community, this means that—minimally—office is indispensable to the public shape of communion in the apostolic gospel. In terms of the church's relation to the world, further, this means that the common life of the church is constitutive of the perfection of human life and culture, and hence that an ecclesiology of communion lies at the center of a comprehensive account of human social goods.[12] In short: "our faith should never make separate what God from the beginning has joined together: *sacramentum magnum in Christo et in ecclesia.*"[13]

With this we move to the second aspect of communion ecclesiology, namely its metaphysical substructure. The key text here is Henri de Lubac's (still untranslated) work *Surnaturel.*[14] Like most of the *ressourcement* thinkers, Lubac was not a philosophical theologian but an exegete of the tradition. In *Surnaturel,* however, he gave sustained attention to the borderlands of doctrine, spirituality and philosophy, and the work has had an extraordinarily wide impact on Roman Catholic[15] theology in the last fifty years: the work of figures as di-

---

[11]Yeago, "The Church as Polity?" p. 203.

[12]Most vividly articulated by David L. Schindler, *Heart of the World, Center of the Church: Communio Ecclesiology, Liberalism, and Liberation* (Edinburgh: T & T Clark, 1996); see also Robert Jenson, "Christ as Culture 1: Christ as Polity," *International Journal of Systematic Theology* 5 (2003): 323-29, and (more distantly) John Milbank, *Theology and Social Theory: Beyond Secular Reason* (Oxford: Blackwell, 1990).

[13]Lubac, *Catholicism,* p. 28.

[14]Henri de Lubac, *Surnaturel* (Paris: Aubier, 1946). For useful background here, see Fergus Kerr, *After Aquinas: Versions of Thomism* (Oxford: Blackwell, 2002), pp. 134-48.

[15]And not only Roman Catholic—as can be seen again from the work of John Milbank: see, for example, "The Name of Jesus," in *The Word Made Strange: Theology, Language, Culture* (Oxford: Blackwell, 1997), pp. 145-68; "Ecclesiology: The Last of the Last," in *Being Reconciled: Ontology and Pardon* (London: Routledge, 2002), pp. 105-37. But Milbank's thought is more tragic, and so lacks Lubac's confident and loving description of the tradition ("my ambition is simply to be [tradition's] echo—that is all. I want to share with others the recurrent thrill which comes from recognizing that impressive and undivided voice in all its modulations and all its harmonics": Henri de Lubac, *The Splendour of the Church* [London: Sheed and Ward, 1956], p. ix).

verse as von Balthasar and Milbank is unthinkable without the possibilities
which Lubac opened. For Lubac, an ecclesiology of communion—in his par-
lance, "catholicism"—stands opposed not only to a "separated theology" but
also to a "separated philosophy"—that is, a metaphysics constructed around
a systematic separation of nature from supernature. Like its more dogmatic
counterpart *Catholicism*, *Surnaturel* attempts to dismantle the edifice of Neo-
Scholastic dogmatics and apologetics which Lubac believed had been
erected on the foundation of a duality between nature and grace, a duality
absent both from the fathers and from Thomas, and which led inexorably to
the secularization of nature and its alienation from the reality of God. Nature
considered on its own comes to acquire an immanent finality, having purely
natural ends, and so as "pure" nature can be conceived apart from any transcendent ordering toward participation in God. The resultant dualisms—
between supernatural and natural, between time and history, between material form and inner substance—not only render impossible a Christian ontology of creatureliness; they also have destructive ecclesiological effects:
Christ as supernature and the church as nature as placed in a purely extrinsic
relation. Corresponding to the invention of natural philosophy, natural law
and natural theology, that is, we have in effect a natural ecclesiology, shared
by both Trent and the Reformers. In Catholic form, this natural ecclesiology
abstracts the church's hierarchical and juridical institutions from the incarnational and Eucharistic self-communication of God in Christ; in Protestant
form, it is expressed as a drastic internalism, in which the visible forms of the
church can never be anything other than secular occasions for the occurrence
of unmediated grace.

In terms of our theme, the central question raised by both the dogmatics
and the metaphysics of communion ecclesiology is this: does an ecclesiology
which starts from a theology of the perfection of God have built into it from
the beginning the corrosive dualisms which Lubac sought to expose and
which lead inexorably to an ecclesiological extrinsicism? Put the other way
round—as a question to communion ecclesiology, the matter becomes: does an
ecclesiology centered on communion of necessity compromise the imparticipable perfection of God's triune life, and so disturb the fundamental asymmetry of Christ and the church? The issues can be introduced by some critical ob-
servations on the ecclesiology of communion.

The most pressing questions to be asked concern the distinction between
God and creatures. It would be entirely improper to interpret communion ecclesiology as a systematic attempt to subsume God and creatures under a single reality of "communion." Nevertheless, the confluence of two factors—a

mistrust of the category of "pure nature," and a potent doctrine of the church's relation to God as both participatory and mediatorial—makes communion ecclesiology rather uneasy with at least some ways of speaking of the "originality" of God, that is, of God's utter difference from creatures even in his acts toward and in them. In a telling passage, Lubac suggests that "nowhere within our world is there any absolute beginning of any kind, and if, *per impossibile*, everything could be destroyed it would be impossible to create all afresh."[16] At the very least, it is not self-evident that such an account can be coordinated with an account of *creatio ex nihilo*, still less with a theology of incarnation and atonement, resurrection, Spirit, justification and sanctification. For what are such acts if not absolute beginnings, the introduction into creation of an absolute *novum*, unconditioned and unexpected?

A test case here is, of course, Christology, and especially the perfection of Christ. Because communion ecclesiology is heavily invested in a theology of the ontological union between Christ and the body of the church, it is characteristically insecure (even casual) about identifying Christological boundaries: it is not possible to determine the point at which Jesus stops and the church begins. A maximal instance is Milbank's rendering of the person and work of Christ as wholly resolvable into the church. The motive of this "ecclesiological deduction"[17] of incarnation and atonement is (presumably) the avoidance of a merely external Christology and soteriology, on the principle that "the only thing that will really remove us from extrinsicism is the primacy of ecclesiology."[18] But the result is an account of Christ and the church as co-constitutive, even, perhaps, of Christ as ecclesially constituted, and so having no substantial subjectivity proper to him. Milbank is an extreme example, but similar patterns of thought can often be found elsewhere. Thus Robert Jenson proposes that the church as the body of the risen Christ is the sole means of his presence: "That the church is the body of Christ . . . means that she is the object in the world as which the risen Christ is an object for the world, an available something as which Christ is there to be addressed and grasped. Where am I to aim my intention, to intend the risen Christ. The first answer must be: to the assembled church, and if I am in the assembly, to the gathering that surrounds me."[19] Or again: "The church with her sacraments is the object as which we may intend Christ because she is the object as which he intends himself. The relation

---

[16]Lubac, *Catholicism*, p. 145.
[17]John Milbank, "Name of Jesus," p. 159.
[18]Ibid., p. 165.
[19]Robert Jenson, *Systematic Theology*, 2:213.

between Christ as a subject and the church with her sacraments is precisely that between transcendental subjectivity and the objective self . . . the church is the risen Christ's Ego."[20] Jenson does offer a qualification to this startling statement of the identity between the church and the risen Christ in these terms: "Within the gathering we can intend the identical Christ as the sacramental elements in our midst, which are other than us. . . . [T]he church as community is the object-Christ for the world and her own members severally, in that the church as association is objectively confronted within herself by the same Christ."[21] But it is very doubtful if the distinction between Christ and the church is adequately secured by reference to the Eucharistic elements as a transcendent presence of Christ to his body: much more is needed by way of specification of Christ's personal will and action ("availability" is a curiously passive term for Christ's gratuitous and authoritative presence). And it will not do for Jenson to gesticulate at potential critics by saying that they are merely repeating "the metaphysics of Mediterranean antiquity. . . . Therefore they are in error":[22] traditions of Christian thought surely deserve a bit more pondering? Lubac is a good deal more measured.

> If God had willed to save us without our co-operation, Christ's sacrifice by itself would have sufficed. But does not the very existence of our Saviour presuppose a lengthy period of collaboration on man's part? Moreover, salvation on such terms would not have been worthy of the persons that God willed us to be. God did not desire to save mankind as a wreck is salvaged; he meant to raise up within it a life, his own life. The law of redemption is here a reproduction of the law of creation: man's cooperation was always necessary if his exalted destiny was to be reached, and his cooperation is necessary now for his redemption. Christ did not come to take our place—or rather this aspect of substitution refers only to the first stage of his work—but to enable us to raise ourselves through him to God. He came not to win for us an external pardon—that fundamentally was ours from all eternity and is presupposed by the Incarnation itself; for redemption is a mystery of love and mercy—but to change us inwardly. Thenceforth humanity was to cooperate actively in its own salvation, and that is why to the act of his sacrifice Christ joined the objective revelation of his Person and the foundation of his Church. To sum up, revelation and redemption are bound up together, and the Church is their only Tabernacle.[23]

Yet even here all is not well. "Christ did not come to take our place" is just

---

[20]Ibid., p. 215.
[21]Ibid., p. 213.
[22]Ibid., p. 215.
[23]Lubac, *Catholicism*, pp. 111-12.

possible as a rejection of pure soteriological extrinsicism; but the emphasis on collaboration and cooperation, on raising ourselves through Christ, and the hostility to "sufficient sacrifice" and "external pardon" all suggest a porous Christology, one which is a function of "the leavening of the Gospel within the Catholic community."[24]

Much more could be said along these lines: the negative effects upon Christology of an over-elaborated theology of the spousal union between Christ and the church;[25] the elevation of the church beyond creaturely status;[26] an apparent transference of agency from Christ to the church.[27] All of this, it should be remarked, is not unconnected to a decidedly thin theology of the cross. At the end of *Catholicism*, Lubac has a tantalizingly brief section on "Mysterium Crucis": "There is," he writes, "no smooth transition from a natural to a supernatural love. To find himself man must lose himself, in a spiritual dialectic as imperative in all its severity for humanity as for the individual."[28] But the cross, we should note, is quickly assimilated into the church's spirituality or ethics of self-loss; it is not explicated in terms of *solus Christus* or *sola fide*; and the Eucharistic representation of the cross is not so much a figure of the divine "ephapax" as of the enduring communion between Creator and creature.

To criticize the ecclesiology of *koinonia* along these lines is not simply to regress to the polarities of nature versus supernature: the theology of Christ's perfection surely transcends any such duality. But for evangelical ecclesiology— that is, for an account of the church which tries to sit under the governance of the gospel—the options are not restricted to either a theology of *koinonia* or the drastic dualism which Lubac and others rightly sought to scour out of modern Christianity. A fresh set of possibilities is opened for us by a dogmatics of the mutuality between God and creatures. Such a dogmatics attempts to articulate the difference between God and his human partners, not because it is infected by naturalism or extrinsicism, but because the theologies of creation and of reconciliation alike require us to conceive of the relation of God and creatures as a relation-in-distinction, that is to say, as *covenant fellowship*. Our next task is to outline some of the crucial features of such a dogmatic account.

---

[24]Ibid., p. 111.

[25]Exemplified in Schindler, *Heart of the World*, pp. 18-29.

[26]See here Susan K. Wood, "Robert Jenson's Ecclesiology from a Roman Catholic Perspective," in *Trinity, Time and Church*, ed. Colin E. Gunton (Grand Rapids: Eerdmans, 2000), pp. 178-87.

[27]Thus Lubac: "If Christ is the sacrament of god, the Church is for us the sacrament of Christ; she represents him . . . she really makes him present. She not only carries on his work, but she is his very continuation" (*Catholicism*, p. 29).

[28]Lubac, *Catholicism*, p. 206.

IV

Two things are by now clear: first, that the doctrine of the church may not be developed in such a way as to compromise the perfection of God and Christ; second, that theology cannot protect itself from the compromise by the draconian measure of eliminating the church from the economy of salvation. What is required is not a reduction of ecclesiology to a vanishing point, but a more precise specification of God's perfection, out of which an ecclesiology of fellowship can be generated. We must return, therefore, to the doctrine of God.

God is perfect; but his perfection includes a movement outward, a turning to that which is not God, as its lordly Creator, reconciler and consummator. Of this turning—wholly miraculous, beautiful beyond expression—we need to say at least three things. It is not the first but a second movement of the being of God. The first movement is the eternally mobile repose of the Holy Trinity, the life, peace and love of Father, Son and Spirit. This is the movement of God's majestic repleteness. To this movement there corresponds a further movement in which the fullness of God is the origin and continuing ground of a reality which is *outside* the life of God: "outside," not in the sense of unrelated, but in the sense of having its own integral being as a gift rather than as an extension of God's own being. This second movement, in which God wills and provides for free creaturely being, is a necessary movement. It is not *externally* necessary, for then it would not be a divine movement but a divine reaction (and therefore not divine); rather, it is internally necessary, because it flows from the eternal divine counsel to be himself also in this second movement. (2) This movement is a movement of holy love. God's holy love is the perfect integrity with which he consecrates creatures for fellowship with himself. He consecrates first by willing the creature, then by creating, by preserving the creature, by reconciling it to himself, and by directing it to its perfection. God's holiness is loving because it is not mere divine self-segregation but God's self-election for integrity in loving fellowship with what is not God; God's love is holy because it sanctifies creatures for fellowship with the Holy One. (3) This movement is, therefore, most properly and fundamentally a movement of God's grace. Grace is sovereignty directed to the creature's wellbeing. The perfection of God's lordship—his unbroken, effortless rule—is wholly to the creature's good. Through it, God wills, allows and nourishes the creature's being and so gives life.

In this second movement of holy love and grace, then, God's perfection is actual as his determination for fellowship. It is this movement which is the ground of the church. The basis of the church's being is the very simple and entirely unfathomable divine declaration: "I am the Lord your God." Expressed dogmatically, ecclesiology is a function of the election of the saints, and the first statement in ecclesiology is: *credo sanctorum communio*. Accordingly, rather than using *communion* as an ecclesiological master concept, there is much to be gained from explicating the doctrine of the church through the twin notions of election and holiness. What is gained in this way is the retention of a sense of God's perfection, and thus of the distinction of the church from God, a distinction which is the primary condition for fellowship.

In deploying these doctrines, however, we need to extricate them from some of their more familiar uses in the context of ecclesiology. Though holiness has an established place as a creedal mark of the church, it has attracted relatively little modern discussion, especially in ecumenical ecclesiology, where unity, catholicity and apostolicity have commonly been at the forefront of the discussion, because they act as markers of confessional divergences. Where the holiness of the church is discussed,[29] it is usually in the context of sanctification. However, holiness as ecclesial sanctity is properly a derivative aspect of the church's holiness; primarily, to speak of the church as holy is to indicate that it is the assembly of the elect. To be the saints is to be those summoned by the divine call: "You will be my people." This association of the church's holiness with its election entails, in turn, a refocusing of the ecclesiological use of the doctrine of election. The near-exclusive association of election with the inscrutability of divine choice in high Protestant orthodoxy meant that in ecclesiology, election served to emphasize that mere membership in the visible "mixed" church is no guarantee of eternal security. The consequence which was ready to hand was a moralization or subjectivization of election, its enclosure within the drama of Christian selfhood. This "concealed naturalism"[30] is deeply distorting, because it coverts an affirmation about God into a knot of anxiety. Most properly, election concerns the sovereign directedness of the being of God to us, the divine self-determination to summon, protect and bless a people for himself. In short, the church "stands by God's election."[31] As with holiness, the ecclesiological force of the doctrine of election is to emphasize the twofold truth of the divine originality of fellowship with God, and the directedness of the ways of God to the church as "God's own people."

What, then is meant by the church's confession, "we believe in the com-

---

[29]Authoritatively in *Lumen Gentium*, "The Call to Holiness," in *Vatican Council II: The Conciliar and Postconciliar Documents*, ed. Austin Flannery (Northport: Costello, 1987), pp. 396-402.

[30]Karl Barth, *The Theology of the Reformed Confessions* (Louisville, Ky.: Westminster John Knox, 2002), p. 142.

[31]Calvin *Institutes of the Christian Religion* 4.1.3.

munion of saints"? (1) In theological talk of the church we are in the realm of
the confession of faith. Truthful apprehension of the church's existence and nature cannot be derived from consideration of its natural history in and of itself,
but only from the knowledge of the electing and consecrating work of God.
The church exists by virtue of that work, having no naturally spontaneous
source of life and no immanent capacity to sustain itself as a spiritual company. The church's nature as the creaturely sphere in which we are in the society of God derives wholly from God's electing and consecrating presence. So
it is only in faith's knowledge of the works and ways of God that the church
can be seen for what it is: the fellowship of the saints. In formal terms, the concept of church is not deducible from or resolvable into the concept of sociality
(even Christian sociality). Though the life of the saints necessarily is a social
form, it is this only by God's choice and calling. In a sense, therefore, to confess
the communion of saints is simply to repeat the confession of God, Father, Son
and Spirit. (2) The object of the confession is the communion of *saints*. God's
saints are God's elect. God's elect are a human assembly which has its existence solely on the basis of a divine decision, not on the basis of creaturely
prestige. "It was not because you were more in number than any other people
that the Lord set his love upon you and chose you, for you were fewer than all
peoples; but it is because the Lord loves you" (Deut 7:7-8). God's election is enacted in the work of salvation, which gathers a people by extricating them
from absolute jeopardy (bringing the people out of the land of Egypt, out of
the house of bondage [Deut 5:6]; being summoned out of the condition of being "no people" into the condition of being "God's people" [1 Pet 2:10; Hos
2:23]). That work sets the newly created people of God apart from all other
possibilities, for consecration closes off any other avenues along which the
people might be; to depart from this God is simply to revert to the non-state of
being "not my people." In so doing, election places the people in the sphere of
God's blessing, since it is determination for life. And blessed in this way by
their election, the people are summoned to obedience, to live in accordance
with the law—that is, the given shape—of their nature as the people of the covenant. To sanctity as consecration there corresponds sanctity as active holiness.
(3) The object of the church's confession is the *communion* of saints. Election
generates a polity, a common life. Yet it is a common life of a distinctive kind,
not just a modulation of sociality in general. It is the communion of the saints,
and so determined at every point of its life by the shockwaves which flow from
God's reconciling work. It is regenerate, eschatological communion, common
life transfigured. At the heart of its polity is an event and presence which cannot be assimilated, of which the community is no extension, and in which it

may not participate. That event and presence is the perfect being and work of the community's Lord, the Holy One in its midst.

But what is meant by a human common life which has the Holy One in its midst? In particular: how does this common life relate to its Lord? What is the relation between the Holy One and the saints? Because the relation is most properly conceived as a relation-in-distinction, the "communion" between the church and its Lord is best articulated as *fellowship* rather than *participation*. Here we may follow the instruction to be found in Calvin's account of the union of Christ and the church. That there is such a union is for Calvin a deep truth of the gospel: "that joining together of Head and members, that indwelling of Christ in our hearts—in short, that mystical union—are accorded by us the highest degree of importance, so that Christ, having been made ours, makes us sharers with him in the gifts with which he has been endowed. We do not, therefore, contemplate him outside ourselves from afar, in order that his righteousness may be imputed to us but because we put on Christ and are engrafted into his body—in short, because he deigns to make us one with him. For this reason, we glory that we have fellowship of righteousness with him."[32] But this "fellowship of righteousness" is utterly different from the *crassa mixtura*, the gross admixture of deity and humanity which Calvin abhors in Osiander.[33] It is, rather, "spiritual bond,"[34] not "essential indwelling."[35] That is, the church's relation to Christ is a fellowship in which distance or difference is as essential as union, for it is a mutuality ordered as precedence and subsequence, giving and receiving, and so one from which any identification is excluded. Later in the *Institutes*, Calvin gives this exquisitely condensed trinitarian statement of the matter: "[A]ll those who, by the kindness of God the Father, through the work of the Holy Spirit, have entered into fellowship with Christ, are set apart as God's property and personal possession; and . . . when we are of that number we share that great grace."[36]

There are Christological ramifications here to which we will shortly turn;

---

[32]*Institutes of the Christian Religion* 3.11.10. For a somewhat different account of Calvin's theology of "non-substantial participation" in Christ, see recently Julie Canliss, "Calvin, Osiander and Participation in God," *International Journal of Systematic Theology* 6, no. 2 (2004): 169-84.

[33]Ibid.

[34]Ibid.

[35]Ibid.

[36]*Institutes of the Christian Religion* 4.1.1 (p. 1015). Further here, see G. C. Berkouwer, *The Church* (Grand Rapids: Eerdmans, 1976), pp. 77-102; Karl Barth, *Church Dogmatics* 4/2, pp. 653ff.

but before doing so, we should not fail to note that more is at stake than establishing the precise nuances of the term *koinonia*. At its core, the matter concerns the right relation of God and creatures; so, as often in fundamental ecclesiology, the ontological dimension has once again to claim our attention. Ecclesiologies which make much of the notion of communion commonly assume a particular understanding of the ontological difference between God and creation. "The patristic concept of theosis is the most precise and compendious possible evocation of the end for which God creates us. The difference of Creator and creature is indeed absolute and eternal, but precisely because God is the infinite Creator there can be no limit to the modes and degrees of creatures' promised participation in his life."[37] From this vantage point, to lay emphasis upon fellowship (rather than mutual participation) between the Holy One and the saints is simply to repeat an ontological error, one in which God and creatures are conceived in extrinsicist and therefore competitive fashion, such that they are considered to be inversely rather than directly proportional. God's infinity is conceived as exclusive, and therefore precisely *not* as infinity. But, tempting though the argument is, it collapses too much together. For, on the one hand, it is a basic entailment of the doctrine of creation ex nihilo that God and creatures are in a certain sense inversely proportional. But—on the other hand—this is not to deny *any* relation between God and creatures. Rather, it is to say, first, that at key moments in the drama of God's ways with the world—in establishing his covenants, in taking flesh, in the Son's glorification and in the outpouring of the Holy Spirit—God acts alone. And it is to say, second, that even in God's uniting himself to the communion of the saints and in his acting through the church, there is no transgression of the boundary between the Holy One and his saints. God may choose to act through creatures; in doing so, he elevates the creature but does not bestow an enduring capacity on the creature so much as consecrate it for a specific appointment. And in its acts, the creature remains wholly subservient, ministerial and ostensive. The ontological rule in ecclesiology is therefore that whatever conjunction there may be between God and his saints, it is comprehended within an ever greater dissimilarity. That, in brief, is what is meant by the saints' communion with the Lord who is the Holy One.

To sum up so far: a theology of the church needs to be undergirded by a theology of divine perfection; this is accomplished by tying ecclesiology to election, thus generating an account of the church as differentiated, asymmetrical fellowship with God. We turn finally to the Christological dimensions of God's

---

[37]Robert Jenson, "The Church as *Communio*," p. 3.

perfection in relation to the church: what does it mean for ecclesiology that God's fullness dwells in Christ?

In his extraordinary early book *The Gospel and the Catholic Church*—with Lubac's *Catholicism* one of the magisterial ecclesiological texts of the last century—Michael Ramsey argued with characteristic economy and cogency that "the meaning and ground of the church are seen in the death and resurrection of Jesus and in the mysterious sharing of the disciples in these happenings."[38] It seems, he wrote, "not only that Christ creates the Church by dying and rising again, but that within Him and especially within His death and resurrection the Church is actually present. We must search for the fact of the Church not beyond Calvary and Easter but within them."[39] "*One died for all, therefore all died.* To say that is to describe the Church of God."[40] But can this notion of the church's sharing in Christ be coordinated with an affirmation of the perfection of God? Can we say with Ramsey that "the history of the Church and the lives of the saints are acts of the biography of the Messiah"?[41]

A first line of reflection concerns the manner of Word's becoming flesh. The incarnation is a wholly unique, utterly nonreversible divine act; in it the Son of God unites himself to the man Jesus. It is an instance of itself; it is not a figure in some more general union of divinity and humanity. Its origin lies wholly outside creaturely capacity, and there is no preexisting creaturely coordinate of its occurrence. The humanity of Jesus is thus not a creaturely quantity which is annexed or commandeered by God, for then it would precede the incarnation as its creaturely condition. The incarnation is unilateral; it rests on the unqualified freedom of God to be and do this. Moreover, because it is irreversible, the incarnation is not extensible. It is categorically dissimilar from (for example) the providential presence of God in and through creatures, and has no analogies or repetitions in other realities. Nothing can qualify its insistent singularity. It is for this reason that the incarnational union is a *personal* or *hypostatic* union, not a union at the level of the natures in some general conjunction of deity and humanity. Only as such can its perfection be grasped.

This is not, of course, to deny the genuineness and integrity of the humanity of Christ, but simply to specify the conditions of its occurrence. Nor is it to deny the consubstantiality of the incarnate one with us. In Christ, God unites himself to us; but he does so only in this one person, and this one person is not the sym-

---

[38]A. Michael Ramsey, *The Gospel and the Catholic Church* (London: Longmans, Green, 1936), p. 6.
[39]Ibid., p. 19.
[40]Ibid., p. 27.
[41]Ibid., pp. 35-36.

bol of some more general communion or identity. He is the one mediator; he alone is the place of union between God and creatures. But what kind of union? It is a union in which he elects to share with us the benefits of fellowship with God. He acts as our reconciler, taking upon himself our alienation from God, and so taking it away. He assumes our humanity; but he does not do this by absorbing it into his own and so enabling us to partake of his union with the Father. Rather, he assumes our humanity by freely taking our place, being and acting in our stead. His humanity only gathers all others into itself as substitute; it includes all in itself only as it also excludes them. Whatever else may be meant by speaking of the mystery of the church as the marital union between Christ and his body, it cannot mean any subtraction of the incarnation's uniqueness.

Second: Christ's perfection is enacted in his death and resurrection. To the incarnational *filius unicus* there corresponds the soteriological *solus Christus*. In the mystery of salvation, Christ acts alone, and acts with finality and sufficiency. Of that action, no ecclesial repetition is possible, because none is needed. That the incarnate Son's death and resurrection constitute the baptismal figure of the church's existence is, of course, indisputable. But the church's dying and rising are wholly contingent on the nonrepresentable death and resurrection of its Lord. To talk of the church "entering into the movement of his self-offering" is possible only if by that we mean that the moral life-act of the church is a faint analogy to Christ's saving intervention; as a Eucharistic motif it undermines the *alien* character of Christ's person and work, and so compromises their perfection and grace.

Third, therefore, great ecclesiological significance is to be attached to the resurrection and ascension. In an important way, those events indicate the proper distance between Christ and his saints, even as the saints are "in" him. Christ's exaltation at Easter and after the forty days enacts his over-againstness to the church. The church is risen with Christ, but it is not risen as Christ. He himself is properly withdrawn at the ascension, which marks his transcendence as the enthroned Lord who is the object of the saints' worship. The saints, to be sure, are made alive together with him, and are raised up to sit with him in the heavenly places (Eph 2:5-6). But the undergirding principle here is: "by grace you have been saved" (Eph 2:5); even as the church is raised with him and sits with him in heaven, it is only as the creature of resurrection mercy and as the subject of his lordly rule. "Christ is indeed properly called the sole Head," says Calvin, "for he alone rules by his own authority and in his own name."[42] Calvin makes the point against the trespass of the re-

---

[42]*Institutes of the Christian Religion* 4.6.10.

deemer's rule which can attend some views of ministerial order in the church; but beneath it lays a theology of Christ's perfection in which, as the risen and ascended Lord who in the Spirit exhibits his benefits, he transcends the church even as he enters into intimate fellowship with it.

All this, then, amounts to a cumulative suggestion that the notion of the *totus Christus*—of Christ's completeness as inclusive of the church as his body—will be impermissible if it elides the distinction between Christ and the objects of his mercy: impermissible on the grounds of the doctrines incarnation, salvation and the exaltation of Christ. Christ, says Lubac, bears "all men within himself. . . . For the Word did not merely take a human body; his Incarnation was not a simple *corporatio* but . . . a *concorporatio*."[43] At this point, a responsible evangelical ecclesiology must beg to differ: any attempted synthesis of Christology and ecclesiology must be broken by "the all-shattering truth of *unus solus creator*."[44] Christ's perfection is not integrative or inclusive, but complete in itself, and only so extended to the saints in the work of the Spirit who shares "the immeasurable riches of his grace toward us" (Eph 2:7).

But does not this leave us with an essentially negative ecclesiology, a church without enduring, active form in the world? Is there a real ecclesial horizontal which corresponds to the incarnational and soteriological vertical? Is there a perceptible history of the saints? To those questions we shall turn in the next chapter, on the church's visibility.

---

[43]Lubac, *Catholicism*, p. 8.
[44]Barth, *Theology of the Reformed Confessions*, p. 80.

5

"THE VISIBLE ATTESTS THE INVISIBLE"

JOHN WEBSTER

$\quad$ The Body of Christ takes up physical space here on earth"[1]—thus writes Bonhoeffer at the beginning of a remarkable set of reflections on "the visible church community" in *Discipleship*. The consensus of much recent ecclesiology has been to confirm the correctness of Bonhoeffer's judgment: no ecclesiology can be adequate which does not give primacy to the church's *visibility*. In what follows, I want to propose an evangelical *sed contra:* rather than focusing on the church as a visible community of practices, contemporary ecclesiology would do well to recover a proper sense of the church's *invisibility*—that is to say, of the "spiritual" character of its visible life. And as a corollary, I suggest that the active life of the church is best understood, not as a visible realization or representation of the divine presence but as one long act of testimony—as an attestation of the perfect work of God in Christ, now irrepressibly present and effective in the Spirit's power. This combination of emphases—on the "spiritual visibility" of the church, and on the character of its acts as attestations of God—reflects an orderly account of the relation between God's perfection and creaturely being and activity, neither separating nor confusing the divine and the human. The church is the form of common human life and action which is generated by the gospel to bear witness to the perfect word and work of the triune God.

I

We begin with some analysis of the significance of the theme of the church's visibility in contemporary ecclesiology. Like the concept of communion, that of visibility is pervasive. They are, of course, correlative notions, for both are rooted in a rejection of the inherited dualisms which separate the natural his-

---

[1]Dietrich Bonhoeffer, *Discipleship* (Minneapolis: Fortress, 2001), p. 225.

tory of the church from its life in God, and both therefore refuse to sever the church as the sphere of divine grace from the public existence of the church as "political" community in time. The church's essence is participation in the divine communion; but this does not in any way entail its removal from the negotiations of temporal, social and material existence, precisely because it is as such—as a visible social form—that the church is in God. The issues could be broached in a number of ways, especially through looking at developments in ecumenical ecclesiology over the last couple of decades;[2] here, however, I want to explore Bonhoeffer's thoughts a little more, and then move to recent ecclesiological use of the notion of practice.

Bonhoeffer reflects twice on the church's visibility in *Discipleship*,[3] and on both occasions what he has to say betrays his profound mistrust of the way in which the notion of the invisibility of the church can be used to resist the church's calling by assimilating itself to or hiding itself within the civil order.[4] Unlike contemporaries such as Althaus, Hirsch or Brunner, or later existentialist Lutherans like Ebeling, Bonhoeffer insists that the church's distinction from the world necessarily takes visible, bodily form. "The followers are the visible community of faith; their discipleship is a visible act which separates them from the world—or it is not discipleship. . . . To flee into invisibility is to deny the call. Any community which wants to be invisible is no longer a community that follows him."[5] Returning to the same themes later on in the book, Bonhoeffer grounds the church's visibility in a theology of incarnation, for "the incarnation does entail the claim to space on earth, and anything that takes up space is visible. Thus the body of Jesus Christ can only be a visible body, or else it is not a body at all."[6] Why? Because "a truth, a doctrine, or a religion needs no space of its own. Such entities are bodyless. They do not go beyond being heard, learned, and understood. But the incarnate Son of God needs not only ears or even hearts; he needs actual, living

---

[2]On recent developments, see M. Tanner, "The Goal of Unity in Theological Dialogues involving Anglicans," in *Einheit der Kirche*, ed. Günther Gassmann and Peder Nørgaard-Højen (Frankfurt am Main: Lembeck 1988), pp. 69-78; idem, "The Ecumenical Future," in *The Study of Anglicanism*, ed. Stephen W. Sykes et al. (London: SPCK, 1998), pp. 427-46; M. Root, " 'Reconciled Diversity' and the Visible Church," in *Community, Unity, Communion*, ed. Colin Podmore (London: Church House 1998), pp. 237-51. From the earlier literature, see the notable essay by Max Thurian, "Visible Unity of Christians," in *Visible Unity and Tradition*, trans. W. J. Kerrigan (London: Darton, Longman and Todd, 1964), pp. 1-49.
[3]Bonhoeffer, *Discipleship*, pp. 110-15, 225-52; both sections have the same title, "The Visible Church-Community."
[4]For background, see David Yeago, "The Church as Polity?"
[5]Bonhoeffer, *Discipleship*, p. 113.
[6]Ibid., p. 225.

human beings who follow him. His community with them was something everyone could see." And "[t]he body of the exalted Lord is likewise a visible body, taking the form of the church-community."[7]

Bonhoeffer's use of spatial imagery is especially significant: in its acts of proclamation, sacrament and order, the church assumes a specific set of contours, and so claims a particular territory. The church's authority in the world, its representation of a commendable mode of human existence, does not take the form of a doctrine only but of a communal enactment in space, what Bonhoeffer calls (pointedly) "the living-space [Lebensraum] of the visible church-community."[8] "The bodily presence of the Son of God demands bodily commitment to him and with him throughout one's daily life. With all our bodily living, existence, we belong to him who took on a human body for our sake. In following him, the disciple is inseparably linked to the body of Jesus."[9] Whereas for most of his contemporary Lutherans, Christian difference was radically internalized, for Bonhoeffer the church's public, territorial character is essential to its witness, for in its visibility before the world, the church "gains space for Christ."[10]

Thus Bonhoeffer; many of the same themes can be picked up in recent theological interest in the concept of "practice" as it has been developed in social and cultural theory. Some of the discussion has concentrated on epistemological issues, above all, on how theological knowledge emerges out of the practices of the church[11]—a move not unrelated to explorations of the relation of knowledge and virtue which have preoccupied some recent philosophical writing.[12] Here it is important to note that speaking of knowledge of God as carried by Christian communal activity tends to favor a certain theology of the church, one in which the "communion of the church" is to be identified in terms of its forms of life, that is, "the specific practices that make it distinctive among human communities."[13] This stress on practices, it should be noted, is not simply empiricist, a way of getting some kind of descriptive purchase on the actualities

---

[7]Ibid., p. 226.

[8]Ibid., p. 232.

[9]Ibid.

[10]Ibid., p. 236.

[11]See chapter four, note 6 of this volume, and Bruce Marshall, Trinity and Truth (Cambridge: Cambridge University Press, 2000).

[12]See Linda Zagzebski, Virtues of the Mind (Cambridge: Cambridge University Press, 1996); Abrol Fairweather and Linda Zagzebski, eds., Virtue Epistemology: Essays on Epistemic Virtue and Responsibility (Oxford: Oxford University Press, 2001); Alasdair MacIntyre, Dependent Rational Animals: Why Human Breings Need the Virtues (London: Duckworth, 1999).

[13]James Buckley and David Yeago, eds., "Introduction: A Catholic and Evangelical Theology?" in Knowing the Triune God, p. 8.

of church life. It is, at heart, an ontological proposal, undergirded by resistance to what are taken to be modern assumptions about the dialectical relation of inner and outer, and about the way in which the "spiritual" is always tainted by being brought into association with the embodied and public. Controverting these assumptions entails refusing to separate the church as—say—pneumatological reality from its distinctive habits of discourse, its routines of practice and its shape as a temporally extended human polity.

All this is clearly companionable to Lubac's interpretation of the plight of modern ecclesiology: marred by the segregation of natural from supernatural history, it almost inevitably ends up in one or other version of ecclesiological monophysitism—the church is either purely divine or merely human. Worries like these often surface in analysis of Barth's ecclesiology.[14] Barth's doctrine of the church is generally accorded a rather cool reception. If it fails (and many of its interpreters are disposed to think that, for all its glories, it does in some measure fail), it is because Barth will not allow that the church itself is the medium or form of the gospel in the world, and so presupposes the fatal separation of the divine work of reconciliation from the human and the temporal. By thinking of the church as external to the work of the Spirit, Barth leaves himself on the one hand with a pneumatology which lacks a sufficiently concrete historical referent, and on the other hand with a doctrine of the church in which the only significant ecclesial act is that of self-transcending indication of the Word and work of God, which exist in their perfection in another, nonchurchly realm. As von Balthasar put the point (his criticism has all the more substance because of his superbly attentive and sympathetic rendering of Barth's intentions): "The greatest doubts surround what Barth means by Church. . . . Does this space, considered as a concrete reality in the world, suffice to bear witness to the presence of faith and revelation in the world?"[15]

---

[14]See, for example, N. Healy, "The Logic of Karl Barth's Ecclesiology," *Modern Theology* 10 (1994): 253-70; J. Mangina, " 'Bearing the Marks of Jesus': The Church in the Economy of Salvation in Barth and Hauerwas," *Scottish Journal of Theology* 52 (1999): 269-305; idem, "The Stranger as Sacrament: Karl Barth and the Ethics of Ecclesial Practice," *International Journal of Systematic Theology* 1 (1999): 322-39; Reinhard Hütter, *Evangelische Ethik als kirchliche Zeugnis* (Neukirchen: Neukirchener Verlag, 1993); idem, "Karl Barth's 'Dialectical Catholicism': *Sic et Non*," *Modern Theology* 16 (2000): 137-58; James Buckley, "Christian community, baptism, and the Lord's Supper," in *The Cambridge Companion to Karl Barth*, ed. John Webster (Cambridge: Cambridge University Press, 2000), pp. 195-211; Stanley Hauerwas, *With the Grain of the Universe: The Church's Witness and Natural Theology* (Grand Rapids: Brazos, 2001); John Yocum, *Ecclesial Mediation in Karl Barth* (Aldershot, U.K.: Ashgate, 2004).

[15]Hans Urs von Balthasar, *The Theology of Karl Barth: Exposition and Interpretation* (San Francisco: Ignatius, 1992), p. 245.

Now, it is by no means self-evident that the criticism of Barth stands. Barth took very seriously the "horizontal," ethical-political interests of the Reformed tradition, and had a deep commitment to the historical and ecclesial character of Christianity; to think of him as espousing a docetic ecclesiology is, at the very least, counterintuitive. Nevertheless, Barth has often served as an example of where ecclesiology ought not to go if it is to give attention to the enduring shape and active forms of the church as a human, historical reality.

From this "turn to the visible" in contemporary ecclesiology, the questions which emerge for our attention are these: Is the church the visible presence of the new creation, or merely its sign? Does the church indicate a reality which remains beyond visible form, or is the life of the church as a public body itself the temporal realization of salvation? Pursuing these questions is a matter of some importance for the ecclesiological sketch attempted here, precisely because of its orientation to the perfection of God. Does an account of the church which is governed by the theology of God's perfection inevitably underplay social and historical materiality, above all by rooting the ontology of the church in pretemporal election, and in the imparticipable person and work of the incarnate Son? Is not the inevitable result a "spiritualization" of the church, in which the church's social form is extrinsic to its being and its public life is secularized or naturalized as just so much accumulated debris? And does this not lead to an overwhelming emphasis on the *passivity* of the church, segregated as it is from the acts of Christ, of which it is always and only a recipient? Does not the church then become simply a void created by the incursion into time of pure grace as an alien power? In short: what becomes of the church's visibility?

II

We must be clear from the outset: the issue is not *whether* the church is visible, but rather, what *kind* of visibile? Nothing of what has been said so far about the perfection of God, about election or about the unique efficacy and sufficiency of the person and work of Christ should be taken as a denial of the church's visibility. What is required, however, is careful dogmatic specification of a notion of visibility, to ensure that it is demonstrably coherent with the Christian confession of God. This specification will entail (1) an account of the church's visibility as "spiritual" visibility, and (2) an account of the acts of the church as attestations of the Word and work of God.

How is the visibility of the church to be conceived? First, the primary concern of this piece of Christian teaching is not with discriminating between true believers and hypocrites. Along with the corresponding notion of "invisibility," the notion of visibility has often been used (especially in the Reformation tradition) to address the question of how to distinguish the church as the—invisible—community of believers from the—visible—church as a mixed body of saints and false professors. Thus Calvin: "Often . . . the name 'church' designates the whole multitude of men spread over the whole earth who profess to worship one God and Christ. . . . In this church are mingled many hypocrites who have nothing of Christ but the name and outward appearance. There are very many ambitious, greedy, envious persons, evil speakers, and some of quite unclean life. Such are tolerated for a time either because they cannot be convicted by a competent tribunal or because a vigorous discipline does not always flourish as it ought."[16] In the present context, however, I use *visible* in a different, though not unrelated, sense. The "visible" church is the "phenomenal" church—the church which has form, shape and endurance as a human undertaking, and which is present in the history of the world as a social project. The church is visible in the sense that, as genuine creaturely event and assembly, it does not occur in "no-space" and is not a purely eschatological polity or culture. It is what men and women do because of the gospel. The church is a human gathering; it engages in human activities (speech, washing, eating and drinking); it has customs, texts, orders, procedures and possessions, like any other visible social entity. But how does it do and have these things? It does and has these things, and so it is what it is, by virtue of the work of the Holy Spirit. Only through the Holy Spirit's empowerment is the church a human assembly; and therefore only through the same Spirit is the church visible.

The Holy Spirit is the one who brings to completion the work of reconciliation by generating and sustaining its human correspondent; in this way, the Spirit perfects creatures so that they attain that for which they were created. The work of reconciliation is triune. It has its deep ground in the eternal purpose of the Father, who wills creatures for fellowship. This purpose is established by the Son, against all creaturely defiance and in mercy upon creaturely distress, overcoming alienation and reconciling us to God. The office of the Holy Spirit is then to apply to creatures the benefits of salvation, in the sense of making actual in creaturely time and space that for which creatures have been reconciled—fellowship with God and with one another. In perfecting creatures, sanctifying them so that they come to take the form purposed by the Father and achieved for them by the Son, the Spirit is, according to the creedal confession, the "giver of life," for creatures can only "have" life in relation to God who creates and defends life. But as the life-giver, the Spirit is also confessed as "Lord." He perfects creatures through acts of transcendent freedom;

---

[16]*Institutes of the Christian Religion* 4.1.7.

he cannot be folded into creaturely causality as a kind of immanent life-force. Always he is *Spiritus creator*, renewing creaturely existence by the event of his coming, rather than simply being some sort of continuous substratum to created being. The Holy Spirit is the church's God.

This rooting of the doctrine of the church in the doctrine of the Spirit has one crucial effect. It ensures that the third element of the economy of salvation—the making real of reconciliation in human life and history—is as much a divine work as the first element (the Father's purpose) and the second (its accomplishment by the Son). In ecclesiology we are within the sphere of the perfection and sovereignty of God. There can be no sense in which, whilst God's first and second works are pure grace, his third work involves some kind of coordination of divine and creaturely elements. The history of the application within the creaturely realm of God's reconciling will and deed—that is, the history of the church—is the history of the new creation, the history of the resurrection of the dead. The reality out of which the church emerges, and in which alone it always stands, is: You he made alive. This sheer gratuity is fundamental to the church's being: it is what it is because in the Holy Spirit God has completed the circle of his electing and reconciling work, and consummated his purpose of gathering the church to himself. The church, therefore, is natural history only because it is spiritual history, history by the Spirit's grace. And so also for the church's visibility: it is through the Spirit's work alone that the church becomes visible, and its visibility is therefore a "special" or "spiritual visibility," created by the Spirit and revealed by the Spirit.[17]

More closely described, the church's visibility has its center outside itself, in the ever-fresh coming of the Spirit. The "phenomenal" form of the church is therefore the phenomenal form of the *church* only in reference to the Spirit's self-gift. The phenomena of church life—words, rites, orders, history and the rest—do not automatically, as it were *ex opere operato*, constitute the communion of saints; rather, the church becomes what it is as the Spirit animates the forms so that they indicate the presence of God. This is not to fall into the trap famously identified by Cardinal Bellarmine—"they imagine two churches": a visible casing to an inner "spiritual" reality. If visible phenomena are not in and of themselves the final truth of the church, that is not because they are phenomena and therefore unspiritual, secular, pure nature. It is rather because of the kind of phenomena that they are: they are indications of the presence of the Spirit who bears Christ to the church and the world and so fulfills the Father's purpose. And so if the phenomena of the church really are the church's visibility, this is not be-

---

[17]See here Karl Barth, *Church Dogmatics* 4/1, pp. 656-58; 4/2, p. 619; 4/3, p. 726.

cause they constitute a "true epiphany of God's reign in the flesh-and-blood community of the faithful."[18] It is, rather, because through the Spirit they are consecrated, taken up into God's service as the witnesses to his presence and act.

It is for this reason that knowledge of the church cannot be derived in a straightforward way by deduction from its visible phenomena and practices. Once again, this is not because "phenomena" in and of themselves somehow obscure the "real" internal work of the Spirit. It is, instead, because only through the Spirit's agency are the phenomena to be grasped as phenomena of the *church*. The church is known as God is known, in the knowledge which comes from God's self-communicative presence, of which the human coordinate is faith. Only in this spiritual knowledge is the church known and its phenomena seen as what they are. Faith does not, of course, perceive a different, "hidden," set of phenomena, behind the natural-historical realities of the church's visible acts. It sees those acts as what they are: attestations of God. "We need not . . . see the church with the eyes or touch it with the hands," writes Calvin.[19] Why? Not because behind dead nature there lurks the real, supernatural, invisible and intangible church. Indeed, it is only in the church's visible human instrumentality, in the voice of its teachers, for example, that God chooses to be heard. Calvin is very far indeed from any principled separation of the sensible from the spiritual. Rather, the church is visible to the perception of faith, for it is to faith that the church steps out of the obscurity and indefiniteness of an historical phenomenon and becomes fully and properly visible as the creature of the Spirit. "[T]he fact that it belongs to the realm of faith should warn us to regard it no less since it passes our understanding than if it were already visible."[20]

The visibility of the church is thus spiritual event, spiritually discerned. This is not to espouse an ecclesiological occasionalism, as if the church lacks a durable identity and is simply a string of discreet moments in which the Spirit from above seizes dead forms and gives them temporary animation. That would be to deny that the Spirit really is promised and really is given to the church. But how promised and how given? Not in a way which is convertible into something immanent to the church or something which the church fills out or realizes in its action. The Spirit is promised and given as Lord and giver of life. And as Lord and giver of life he is other than the church, the one in whom the church has faith, to whom the church is obedient, and for the event

---

[18]Yeago, "The Church as Polity?" p. 229.
[19]*Institutes of the Christian Religion* 4.1.3.
[20]Ibid.

of whose coming the church must pray, *Veni, Spiritus creator.*

To sum up, the church is visible through the work of the Holy Spirit. Its life and acts are the life and acts of the communion of the saints by virtue of the animating power of the invisible Spirit, and known as such by the revealing power of the invisible Spirit. Such an account of the church's visibility attempts to govern itself according to the fundamental norm of ecclesiology, namely the perfection of God in his works toward the saints. This perfection is as true in pneumatology as elsewhere; the outpouring of the Spirit, his gracious descent upon the community, is not a breach of the Spirit's integrity. But this norm does not assume a secularization of the church through a separation of inner from outer. It simply acknowledges that the Spirit's life-giving and revelatory agency is fundamental to the church's being, including its visibility in creaturely time and space. The church is and is visible because God the Holy Spirit is and acts.

III

If this is the way in which the church "takes up space on earth," then what is to be said of the basic shape of the church's action? What *kind* of visibility does the church have? The suggestion I wish to explore is that the active visibility of the church consists in attestations of the Word and work of the God who is its Creator, reconciler and consummator.[21] In speaking of the acts of the church as acts of attestation or witness, we are trying to answer the question: what is the relation between the visible undertakings of the church and their ground in the perfect work of God? In view of the perfection of God's grace, and in view of the special visibility which the church has on the basis of the fact that it exists in that grace, the notion of witness tries to express the permanently derivative character of the work of the church.

We may orient our explanation of this by returning to the doctrine of election. The church of Jesus Christ is a "chosen race" (1 Pet 2:9). It exists by virtue of the unshakably strong declaration of the Son in which the eternal resolve of the Father is realized: "You did not choose me; I chose you" (Jn 15:16). This

---

[21]On the ecclesiological primacy of witness, see *Church Dogmatics* 4/3, pp. 843ff.; Karl Barth, "The Christian as Witness," in *God in Action* (Edinburgh: T & T Clark, 1936), pp. 94-118; Christoph Schwöbel, "Kirche als Communio," in *Gott in Beziehung: Studien zur Dogmatik* (Tübingen: Mohr, 2002); idem, "The Creature of the Word," in *On Being the Church: Essays on the Christian Community,* ed. Colin E. Gunton and Daniel W. Hardy (Edinburgh: T & T Clark, 1989). See also T. F. Torrance's deployment of the somewhat similar notion of "hypodeigma," in *Royal Priesthood: A Theology of Ordained Ministry* (Edinburgh: T & T Clark, 1993), pp. 94-97—though Torrance envisages a good deal more continuity between divine and human action than I am suggesting here.

being the case, the church is characterized by a particular dynamic or movement. This dynamic is its origin in the determination of God the Father, whose purpose is set forth in the Son and brought to human fruition in the work of the Holy Spirit. Its origin in the divine resolve is what gives the church its specific character, which is fundamentally not one of communion, still less one which is a form of practice, but rather a dynamic of *being chosen*. Divine election, as it unfurls in the economy of God's grace, must not be thought of simply as a background or preliminary reality, perhaps the church's ultimate ground or origin but not an operative factor in giving an account of what the church actually does. Quite the contrary: the dynamic of being chosen determines the modes of common life and activity in which the church is visible. Its forms of life, its principal activities—all the ways in which it disposes of itself in time and space—have to be such that they partake of a reference to the election of God.

A number of demarcations follow from this. First, if the visible life of the church does have this definite and specific dynamic, then a general phenomenology of sociality will not prove particularly serviceable in setting out a doctrine of the church. Some recent ecclesiology has been (alarmingly) relaxed at this point, making free use of social or ethical or cultural theory to frame an account of the church to which talk of divine action is then rather loosely attached. But election and its outworking in the mighty acts of God through which the saints are gathered is not patent of ethnographic or pragmatic description. That is not because the life of the saints is not visible, but because it is spiritually visible, and therefore can be described only by reference to the work of God. Second, the application of the language of "practice" is similarly restricted in a theology of the church, most of all because it can drift into immanentism, in which the doctrine of God threatens to become a function of the church. A representative account suggests that in an ecclesiology oriented to church practices, there is *"one single starting-point:* in the Spirit, beginning with God's action and beginning with the Church and its practices are *one* beginning, in a unity in which the divine and the human are neither divided nor confused."[22] But "Spirit" here becomes broadly identifiable with the acts of the church; the "without confusion" can carry no real weight if Spirit and church together constitute "one beginning"; and the referential objectivity of the church's acts is thereby in some measure threatened.[23] Third, even more di-

---

[22]Buckley and Yeago, eds., "Introduction: A Catholic and Evangelical Theology?" pp. 17-18.
[23]See here N. Healy, "Practices and the New Ecclesiology: Misplaced Concreteness?" *International Journal of Systematic Theology* 5 (2003): 287-308.

rectly theological language of the church's acts as epiphany, realization or mediation of the acts of God is not fully adequate to secure this reference. Such language certainly has a long tradition of usage across the confessions, and ought not to be discarded lightly. And it is genuinely theological, far from the easy pragmatic immanentism which can afflict some theologies of the visible church. Nevertheless it can unravel rather quickly (this often happens when it is used in the context of sacramental theology or the theology of ministerial order). Only with some real vigilance can it be used without some damage to the proper distinction between *opus Dei* and *opus hominum*. Otherwise, the purity and sufficiency of the work of God is in some measure broken down; divine agency, if not suspended, is at least relegated to background status and so in some measure inhibited.

What, by contrast, is involved in speaking of the church's acts as *attestations* of the Word and work of God? Testimony is astonished indication. Arrested by the wholly disorienting grace of God in Christ and the Spirit, the church simply *points*. It is not identical or continuous with that to which it bears witness, for otherwise its testimony would be self-testimony and therefore false. Nor is its testimony an action which effects that which it indicates; the witness of the church is an ostensive, not an effective, sign; it indicates the inherent, achieved effectiveness which the object of testimony has in itself. Strictly subordinate to that which it is appointed and empowered to indicate, raised up not to participate in, extend or realize a reality which lies quite outside itself, the church lifts up its voice and says, Behold the Lamb of God who takes way the sin of the world. As Barth says of John the Baptist (probably Barth's favorite biblical character): "for the very reason that he is a genuine witness. [He] only makes reference to another. He has no subsistence of his own. He is without importance of his own. He only functions as he bears witness of another and points away from himself to another."[24] Crucially, that to which the church's acts point is not something inert—locked in the past or in transcendence. The church points to the prevenient perfection of the triune God. It witnesses to God the Father's omnipotently effective purpose which in Jesus Christ has broken through the realm of deceit and opposition, which is now supremely real and limitlessly active in his risen presence, and which is unleashed with converting power in the Spirit of Christ. Of all this, the church is an attestation.

Developing a theology of the church's visible acts along these lines carries with it the considerable advantage of avoiding the transference of agency from God to the church. It ensures a conception of the church's action in which the

---

[24]Barth, "The Christian as Witness," p. 107.

work of God is not a reality awaiting completion, but a *perfectum* of unrestricted, self-realizing power. Yet this does not mean a reduction of the church to pure passivity, so that its only visible feature is emptiness, waiting upon the self-presenting Word of God. Attestation is human activity bent to the service of God. If the church takes with full seriousness that to which it bears witness, it is not indolent or irresponsible, precisely because the gospel is a summons. But it is a summons to act in particular ways which are shaped by the truth of the gospel. That means that the church is appointed to visible activity which is in accordance with the given fact that the world is the sphere in which the triune God's antecedent grace is wholly victorious and resplendent. To act in accordance with that given fact is, indeed, to *act*: think, speak, judge, assemble, celebrate, suffer, heal, share, bless. But such actions have no center in themselves, no pure spontaneity. They are acts that arise from trust and hope in the action of God in Christ now present through the Spirit. They are wholly defined by the basic statement which underlies and conditions all other statements about the church: the Holy One is in your midst. The church *is* by virtue of the being and acts of another; and its acts are enabled by and witness to the one to whom the church owes itself and toward whom it is an unceasing turning.

IV

The concrete forms of the church's attestation of the gospel are the proclamation of the Word and the celebration of the sacraments. In Word and sacraments, the church sets forth the presence and activity of the living Jesus Christ. Word and sacrament are not "realizations" of Jesus Christ's work, for in the Holy Spirit he is self-realizing. They are, rather, a reference to his being and his work, a work which has been achieved with royal freedom and full effectiveness, and which now sets itself before the church in its converting effect. Word and sacrament are the church's visible acts which let God act.

Time does not permit anything like a full account of the theology of Word and sacrament, and I want to restrict myself to some theological remarks about the ministry of the Word in the church. I do so not to fall in with the sacramental minimalism which has attached itself to some bits of the evangelical tradition. Often espoused as a reaction to what is perceived to be lush sacramentalism, this minimalism is deeply disruptive of the church's exposure to the gospel, and all too often goes along with a dreary moralization of the Christian faith. Here I want to concentrate on Word for a couple of reasons. First, modern ecumenical ecclesiology has shown surprisingly little interest in the topic, and tends to have concentrated its energies elsewhere, on the sacraments (especially the Eucharist) and on the theology of ministerial order. An effect of this has been to promote a theology of the church in which the ministry of the Word does not always play a determinative role in understanding the character of the church's action. Sacramental agency has usually been assumed to be paradigmatic of the church's action, and fundamental questions about the relation of God's work to the work of the church have commonly been approached by trying to sort out a number of issues in Eucharistic theology (a good example is discussion of the "sacrificial" character of the Eucharist as the quintessential ecclesial act). The result is that "Eucharistic ecclesiology" presents itself as self-evidently normative, and I hope to redress the balance a little. My second reason for focusing on the ministry of the Word is that evangelical ecclesiology has a serious dogmatic task to undertake in this matter. To speak of the church as the "community of the Word" involves a good deal more than routine affirmations of the authority of the Bible and the importance of preaching in the church. It rests upon some primary Christological affirmations, affirmations which effect a recharacterization of the church as the community which witnesses to the prevenient presence of the Word of God.

At the beginning of the apocalypse, John writes thus:

> I was in the spirit on the Lord's day, and I heard behind me a loud voice like a trumpet. . . . Then I turned to see whose voice it was that spoke to me, and on turning I saw seven golden lampstands, and in the midst of the lampstands I saw one like the Son of Man, clothed with a long robe and with a golden sash across his chest. His head and his hair were white as white wool, white as snow; his eyes were like a flame of fire, his feet were like burnished bronze, refined as in a furnace, and his voice was like the sound of many waters. In his right hand he held seven stars, and from his mouth came a sharp, two-edged sword, and his face was like the sun shining with full force. When I saw him, I fell at his feet as though dead. But he placed his right hand on me, saying, "Do not be afraid; I am the first and the last, and the living one. I was dead, and see, I am alive forever and ever; and I have the keys of Death and of Hades." (Rev 1:10, 12-18)

What instruction might we receive here for our understanding of the church as the communion of saints which—like John the seer—bears witness to the Word of God (Rev 1:2)?

Jesus Christ is alive, gloriously and resplendently alive, because alive with the life of God. He is risen from the dead, and so he is neither inert nor absent, neither a piece of the past nor one who possesses himself in solitude and remoteness: he is majestically and spontaneously present. And this presence of his is communicative or revelatory, in a way which is wholly free, self-originating and authoritative: he presents himself in royal power and glory, and with axiomatic certainty. He is life and therefore presence. There is no creaturely initiative here; his self-communication is prior to any human seeking. The "loud voice" which John hears (Rev 1:10) is "behind" him, anterior to him; John "turns" (Rev 1:12) to the voice which is already addressing itself to him; the voice is not the voice of a creature but "the sound of many waters" (Rev 1:15); from the mouth of the speaker there issues no human speech but the "sharp two-edged sword" of divine judgment. To see and hear this one is to be utterly overwhelmed: "I fell at his feet as though dead" (Rev 1:17). But the Son of Man does not slay; he *speaks.* And as he speaks, he declares himself: "I am the first and the last, and the living one; I died, and behold I am alive for evermore, and I have the keys of Death and Hades" (Rev 1:17-18). He declares himself to be present to all times and places, catholically real because infinitely alive, spreading abroad the knowledge of himself and of his own repleteness.

Why begin here? Because what John describes is the fundamental situation of the church which seeks to testify to the Word of God. The church is the assembly which is addressed by this Son of Man. The situation in which the church speaks is, therefore, not one in which the church is as it were called upon to fill a silence, or to take some initiative in order to communicate Jesus Christ. No, it is a situation in which this Son of Man, undefeated and alive, is in the church's midst (Rev 1:13), not on the periphery, and is already lifting up his voice and making himself known. The church speaks, because it has been spoken to. Only because there is a word from this Son of Man—only, that is, because there is a Word of God—is there a word to be uttered by the church. And this word of the church is therefore nothing other than "witness to the Word of God" (Rev 1:2). In its word, the church does not activate, demonstrate or justify the Word which has already been spoken; it simply attests that Word in its inherent clarity and self-demonstration, announcing what has already been announced with kingly power.

This, then, is the fundamental dynamic of the Word in the church; this is what occurs when the church hears the announcement of the gospel in Holy Scripture and attests what it hears. For Jesus Christ, the church's Lord, announces himself to the communion of saints in the canon of Holy Scripture. In the words of the prophets and apostles, Jesus Christ declares himself. The crucial factor here is Jesus Christ's personal, nontransferable agency—that is, the fact that he *himself* declares himself. At his glorification to the Father's right hand, Jesus Christ does not resign his office of self-communication, handing it over to the texts of Scripture which are henceforth in and of themselves his voice in the world. Rather, in the texts of Holy Scripture, the living One himself speaks: Scripture is his prophet and his apostle. Holy Scripture is "holy" because it is sanctified: that is, it is set apart by God for the service of his self-announcement. Scripture is the elect, consecrated auxiliary through which the living One walks among the churches and makes known his presence. For this reason, Scripture is a transcendent moment in the life of the church. Scripture is not the church's book, something internal to the community's discursive practices; what the church hears in Scripture is not its own voice. It is not a store of common meanings or a Christian cultural code—and if it engenders those things, it is only because Scripture is that in which Jesus Christ through the Spirit is pleased to utter the *viva vox Dei*. Consecrated by God for the purpose of Christ's self-manifestation, Holy Scripture is always intrusive, in a deep sense *alien*, to the life of the church.

All this is to say that the church assembles around the revelatory self-presence of God in Christ through the Spirit, borne to the communion of saints by the writings of the prophets and apostles. This divine revelation is "isolated"[25]—that is, it is a self-generating and self-completing event. God is known by God alone: this is central to a proper understanding of the church's relation to Scripture. Scripture is not to be thought of as one element of a movement of revelation which is completed by the church's acts of reception and interpretation. Scripture is not an initial stage of a process of divine communication which is only fully realized in the life of the church—whether that life be conceived through a theological notion of tradition or through hermeneutical notions such as readerly reception. Scripture bears witness to divine revelation in its perfection. It is for this reason that Holy Scripture is to be spoken of as possessing the properties of clarity and sufficiency. Both these ways of speaking of Scripture emphasize the completeness of Scripture, the fact that in Scripture the church encounters a fully achieved divine communication: in this sense, they are parallel to the sacramental notion of "real presence." Of course, neither "real presence" nor scriptural clarity and sufficiency eliminate creaturely acts of reception. But they do reorder those creaturely acts. So when, therefore, the church "interprets" Scripture, it does not bestow upon Scripture a clarity which Scripture does not already possess, or bring about a completion of the event of revelation of which Scripture is only the precipitating occasion. Interpretation is not clarification or completion, but recognition, assent to the inherent clarity and adequacy of the prophetic and apostolic witness which bears to us the voice of the church's Lord.

The effect of this is clearly a rather drastic revision of some habitual ways of thinking of the church's relation to the Word. The Word is not *in* the church but announced *to* the church through Holy Scripture. The church is therefore

---

[25]The word is Barth's, from *The Theology of the Reformed Confessions*, pp. 48-49, 56.

not first and foremost a speaking but a hearing community. John the seer says that he turned to the voice that was speaking to him (Rev 1:12); and there are few more succinct statements of the primary dynamic of the Christian assembly. The church *is* that turning. And, further, in making that movement, in fear and trembling, falling at the feet of the Son of Man, the church receives its appointment to a specific task: it is summoned to speech.

But what is the character of its speech? If Jesus Christ is the prophet of his own presence through the texts of the canon, then the speech of the church is an indication or attestation of what he himself says. The church's speech is a second—not a first—move, a responsive act whose aim is achieved when it draws attention, not to what it says itself, but to what it has heard. In concrete terms, this means that the primary public language of the church is the exegesis of Holy Scripture. Exegesis is the attempt to listen to the voice of the Son of Man who "walks among the seven golden lampstands," to hear "the words of him who has the sharp two-edged sword" (Rev 2:1, 12). Christian exegesis of Scripture is neither textual archaeology nor hermeneutical revitalization, because the canon is not a lumber-room of obscure historical data or religious meaning which needs to be unearthed by exegetical or interpretative skill. Both these approaches make the mistake of naturalizing Scripture by extracting it from its place in the communicative economy of Christ and Spirit. Christian exegesis is, properly, listening to the address of Christ in his prophets and apostles, and trying to indicate what has been heard of him through their testimonies. "[A] holy exposition doth give a setting out to the word of God, and bringeth forth much fruit to the Godly hearer," says Bullinger in the *Decades*.[26] His term "setting out" catches exactly the way in which the church's public speech, rooted in its attention to the scriptural declaration, is an attestation of what has been spoken to the communion of saints. To "set out" the Word is not to attempt to extend, enlighten or otherwise improve upon what has been said, as if it required to be made more manifest by some ingenuity on the church's part. Rather, it is simply to let the Word stand as what it is, and therefore to be placed beneath its governance.

My suggestion, therefore, is that as the community of the Word the church will be characterized in all its speaking by a deference to Holy Scripture. Of that deference, the primary expression is the church's act of reading so that it may bear testimony to what has been announced. Deferential reading of the Word—listening to and "setting out" the words of Jesus Christ's apostles and prophets—is the paradigmatic instance of the church's activity as a commu-

---

[26]H. Bullinger, *Decades I and II* (Cambridge: Cambridge University Press, 1849), p. 72.

nity of attestation. This deference, it ought to be added, is not simply secured by a doctrine of scriptural authority. Such a doctrine is necessary, but it cannot be expected to bear the whole weight of the church's life in the Word of God. The church will demonstrate that it is a community of the Word not simply by formal affirmations about the nature of Holy Scripture, important though they are, but by setting itself beneath Holy Scripture as the law by which its mind and actions are ruled. The church's relation to Scripture cannot be settled once and for all by a theology of biblical authority and inspiration—and if we think that it can be so settled, we run the risk of arresting that movement in which the church has its being: that ceaseless turn to the voice of its Lord, and that echoing act of witness.

V

In closing, some summary thoughts on evangelical ecclesiology.

First, evangelicals need an ecclesiology, and the ecclesiology they need is an evangelical ecclesiology, for the gospel is ecclesial. But an ecclesiology has to be a good deal more than a set of inchoate instincts which grab hold of whatever bits of doctrine float in their direction. A properly evangelical ecclesiology has to take its place within the scope of doctrinal affirmations which spell out the Christian confession of God, Christ, the Spirit, election, reconciliation, sanctification and the rest. Evangelical Christianity is nowadays sometimes tempted to think that the remedy for its instinctive ecclesiological indifference or minimalism is to move upmarket. The evangelical tradition has latterly been alarmingly undiscriminating—in its very open attitude to socially immanent theories of atonement, for example, or in its enthusiasm for the concept of "relationality" as a theological panacea. But the evangelical tradition surely has more to offer to catholic Christianity than a soft-focus version of the contemporary ecclesiological consensus. Is it too much to hope that the evangelical tradition will dig a little deeper into the theology of grace? Barth warned Roman Catholics around the time of Vatican II to beware lest they became liberal Protestants; my worry is that evangelicals will become catholicized Protestants who make the mistake of thinking that the only ecclesiological improvement upon individualism and "soul liberty" is a rather ill-digested theology of the *totus Christus*.

Second, in the present unreconciled state of the churches, evangelicals need to offer what they have received from their own traditions to the wider fellowship of the saints. They must do so without stridency or anxiety, with humble confidence and generosity, with attentiveness and a teachable bearing toward those from whom they find themselves separated by reason of confession. But these things can only happen if evangelicals take the time to reacquaint themselves with the deep exegetical and dogmatic foundations of the traditions to which they belong; and, more important still, they can only happen if evangelicals demonstrate the supreme ecumenical virtue of acknowledging that we also need to change. This, at least, the churches in the Reformation tradition ought to know—*ecclesia reformanda, quia reformata:* having been reformed, the church still needs to be reformed.

Third, ecclesiology is secondary. The life of the fellowship of the saints comes first, because it is in that fellowship that we keep company with God. The renewal of the fellowship of the church is not a matter for dogmatics, but for the invocation of the church's God. And that is why we may fittingly close with this prayer: "Almighty God, we beseech thee graciously to behold this thy family, for which our Lord Jesus Christ was contented to be betrayed, and given up into the hands of wicked men, and to suffer death upon the cross, who now liveth and reigneth with thee and the Holy Ghost, ever one God, world without end."

6

THE CHURCH AS MISSIONAL COMMUNITY

DARRELL L. GUDER

The research project that generated the book *Missional Church*, published in 1998, must be held accountable, it appears, for the rapid spread of the term *missional* in many circles of discussion dealing with the situation of the church in North America.[1] Our research team chose the term precisely because it was a relatively unknown word. We wanted to stimulate a theological conversation about the church which took seriously the premise that, to use the language of Vatican II, "the church is missionary by its very nature."[2] Within the Gospel and Our Culture Network, which sponsored that particular project, this was our working consensus.[3] We needed, somehow, to find a way to talk about the fundamentally missional nature of the church without using terms freighted with all kinds of baggage. By proposing the term "missional" we wanted to claim the right to define what it means. Of course, since then the word has taken on so many meanings that any discussion must always begin with yet another clarification of terms! It is almost comparable to the terminological confusion that always surrounds the term "evangelical," for perhaps many of the same reasons.

Proliferation of possible meanings for the word "missional" complicates the terminological challenge we face when we approach the task of doing an "evangelical ecclesiology." The modern missionary movement of the last three centuries has generated a lot of vocabulary. It has restored the term "mission" to Western theological discourse, along with "missionary" and "missioner,"

---

[1]The term is not a neologism (the *Oxford English Dictionary* records its first usage in English in 1907), but has been rarely used until the last few years. See Darrell Guder et al., eds., *Missional Church: A Vision for the Sending of the Church in North America* (Grand Rapids: Eerdmans, 1998).
[2]See *Ad Gentes* 1; *Lumen Gentium* 1.
[3]See <www.gocn.org>.

"mission society," "mission field" and the problematic plural term "missions." And it fostered that more intimidating neologism, "missiology." Here in the West, in the old territories of established Christianity whose history and complexities we lump together under the term "Christendom," the emergence of the term "evangelism" parallels the growth of mission language. For centuries, Western Christendom rarely spoke of "mission," except as a technical term used by medieval theologians to discuss the internal dynamics of the Trinity. We had no need for a verb such as "to evangelize," if we could assume that everyone was a Christian by virtue of birth, baptism, social conditioning and geography. One still finds lexical definitions that speak of "mission" as that activity done by agents of Western Christendom when they are planting churches in non-Western cultures, and "evangelism" as that activity within Christendom which strives to make people who are culturally Christian into active and practicing Christians.[4] In either instance, the language of mission and evangelism has referred to one of the several programs that Christian communities may be involved in, perhaps even to one of several primary emphases of the church. We often find "mission" listed next to things like "worship" and "service" in contemporary discussions of the church's purpose and practice. Rarely, however, would either "mission" or "evangelism" appear in any classical discussion of the doctrine of the church emerging from the Christendom tradition.

There is, of course, a very different attitude out there in our late modern society with regard to the language of mission and evangelism. We do not have to go far to find wholesale condemnation of the entire vocabulary and practice of mission. Both the secularized intellectual establishment of the West and significant groupings within the theological guild pretty well agree that the missionary movement must be roundly criticized as a major misadventure—and not without some justification. As the sometime partner of colonialism, it is supposed to be regretted as the insensitive imposition of Western religious cultures on captive populations, motivated by the misguided assumption that the benefits of both the gospel and Western civilization were what the world outside Christendom desperately needed. The decline of Western Christendom in the last century has thus been welcomed not only as just desserts but as the only thing that enlightened societies could do after centuries of what Kant called "self-incurred tutelage,"[5] the tutor being the authoritarian tradition of Christianity embodied

---

[4]For a more detailed discussion of mission terminology, see Darrell L. Guder, *The Continuing Conversion of the Church* (Grand Rapids: Eerdmans, 2000), pp. 9-15, and the literature cited there.

[5]Immanuel Kant, "What Is Enlightenment," in *Kant: Selections,* ed. Lewis W. Beck (New York: Macmillan, 1988), p. 462.

in the powerful organization of the established churches. It has come as a great shock to this secularized intellectual establishment that Christendom is not disappearing, but has shifted, as Philip Jenkins documents in his important study of *The Next Christendom*.[6] While Christianity continues to recede in the territories of its former domination, Jenkins chronicles the enormous growth and vitality of the "next Christendom" in Africa, Southern and Eastern Asia, and Latin America. That much maligned Western missionary movement, to everyone's surprise, worked, and the former "daughter churches" are now our "sister churches," many of which are sending missionaries to the now post-Christian societies which, not along ago, sent missionaries to them.

The term *missional* is an attempt to move the discussion beyond too narrow definitions of mission as merely one among the various programs of the church, and to find ways to think about the church's calling and practice today in light of the fact of the multicultural global church, what Archbishop Temple famously called "the great new fact of our time." To describe the church as "missional" is to make a basic theological claim, to articulate a widely held but also widely ignored consensus regarding the fundamental purpose of the Christian church. Rather than seeing mission as, at best, one of the necessary prongs of the church's calling, and at worst as a misguided adventure, it must be seen as the fundamental, the essential, the centering understanding of the church's purpose and action. The church that Jesus intended, to use Gerhard Lohfink's provocative book title, is missional by its very nature.[7] The church that the triune God gathers, upbuilds and sends, to use the profoundly missional outline of Karl Barth's ecclesiology in volume four of *Church Dogmatics*, exists to continue the service of witness.[8]

The church whose planting is witnessed to in the New Testament is properly understood in terms of its missional calling.[9] That was the purpose of the

---

[6]Philip Jenkins, *The Next Christendom: The Coming of Global Christianity* (Oxford: Oxford University Press, 2002).

[7]The original of Gerhard Lohfink, *Jesus and Community: The Social Dimension of Christian Faith*, trans. John P. Galvin (Philadelphia: Fortress, 1984), has the much more evocative title, *Wie hat Jesus Gemeinde gewollt* (Freiburg/Basel/Vienna: Herder Verlag, 1982) = "How Did Jesus Intend the Community."

[8]Karl Barth, *Church Dogmatics*, ed. G. W. Bromiley and T. F. Torrance, trans. G. W. Bromiley (Edinburgh: T & T Clark, 1956-1962), vol. 4; see also David Bosch, *Transforming Mission: Paradigm Shifts in Mission Theology* (Maryknoll, N.Y.: Orbis, 1991), pp. 372-73.

[9]The subject under discussion is "missional hermeneutics," for which a small but important literature is beginning to appear. See, e.g., David Bosch, *Transforming Mission*, pp. 15-55; James V. Brownson, *Speaking the Truth in Love: New Testament Resources for a Missional Hermeneutic* (Harrisburg, Penn.: Trinity Press International, 1998); Richard Bauckham, *The Bible and Mission* (Grand Rapids: Baker, 2003).

apostolic mission: to found missional communities to continue the witness that had brought them into being. The interpretation of the New Testament Scriptures finds its key in that purpose. The apostolic witness preceded the writing of the scriptural documents. The communities were already missional when Gospel authors and epistle writers tackled the task of their continuing formation through these written testimonies. Thus, the Scriptures' collective purpose, we contend, was the continuing formation of already missional communities for faithful and obedient witness. This formation took place in the synoptic Gospels and John by incorporating young missional communities into the discipling process of Jesus, the outcome of which must always be apostolate, "being sent out." The formation took place in the Epistles as the apostolic authors affirmed, prayed for, corrected, argued with and continued to evangelize the missional churches to which they wrote. Their problems became the curriculum of continuing conversion to missional calling and its practice for the benefit of the church catholic.

Defining *missional* in such a way has broad implications for the entire theological task, starting with ecclesiology but not stopping there. It certainly bears upon our understanding of what it means to be "evangelical." There is virtually no attempt to define *evangelical* which does not emphasize, in some way, the priority of mission and the essential importance of evangelism—however problematically either may be understood in these definitions. In what follows, I would like to suggest, in broad strokes, some aspects of the task of formulating a missional ecclesiology that may contribute to a clearer understanding of what we mean by *evangelical.*

THE REDUCTIONISM OF MISSION IN WESTERN THEOLOGIES

Wilbert Shenk defines "historical Christendom" as "the powerful religio-political synthesis that resulted when Christianity won recognition as the religion of state in the fourth century," with the result that "the church now took its place alongside the other powers controlling society but was thus itself redefined by its new role."[10] As one outcome of the process by which the Constantinian project reshaped Christianity, he then succinctly defines Christendom as "Christianity without mission." As helpful as his general analysis is, this is an oversimplification. It discounts such important movements as the Celtic mission of St. Patrick and the Iro-Scottish mission that it fostered, or the

---

[10]Wilbert Shenk, *Write the Vision: The Church Renewed* (Valley Forge, Penn.: Trinity Press International, 1995), p. 33.

Slavic mission of Saints Methodius and Cyril, or even the missional ministry within European Christendom of the Franciscan and Dominican movements. But it makes a valid point with regard to the formation of Christian *theology* within Christendom. It is not an oversimplification to say that the fundamentally missional nature of the church gradually disappears from the formulations of Western ecclesiology. We can only suggest some of the major reasons for that shift.

Certainly the reduction of mission in Western theology has to do with the so-called Christianization of Western cultures. Once the Christian religion had become the only allowed religion within the boundaries of Christendom, mission was not seen as the central task of the church. Rather, her theological definition gradually came to focus upon the care and tending of the salvation of her members, who were simultaneously citizens of Christendom. This centering on the savedness of the saved reflected another profoundly important shift in thought and practice, relating directly to the gospel itself. The biblical message of salvation underwent a reductionism that resulted in emphasis upon individual salvation, how it was attained and how it was maintained. The classic definition of Christian existence focused on the benefits the person receives from the gospel, to the neglect of the vocation of witness for which the benefits prepare the Christian.[11] The institutional church was thus construed as essential for individual blessedness, providing the rites which initiated salvation, baptism, and which tended and maintained it, from Eucharist through penance to unction. Diminished or distorted in the process was the biblical understanding of the corporate and cosmic scope of salvation as the healing of all creation, the restoration of all things to the sovereign and gracious rule of God. Together with that loss there was the diminishing of the church's understanding of how it did the minimal mission that remained. Ultimately, only the clergy did that mission—which consisted primarily of the administration of personal salvation—and the members simply received the benefits distributed by the church on behalf of God.

Further, the eschatological shaping of the gospel, so central to the New Testament, was distorted and reduced. Jesus' message was the inbreaking reign of God, and the early church confessed him as the one who is and brings that reign into human reality. He is enthroned and rules as Savior and Lord, wit-

---

[11]This is the focus of Karl Barth's critique of the "classic definition of a Christian," *Church Dogmatics* 4/3, pp. 561-73; see also my *Be My Witnesses: The Church's Mission, Message, and Messengers* (Grand Rapids: Eerdmans, 1985); idem, *The Continuing Conversion of the Church*, pp. 121-41.

nessed to by his church through the empowering of the Holy Spirit. The church's empowered witness has, in the New Testament, a dynamic sense of God's work begun, God's work promised, and God's work being carried out now in the pilgrimage of faith and healing. The evidence of that inbreaking reign takes shape within the "community of the Word" in the reality of continuing conversion and healing, and in the empowering of the community to live publicly in ways that point to God's rule. God's future will, to be sure, bring the end of history, the judgment of humanity, the abolition of all opposition to God's rule and the "new heavens and new earth." But the community's common witness is so energized and focused by its confidence in God's future that its life now is already transformed and informed by the "living hope" established by "the resurrection of Jesus Christ from the dead." It looks forward to "an inheritance which is imperishable, undefiled, and unfading, kept in heaven" for God's children. Now, in this time of testing, God's power guards the community through the gift of faith "for a salvation ready to be revealed in the last time" (1 Pet 1:3-5). And during this passage through time, the community experiences the healing power of the gospel and witnesses to this new reality as it looks forward confidently.

That sense of radical and transforming anticipation, of living hope that profoundly shapes the "now" of the corporate Christian witness, was gradually reoriented to an individualistic emphasis on the second coming at the end of time with its threatening judgment that determines where each soul will spend eternity. The biblical emphasis on the "resurrection of the body" is replaced by the Hellenistic concept of the immortality of the soul, which changes the nature of Christian eschatology and diminishes the strong biblical emphasis upon the integrated wholeness of the human person as body, spirit and soul. Life now was understood not so much as faithful witness in hope but as wearisome and often anxious preparation in this vale of tears for what must come hereafter. Salvation is a question of where one spends eternity rather than the larger biblical witness to the restorative and salvific reign of God breaking in now, whose consummation is yet to come.

As heirs of the Christendom legacy, we inherit these tendencies toward reductionism both of the gospel of salvation (soteriological reductionism) and of the church's purpose and practices (ecclesiological reductionism). We struggle with the compromises made in the name of the gospel over the centuries that have gradually domesticated the gospel and produced what Dietrich Bonhoeffer so aptly called a gospel of "cheap grace."[12] The individualism of such a re-

---

[12]Dietrich Bonhoeffer, *The Cost of Discipleship* (New York: Macmillan, 1959), pp. 35ff.

ductionist soteriology has only intensified in the self-centered and consumerist culture of present-day North America. The church's focus on the tending and maintenance of the savedness of the saved is well attested today in churches that advertise themselves as "full-service" congregations and function as purveyors of the religious programs and products their member-consumers want. The partnership of church and state has, after the end of Christendom, effectively been replaced with the partnership of church and marketplace.

It is, however, an act of theological dishonesty to present the reductionist legacy of Christendom in monotonously somber tones. God has not been absent but graciously and powerfully present through this long history—God has been no more absent than he was from the long and unedifying history of Israel's kings. We are heirs of both our human reductionisms and of divinely empowered resistance to such disobedience. One of the pressing requirements for the development of a missional ecclesiology today is the task of learning how to read and interpret our history dialectically. We need to discern how God has been faithful in and through the lives and activities of both the known and anonymous mentors of witness and obedience, those "special individuals" whom Karl Barth describes as "models and examples" for the church in their "special calling and endowments."[13] We trace God's formation of his people in the prayers and liturgies, the neighborly love and innovative charity, the theological scholarship, the gifts for music and architecture, and the courage of public witness of so many members of the cloud of witnesses that surrounds and supports us. That dialectical realism allows us, constrains us, to speak without hesitation of the missional vocation and purpose of the church, in spite of the unquestioned fact that so much of our modern mission history is a very mixed and even questionable story. We did, in fact, confuse the message of the gospel with our own inflated sense of the normativity of our enlightened Western civilization. A reductionist soteriology did generate a reductionist vision of mission and a highly compromised understanding of the purpose of the church. But God has graciously overruled those shortcomings and allowed the message to be planted and the missional church to be formed in every major cultural area of the world. We are comforted by the wise word of the pastor from Malawi who told my class one day about all the changes the gospel had brought when the missionaries came to his tribe. "And," he concluded, "you must realize that we could always tell the difference between Jesus and the missionaries."

---

[13]Barth *Church Dogmatics* 4/3, p. 888.

THE WESTERN SHIFT TO POST-CHRISTENDOM AND THE EMERGENCE OF THE THEOLOGY OF THE *MISSIO DEI*

Now, however, we are coming to terms with the obvious fact that Christendom has ended—although, in some places it is more accurate to say that it is ending (there is a significant difference in the "state of Christendom" between Atlanta and Seattle!). Historians and social scientists must date and analyze the complex process of its ending and the character of the paradigm shift in which we find ourselves. Pastors must accompany their congregations through the painful recognition that we as the Christian church have indeed lost much, and that we are truly in a situation like that of Israel in exile, as Walter Brueggemann frequently has said.[14] Counselors must help parents deal with the challenge and the sadness of living with the decisions made by their adult children and their grandchildren to leave their faith behind and embrace our modern secularism or the growing variety of new age religions. Students of culture must help us learn and understand the changes, the new languages, the values and goals of our rapidly changing society in all its subcultures. And theologians must recognize anew that, as Martin Kähler said over a century ago, "mission is the mother of theology."[15] We find ourselves as heirs of Christendom in a radically changed territory, the Western mission field, which by any standards is one of the world's most difficult and complex arenas for Christian witness.

We are handicapped by some of the assumptions and attitudes of Christendom that are still very powerful in our minds and congregations. Our ecclesiologies of institutional maintenance and the tending of savedness are not adequate to the task that faces us now. We cannot evangelize under the assumption that most of what it means to be a practicing Christian is already handled by one's being born and raised in so-called Christian North America—so that all one needs to do is accept Jesus, join a church and perhaps start tithing. Nor can we evangelize under the assumption that our culture prepares people for Christ, so that we merely need to recognize the "felt needs" that people bring to church with them. The "felt needs" of a society shaped by consumerism and the entertainment industry may, instead, generate a kind of church that continues the gospel reductionism already so deeply engrained in Western Christianity. What may then happen could be nothing more than a last, desperate attempt to recover the popularity by other means that Chris-

---

[14]See, e.g., Walter Brueggemann, *Cadences of Home: Preaching Among Exiles* (Louisville, Ky.: Westminster John Knox, 1997).

[15]Martin Kähler, *Schriften zur Christologie und Mission* (1908; reprint, Munich: Chr. Kaiser Verlag, 1971), p. 190.

tianity seemed to enjoy during Christendom, popularity that Christians continue to confuse with faithful witness and genuine mission. Genuine missional vocation today must take seriously that process of dilution that David Bosch aptly described when he commented that Western theology could be characterized as a process of explaining why the Sermon on the Mount does not apply to us.[16] Much of our evangelism is based upon unquestioned, undoubted versions of "cheap grace." And much of our understanding and practice of the church's calling and ministry is based upon a reductionist ecclesiology that cannot pretend to be "evangelical" because it is not "missional."

That process of theological reorientation has been emerging for a long time. Although the Reformation does not generate an explicitly missional theology for Christendom, the first resources for such a theology can be traced in Luther's vision of the priesthood of all believers and Calvin's radical understanding of God's grace effecting our justification, our forgiveness and our sanctification in an inextricably intertwined process that generates public witness affecting very area of the community's life. It advances in Kierkegaard's attack upon Christendom[17] and P. T. Forsyth's comprehensive understanding of the formation of the congregation of believers for faithful witness as service.[18] It is certainly accelerated by the beginnings of the Ecumenical Movement at the Edinburgh Conference of 1910 and the subsequent study and exploration under the aegis of the Faith and Order movement, the Life and Work movement and the International Missionary Council.[19] Karl Barth recognized by the early 1920s that "the idol is tottering,"[20] and that it was time to rethink all of Christian doctrine from the perspective of what serves the formation of the church for its faithful witness in an increasingly post-Christian and even hostile world—the result is *Church Dogmatics* rather than a "systematic theology."

With regard to the challenge of developing a missional ecclesiology, there

---

[16]"Indeed, this sermon expresses, like no other New Testament passage, the essence of the ethics of Jesus. Through the ages, however, Christians have usually found ways around the clear meaning of the Sermon on the Mount" (Bosch, *Transforming Mission*, p. 69).

[17]Søren Kierkegaard, *Attack Upon "Christendom,"* trans. W. Lowrie (Princeton, N.J.: Princeton University Press, 1968).

[18]See, e.g., P. T. Forsyth, *The Church and the Sacraments* (London: Independent Press, 1947, 1917).

[19]A comprehensive survey of these ecumenical developments is found in W. Richey Hogg, *Ecumenical Foundations: A History of the International Missionary Council and its Nineteenth Century Background* (1952; reprint, Eugene, Ore.: Wipf & Stock, 2003).

[20]Letter from Karl Barth to Eduard Thurneysen of April 20, 1920, in Ernst Wolf et al., *Antwort: Karl Barth zum siebzigsten Geburtstag am 10. Mai 1956* (Zollikon-Zürich: Evangelischer Verlag AG, 1956), p. 856.

appear to have been two major factors that have shaped the process. On the one hand, there was the theological significance of the emergence of new and autonomous churches in the non-Western world, as the result of the modern missionary movement. It is widely acknowledged that the planting of new churches in previously unevangelized cultures was undertaken with a very inadequate ecclesiology. Most modern mission was undertaken by voluntary societies, not by the established churches of the West. There was virtually no theological attention given to mission by the Western academic guild, and so the mission societies had little ecclesiological equipment to guide the formation of new churches. Thus, Christendom's focus on the salvation of individual souls shaped the proclamation of the modern missionary movement, and so the newly formed mission churches figured largely as a kind of ecclesiastical receptacle for converts. Since Western ecclesiology did not operate under the fundamental principle that the church is called, gathered, formed and sent to be God's witnesses in the world, we did not initially form churches with that sense of missional vocation. The question of missional calling was really forced upon the emerging global church by the reality of being minority churches in completely non-Christian settings and illumined by their own interaction with Scripture as translations into vernacular languages made this possible.

As representatives of Christendom, used to the privileges and protections of majority status, we had little to offer our new sister churches as they began to take up the challenge of their calling in their contexts. But as they received the Bible in their own languages and began to grasp how this story was now their story, and that the missional mandate of the New Testament church defined them as well, they began to address the ecclesiological deficiencies exported by Christendom. The urgent concern for Christian unity pressed upon the complacent denominations of Christendom by the sister churches in the non-Western world grew out of their clear understanding that their divisions invalidated their witness. The issue was well summarized in the statement on mission and evangelism drafted by the Commission on World Mission and Evangelism of the World Council of Churches and adopted in 1982: "The present ecumenical movement came into being out of the conviction of the churches that the division of Christians is a scandal and an impediment to the witness of the church. There is a growing awareness among the churches today of the inextricable relationship between Christian unity and missionary calling, between ecumenism and evangelization. 'Evangelisation is the test of our ecumenical vocation.'"[21]

<hr>

[21]World Council of Churches, *Mission and Evangelism: An Ecumenical Affirmation* (Geneva: World Council of Churches, 1983), §1.

The other factor forcing the issue of a missional ecclesiology has been the disintegration of Christendom in the West, and with it a growing sense of the deficiency of the ecclesiologies we inherit. It is gradually becoming clear that the Christian church in the West can no longer assume that it has a cordial Christian context within which it can go about its duties. When confronted by secularism and paganism today, both the traditional inherited church structures and the theological systems that inform them find themselves largely at a loss. But our theologies of the church do not prepare us for this missional challenge in our own previously Christianized territory. Before we can turn our theological attention to themes like ordered ministry, sacraments and spiritual disciplines, we have to grapple with the basic questions: Who is the church of Jesus Christ and what is it for? As I have shown, the ecclesiological mindset we inherit tends to define the church in terms of the benefits it provides its members, as Avery Dulles explained in his classic discussion of the *Models of the Church*.[22] Thus, mission had to be interpreted as all those activities that build and expand the church. Such ways of thinking, which we group together as ecclesiocentric theologies of the church, are necessarily having to give way to another theological center of gravity. Since the 1930s, the consensus has gradually emerged that the church is not about itself, as though it were a self-justifying end, but the church must be defined and must act as part of the larger mission of God.

The theology of the *missio Dei* defines the church within the framework of the doctrine of the triune God. David Bosch has described this theological consensus succinctly, explaining that mission is "understood as being derived from the very nature of God. It was thus put in the context of the doctrine of the Trinity, not of ecclesiology or soteriology. The classical doctrine on the *missio Dei* as God the Father sending the Son, and God the Father and the Son sending the Spirit was expanded to include yet another 'movement': Father, Son, and Holy Spirit sending the church into the world."[23] The fundamental assumption here has to do with the revealed nature and purpose of God: "mission is not primarily an activity of the church, but an attribute of God. God is a missionary God."

It is not possible in this paper to explore all the twists and turns of the *missio Dei* debate since it became a focusing theme of missiological discus-

---

[22] Avery Dulles, S.J., *Models of the Church* (Garden City, N.Y.: Doubleday Image Books, 1978), pp. 45ff.
[23] Bosch, *Transforming Mission*, p. 390.

sion in the 1950s.[24] It is intriguing, however, that this theological consensus emerges as Christendom is unraveling in the West. Scripture discloses that God's mission is the outworking of God's love for his entire creation, which God translates into purposeful action to bring about the healing of his broken creatures, restoration to himself and to his good design, and incorporation into his kingdom as its witnesses and servant. The theology of the *missio Dei* is making clear that our ecclesiology, if it is truly to be a doctrine for the church that is continuing the apostolic witness, must be rooted in God's nature, purpose and action. It must be developed out of the mission of God as the One who calls and empowers his people to be the sign, foretaste and instrument of God's new order under the lordship of Christ. This ecclesiology understands the church as Christ's witness, living in continuing community with him in its midst, prepared by his Word through Scripture to be sent into the world which he loves and for which he died. Such a doctrine must serve the formation of the "community of the Word" for comprehensive missional witness.

TO BE AUTHENTICALLY "EVANGELICAL," OUR ECCLESIOLOGY MUST NECESSARILY BE "MISSIONAL"

If our concern is faithful witness to the gospel, then our doctrine of the church must be built upon and expound the mission for which the church is called, formed and sent, according to the biblical witness. As I said, the point is God's love for the world and the concrete demonstration of that love in the incarnation, ministry, death, resurrection and ascension of Jesus Christ. The divine strategy for the healing of the world is the calling, setting apart, formation and sending of a particular people whose witness has, as Newbigin puts it, "universal intent." God's gospel is to be made known to all people as an invitation to healing and to enlistment in the service of God as part of his witnessing people. Christian vocation is not merely to individual savedness, but to the service of God's mission to bring healing to the nations. Therefore, Christian witness is corporate in order that it can also be individual and personal. God calls a people into discipleship, formation by Jesus, in order to send it out as an apostolic community, so that each of its members can be an apostolic witness with that flame of the Spirit ignited on every head. The community of the Word is

---

[24]For a thorough review of the *missio Dei* discussion in the latter half of the twentieth century, see the edition of the *International Review of Mission* 92, no. 367 (2003) titled *Missio Dei Revisited: Willingen 1952-2002,* for a series of informative articles examining this tradition from diverse perspectives.

neither a safe enclave nor a colony walled off from the world, although it is, to be sure, always an alternative community within its context. It is a people *in via*, en route, on a pilgrimage definitively shaped by the incarnation, ministry, message, death, resurrection and ascension of Jesus, moving with him along his narrow path toward the certain consummation of God's work of salvation. The church that Jesus intended is a community that lives its message publicly, transparently, vulnerably—that is why it is called *ecclesia*, an assembly set apart to do public business in view of the watching world.[25] Its public witness has its dynamic focus on its gathered worship and proclamation of the Sent One. In Word and sacrament, Jesus encounters us in this central event of inward and focused devotion with the explosive outwardly thrusting commission, "So I send you." The ancient greeting that ended the liturgy, *"Ite missa est"* must be understood not merely as "Go, you are dismissed," but rather, "Go, you are sent."

To be authentically evangelical, I repeat, our ecclesiology must be missional. Such an ecclesiology will function then theologically as an integrative discipline, drawing all of the theological discourses into constructive interaction for the sake of building up the body of Christ and equipping it for its ministry (Eph 4:11-12). Rooted in the trinitarian nature and action of God, this ecclesiology derives its purpose from God's mission. It defines the way it goes about its work by means of God's self-disclosure in the history of Israel and supremely in the earthly ministry of Jesus. As an ecclesiology of Pentecost, this doctrine confesses the church's dependence upon the empowering work of the Spirit as it enables witness to Christ in all that the church is, does, and says. It will be the work of the Spirit to guide the missional church in its disciplined engagement with God's Word as the instrument God uses for the continuing formation of the community of the Word for its vocation. As a result of that biblical formation, the community will grow in its understanding of how its corporate public witness must be practiced, and at the same time, how each member will lead his and her life as an apostolic missionary in the daily neighborliness of witness to Jesus Christ.

Such an ecclesiology pays particularly close attention to the "as" and the "so" in John's missional summary: "As the Father has sent me, so I send you" (Jn 20:21). God's incarnational action in history provides the church the content of its witness and defines how it is to be carried out. "Mission in Jesus' way" has become a much-explored theme in missional theology these last dec-

---

[25]John Howard Yoder, *Body Politics: Five Practices of the Christian Community Before the Watching World* (Nashville: Discipleship Resources, 1992, 1997).

ades, and such thinking must shape our missional ecclesiology.[26] Theological ethics must school the missional church to practice witness with integrity, must guide the community to discern how, in fact, we are to "live our lives worthy of the calling with which we have been called."[27] The dominical and apostolic formation of the missional church focuses upon the concrete obedience of the called community and of all its members; it works intentionally on the transparency and integrity of its common life and its scattered life in an often-hostile world.

There is particular urgency today for a missional ecclesiology to reclaim the profoundly eschatological character of the church's calling. The theological reductionism of both gospel and church has been accompanied, over the centuries, by a great loss of that future tense of faith that should powerfully shape our present life and action. In place of fruitless speculation about events that have not yet happened, we must focus upon the certainty of our hope that enables us now to witness to Christ fearlessly and point away from ourselves modestly. A missional ecclesiology will always be candid about its penultimate nature; the continuing conversion of the church will necessitate obedient and serendipitous re-visiting of all our theological formulae and propositions. This does not mean that the gospel is not sufficient to the task; it means that the church lives with the open confession that its grasp of and response to the gospel is always partial, that there is yet more healing to be done, more conversion to submit to, more wonder to worship.

◆ ◆ ◆

Paul wrote to the Corinthians, after a particularly evocative exposition of the gospel's vocation (in 2 Cor 4:1-14), "Everything is for your sake" (2 Cor 4:15)— and Christendom would like to stop there, would like to leave us as Christians enjoying the benefits of our salvation and working away at the threats to our blessedness that arise both out of the world and our own rebellions. But the text has no period there. It says, "Everything is for your sake, so that grace, as it extends to more and more people, may increase thanksgiving, to the glory

---

[26]Commission on World Mission and Evangelism, *The San Antonio Report: Your Will Be Done: Mission in Christ's Way* (Geneva: WCC Publications, 1990); Lesslie Newbigin, *Mission in Christ's Way* (New York: Friendship Press, 1988); "Turn to the Living God: A Call to Evangelism in Christ's Way," in Office of Theology and Worship, *Selected Theological Statements: Presbyterian Church (U.S.A.) General Assemblies (1956-1998)* (Louisville, Ky.: Presbyterian Church [U.S.A.], 1998), pp. 617ff.

[27]Eph 4:1; see also this fundamental theme in Paul's community formation in Phil 1:27 and the theme of imitation generally in that epistle; 1 Thess 2:11-12; 2 Thess 1:11; Col 1:9.

of God." The purpose of God's mission is ultimately the acknowledgment and enjoyment of the glory of God; it happens as grace extends to more and more people; the evidence of that spread is growing thanksgiving to God which displays before the world the loving character and purposes of our God. It is the task and privilege of a missional ecclesiology to serve God's glory by guiding the church to an ever-growing understanding of who it is and what it is for. Thus, every classical theme of ecclesiology—the doctrine and practice of the sacraments, of proclamation, of ordered ministry, of membership, of stewardship, of spiritual disciplines—will be drawn into and redefined by the foundational vocation of the church to be Christ's witness, to lead its life worthy of its calling, to be Christ's letter to the world, to be, as Peter summarized it, "a chosen race, a royal priesthood, a holy nation, God's own people, in order that you may proclaim the mighty acts of him who called you out of darkness into his marvelous light" (1 Pet 2:9).

PART THREE

THE CHURCH AS
MORAL COMMUNITY

7

INCLUSIVISM, IDOLATRY AND THE SURVIVAL OF THE (FITTEST) FAITHFUL

WILLIAM J. ABRAHAM

The quest for diversity and inclusion is a persistent feature of modern Christianity in North America.[1] Inclusivism in fact trumps postmodernism and pluralism as the working ideology of many of our churches, most especially the "mainline" churches. It also, of course, shows up within Roman Catholicism and evangelicalism. In the latter case there tends to be a time lag, in that evangelicals readily pick up on the agendas of the mainline a decade, or maybe a generation or so, after they have been readily accepted elsewhere. In this paper I shall focus on inclusivism in my own tradition.[2] I shall leave it to the reader to make the necessary adjustments for his or her own ecclesial and theological tradition. I think there is much that evangelicals can learn, but I will not venture into that terrain here.

Inclusivism is at once a theological commitment and a network of practices. Unlike postmodernism, an esoteric and systematically ambiguous philosophical movement, inclusivism is both a slogan of action and the code word of an amorphous ideology. For my own tradition, the commitment to inclusivism has become embedded in our primary discourse, in our long-range planning, in our policy documents, in our structural arrangements, in our favorite theological code words, in our reward systems, and in the language and disciplines of our self-evaluation. Thus the obligation to inclusivism is subject to official audit; watchdog commissions keep a close eye on failure; its advocates do not hesitate

---

[1] In a paper on the church as a moral community there are two ways to proceed. If one already possesses a robust, comprehensive doctrine of the church, one can proceed from above and deal with the issue as a relatively abstract theological issue. If one does not, then one can begin from below and work upward from a significant moral conundrum present in the contemporary church. I have chosen to work from below.

[2] I will draw extensively on my experience within the United Methodist Church.

to take appropriate action against failure or backsliding. At a more political level, the term shows up in the propaganda and buttons of activists, for whom it has become a nonnegotiable moral and theological crusade. Innovations, however controversial or ill-judged, are hitched to its aura of persuasion. In some circles inclusivism has become a worldview, underwritten by claims to epistemological privilege. It has traveled sufficiently far to show up in the political posters of Sinn Fein, the political arm of the IRA in Ireland. In a trip to my hometown of Enniskillen last year I found a poster lauding the quest for "an inclusive peace" in the local offices of Sinn Fein. It was this experience that first triggered the turn to take a hard look at the idea of inclusivism. A concept that has achieved this level of internalization and use deserves to be examined with some care.

My aim here is to conduct a theological audit of our commitment to inclusivism. What does it mean? How did it arise? What are its strengths and weaknesses? Can we move beyond it into a better future?

What does inclusivism mean? At one level it is a thesis about power. Negatively, it begins with the observation that various networks of people have been excluded from the critical organs of decision-making in the culture and in the church. Positively, inclusivism is a call for radical action focused on the redistribution of power. Here is the heart of the matter: inclusion is constituted by the appropriation of power by excluded minorities.[3]

Necessarily, inclusivism requires the naming of victims and oppressors. The victims are readily identified in terms of race, ethnicity, gender, age, class and even culture. The identification of oppressors is relative to the identification of victims. Blacks are oppressed by whites, Hispanics by Anglos, the poor

---

[3]Note that inclusivism does not mean here the claim that all religious roads lead to salvation or to God. My usage is much more restricted and delimited, focused on a moral and political proposal central to mainline modern Protestantism. Of course, it would not take much for inclusivism in my more narrow, morally constrained sense to be transformed into a claim about inclusivism in the wider sense. I attend to inclusivism in the wider sense in the last chapter of *The Logic of Evangelism* (Grand Rapids: Eerdmans, 1989). For a recent incisive analysis of inclusivism in the wider sense see Russell Reno, "At the Crossroads of Dogma," in *Reclaiming Faith,* ed. Ephraim Radner and George Sumner (Grand Rapids: Eerdmans, 1993), pp. 105-37. The core idea of inclusivism in a broader sense than is intended here is made clear by Reno in the following section. "The motto of the dogma of inclusivism is broadly this: One God, many paths. The proponents of inclusivity think along the following lines. If God is truly a God of love, then his love must extend to all his creatures. Moreover, if his love is an affirmation (and if love is anything, then surely it is an affirmation of the beloved), then God's pervasive love must be an affirmation of us all. Finally, if who we are is diverse (Jewish, Christian, Buddhist, or Hindu), then God's universal love must be an affirmation of us all in our diversity. Ergo, God's love affirms the integrity of our Christianness, Jewishness, Muslimness, etc. In other words, God's love is inclusive; it vindicates and makes efficacious the many paths that humans have historically taken to the divine" (ibid., p. 128).

by the rich, Jews by Gentiles, women by men, homosexuals by straights, Palestinians by Israelis, the old by the young and middle-aged, lower classes by upper classes, and adherents of popular culture by cultural elites. The core of inclusivism is a normative thesis: the oppressors must be confronted and the captives must be set free. Power within church and society must be redistributed so as to provide room for the excluded and the marginalized.

This theme, of course, is also the heartbeat of liberation theology. How exactly this theology is to be related to the great tradition of liberal Protestant theology is a contentious issue. Is it a continuation of liberal Protestant theology's concern with injustice and transformation, as updated by Reinhold Niebuhr? Or is it a radical departure from liberal Protestant theology on the grounds that liberal Protestant theology was inescapably enmeshed in the ideology and practice of oppression?[4] How it relates to the classical theology of the church is also contentious. Is liberation theology itself an extension and enrichment of classical theology, or is the classical theology of the church itself in need of liberation? Both options are clearly possible and available in the literature. However these disputed matters are resolved, the call to inclusivism is a call to repentance, disruption, redirection and reorientation.

How did this call to inclusivism arise? Clearly the origins of inclusivism lie, as far as the recent past is concerned, in the quest to rid the world of racism and patriarchy in the social revolution of the sixties. Inclusivism began life as a response to racism, the doctrine that white races are superior to black races, and to patriarchy, the doctrine that men are essentially superior to women. Twinning these evils, we might say that inclusivism began life as a protest against the white, male leadership embedded in the power structures of society and church. Thus it was deeply linked to the exclusion of racial or ethnic minorities and women. In time inclusivism migrated as a solution to other forms of oppression and exclusion.

It is the originating circumstances that explain the pain and rage on the part of the victims and the guilt and readiness to comply on the part of those accused of oppression. The evils of racism and patriarchy were (and are) so obvious that change was inescapable; opposition was morally odious and understandably called forth protest and prophetic fervor. The originating circumstances also explain the ready compliance to change in both thought and practice. Racism and

---

[4]Niebuhr persistently warned that love without justice is sentimentality and that justice without love is simply balance of power. In the current quest for inclusivism we certainly have plenty of sentimentality, but the crucial observation to make is that the quest for justice has been replaced simply by the reallocation of power.

patriarchy are morally wrong; they are incompatible with the gospel; and they are at odds with any robust doctrine of creation. Only those who are self-deceived, or who are caught in the grip of morally corrupt forms of reasoning, would dare to oppose the call to inclusivism. Hence, as the boundaries of exclusion were extended and other victim groups were added to the initial list, it is easy to see how inclusivism became de facto the orthodoxy of modern mainline Protestantism. Challenges to inclusivism come across as a return to the evils of the past; they cannot but be a backlash motivated by a hidden quest for power and domination; they are racism and patriarchy in a new garb.

The morally charged nature of our situation makes it virtually impossible to question the place of inclusivism in the life of the church, society or academy. Reformers will immediately be castigated as racists and oppressors. The situation is often compounded by the tacit claim that the oppressed and those on the margins have privileged access to the truth. Anyone outside these zones who raises critical questions may well be accused of various forms of cognitive malfunctions due to the place of self-interest in their deliberations. Yet underneath the surface there are rumblings; it is only a matter of time before they will come to the surface and cry out for attention. I think it is high time we opened the books to take a fresh look.

We are aware, of course, that rumblings have been around for decades. Charges of the injustice of affirmative action, worries about the inequity of using quota systems, and complaints about the culture of political correctness, have long been with us. However, these strike me as slogans in search of truth rather than effective criticism. They are blunt instruments that tend to be taken back to the armory as soon as they are used rather than icons of illumination that can move us forward beyond our current worries. It is the more subtle worries, worries that folk are reluctant to voice, at least in public, which deserve our initial attention.

Consider the following observation. It is a marked feature of our life together that people watch very carefully what they say and how they say it. It is as if folk are walking on eggshells, treading carefully lest they bruise what is vulnerable and fragile. Changing the trope, folk constantly keep an eye over their shoulder; they expect to get hit from time to time. People fear that they will fail to communicate. Perfectly innocent remarks that happen to use certain critical code words can easily be misinterpreted. Ideas and topics far removed from the neighborhood of exclusion suddenly get conscripted into a name, blame and shame game. Folk begin to internalize their fears to the point where they appoint their own inner thought-police who keep watch on their ideas and thereby destroy intimacy, freedom, spontaneity and creativity. Furthermore, astute observers often wait patiently to see how long it will take before the charge of exclusion will be made, before some victim group complains, or before some new victim group calls for inclusion in the conversation. We might say that the theme of exclusion/inclusion has become the background music that sets the tone for conversation and action together. There is a subterranean note of judgment and accusation lurking below the surface.

Matters become even more acute when it comes to selecting speakers, panel participants and modes of worship at meetings. With speakers and panelists, the solution is clear: simply ensure inclusivism in terms of gender, race and the like.[5] With the actual content of worship the problem is much more difficult. It is clear that certain phrases and words are simply not usable: "Father," "Son," "Lord," "King," "Master," "kingdom," "he," "Old Testament" and "Jesus" are shunned. This is a very short list of words, but they crop up so persistently in Scripture, in the creeds, in hosts of hymns, in the doxology, in the benediction and in the sacraments that finding the right discourse turns out to be a recurring problem. For a time it was popular to refer to the Old Testament as the Hebrew Bible, but this is historically problematic, and it leaves the New Testament dangling without a complement. The most recent effort I have noted is to announce the Old Testament readings as coming from the first part of the canon.[6] "The Christ" is pressed into service as proxy for "Jesus," but the expression is opaque, stilted and unnatural. Substituting "realm" and "reign" for "kingdom" takes the political edge off the language of the gospel. Replacing "Creator, Redeemer and Sustainer" for "Father, Son and Holy Spirit," has turned out to be hopelessly modalistic rather than trinitarian. The more changes we make in language, the more it becomes clear that either we have a terribly thin theological diet to offer, or that we have a whole new theology being pressed into service. The obvious theology to deploy is some version of liberation theology.[7]

Naturally alienation begins to emerge, as folk find the neologisms and changes unconvincing. For those committed to liberation, they see such alienation as a sign of unease, and this unease readily comes across to them as re-

---

[5]Ironically, the result is not diversity but monotonous uniformity. I have served on national panels where in a group of, say, six, I was the only different voice in a chorus of voices intended to represent diversity.

[6]Thus a reading from Genesis was introduced as "A reading from Genesis, the first book of the canon," rather than something like "A reading from the Old Testament in the book of Genesis."

[7]The effort to use the suffering of children in church circles as the point of entry to the themes of liberation theology has now become somewhat hackneyed and predictable. On very good anecdotal evidence I am convinced that the appeal to children on recent occasions by the Council of Bishops originated in a concerted effort to introduce the themes of liberation theology into the bloodstream of the church.

jection of inclusion or refusal of the truth. For those designated formally or informally as oppressors, the potential for alienation has been there from the start, despite the fact that those accused of oppression have an enormous capacity to absorb criticism. Generally they reserve their grief and alienation for the closet or for a circle of trusted friends. Many people, and this includes some victim groups, feel that the goal posts keep moving. New victims arise to challenge the status of the old ones. The criteria of success keep shifting. A narrative of success suddenly does a U-turn and becomes a litany of hidden failure. Diversity audits provide ample opportunity to keep score and to locate gaps in the inclusivist agenda. The end result is the Balkanization and fragmentation of the church as a whole. Reversing the extraordinary claims to unity depicted, say, in Ephesians 2, dividing walls are set up and guards posted to prevent dismantling. Within the ensuing dysfunction, inclusivism becomes a weapon of assault or of criticism against anyone who cannot go along with the latest call for justice and inclusion. What began as an effort to include excluded minorities and women becomes over time an instrument of exclusion silencing those who want to raise fundamental questions about crucial moral, educational and theological proposals in the church.[8] At this point the danger of serious institutional dysfunction lies close to hand.

There is also the clear danger that the oppressed may become the oppressor. Truth be told, some among the oppressed have rapidly turned into oppressors. Given the moral privileging of antiracist and antipatriarchal modes of speech, once this or that favored cause has been housed within this horizon, it is very tempting to use the new power gained to press home the cause.[9] The march to progress becomes relentless, systematic, blind, pharisaical, self-righteous and manipulative.[10] Crucial information can be withheld, due process can be set

---

[8]This applies even more forcefully in the academy where charges of exclusion are used to fend off commitment to intellectual virtue and rigor. The most egregious case I have come across in the academy is the charge of racist grading. The most egregious case in the church operates in the neighborhood of debates about homosexuality.

[9]One of the persistent sins of would be reformers is to assume that because they managed to get it right on one big issue, say, racism, then they will certainly get it right on the next, and then on the next.

[10]For a fine analysis of the concept of manipulation see Marcia Baron, "Manipulativeness," *Proceedings and Addresses of the American Philosophical Association* 77, no. 2 (2003): 37-54. One of the crucial strategies of the manipulator is to "reconceptualize something in a way that serves one's goals, and doing so in order to secure . . . acquiescence." It is hard to doubt that the prominence of the language of inclusivism fits the bill neatly at this point. Another strategy noted by Baron is common. "A may browbeat B by demanding a reason, as if B owes A an explanation and is obliged to do A's bidding unless B has an adequate reason. When a reason is put forward, A challenges either its adequacy or B's sincerity in claiming it as a reason."

aside, and convenient lies can be told and then explained away. Good leaders, caught in a potential line of fire, readily develop political myopia as a strategy of success and survival. Those leaders who resist are punished. I have seen two distinguished white male leaders in two different seminaries (one a dean, the other a president), both of whom were unapologetically liberal in disposition and totally committed to the cause of inclusivism and diversity, summarily dumped and despised by those who replaced them. They were subject to humiliating votes of no confidence, sent packing to the margins to lick their wounds, methodically shunned, and then (among other indignities) systematically barred from serious committee assignments.

Inclusivism is indeed a matter of power. One cannot but wonder that inclusivism has become so popular and widespread precisely because it provides cover for the exercise of raw power. What is at stake is the control of pivotal institutions, access to patronage, promotion, honors, status and money, and ownership of the social, moral and spiritual capital of the church. If there is any truth in this, then we have a very serious moral problem at the very core of the church.

My own theological worries go beyond the problem of power and the corruption (and the complicity in corruption) one encounters from time to time. Consider this simple observation. When we worship together now in mainline corporate settings, the first question before us is not whether God is present but whether the right range of diversity is present. We have the functional equivalent of what some churches that are committed uncritically to church growth do when they make it clear that visitors are far more important in the worship service than God is. The first thing we do is look at who occupies the best seats in the sanctuary. We have collapsed the church into a mutual admiration society, and, when that fails, we turn it into a mutual criticism society. One T-shirt recently captured the limiting case for me when it noted that embracing diversity was embracing God. At this point we are on the edge of idolatry. We have made a god of ourselves, putting our varied identities at the core of our worship. In Luther's and Tillich's terms, we have made the recognition of our identities the ultimate value in our universe.[11] The move from that to the straight theological claim that in embracing diversity we embrace God is surely a short one. We have indeed crossed the threshold from anthropocentrism into idolatry.

---

[11]On one unforgettable occasion I found it quite impossible to participate in a Eucharist that had become in effect a political broadcast focused on a favored set of victims. I quietly withdrew from the service as soon as I could.

One influential leader made the point with telling if evasive simplicity in an address to the United Methodist Council of Bishops on April 30, 2001.

> Some say we have made a God of diversity. They say that, whereas "inclusivity" should be a symptom of our Godliness, the "fruit," if you will, we have made inclusivity our God. It doesn't matter what you believe, they say, it only matters that everyone is at the table.[12]

What has happened overall is that a virulent form of moralism has poisoned the church. This is not easy to detect, especially in those Christian communities that were born to serve the cause of holiness. Generally speaking these communities have no difficulty spotting the trouble that stems from, say, Christian forms of erastianism, ritualism, aestheticism, dead orthodoxy or asceticism. They can immediately discern when the prevailing political powers use the church for their own ends. They can readily see when the obsession with precise ritual turns into a weapon against the spirit of the gospel. They pounce on connoisseurs of church music who impose musical standards of the elite on ordinary believers.[13] They can see the perils of barren assent to orthodox doctrine a mile away. They promptly observe the silliness of imposing harsh standards of, say, fasting on fragile newcomers to the faith. However, those driven by moralism have great difficulty seeing that their moralism can readily turn into self-serving idolatry. A spiritual egocentrism develops that becomes virtually incurable; it is as if moral endeavor excuses moral blindness. We might say that "a unique form of self-poisoning by spiritual values takes place."[14]

In these circumstances, we will not be able to deal with the problems thrown up by inclusivism in a merely cosmetic or procedural fashion. Stringent calls for constructive dialogue, or little homilies about diversity in unity, or moralistic efforts at conflict resolution, will not be enough.[15] Nor will we be

[12]Daniel K. Church, "Remarks," in *Vision and Supervision,* ed. James K. Matthews and William B. Oden (Nashville: Abingdon, 2003), p. 163. Church holds the influential position of General Secretary of the General Council on Ministries in the United Methodist Church.

[13]Happily they also pounce when pious sentimentalists insist that we sing thin theological nonsense.

[14]See Mother Maria Skobtsova, "Types of Religious Life," in *Essential Writings* (Maryknoll, N.Y.: Orbis, 2003), p. 173. This whole essay is a searching analysis of the vices that befall various types of piety.

[15]I have played a very active role in these efforts myself over the years. See William J. Abraham and Donald E. Messer, eds., *Unity, Liberty, and Charity: Building Bridges Under Icy Waters* (Nashville: Abingdon, 1996), and *Dialogues on Differences: Homosexuality and the Nature of the Church* (New York: The General Commission on Christian Unity and Interreligious Concerns, 2004).

able to make appeal to the academy, say, in terms of objective scholarship, analysis or evaluation, as a way forward. The whole idea of critical, objective, scholarship, of the fostering of intellectual virtue, of the elimination of intellectual vice, all these will be reconfigured as bids for dominion and power. There simply are no objective academic brokers. Theory, sometimes presented as "critical theory" of one kind or another, will be invented and deployed to keep criticism at bay.

We can also expect the invention and ready use of diversity audits. Such diversity audits are likely to exacerbate the problem rather than to relieve it. As Onora O'Neill has recently argued with telling effect, the use of audits and increased legislation tends to undermine the kind of trust without which institutions wither and become fragmented.[16] In terms of the problem of idolatry, audits and legislation simply seek to put inclusivism deeper into the hard drive of an institution and thus provide a further protective shield against any kind of criticism; we might see audits as carefully constructed anti-virus programs.

It will not be possible, given these developments, to fix the problem by resort to the conventional means of grace, like prayer, Bible study, preaching, the Eucharist and the like. As we have seen above, the basic practices of the church are themselves the site of debates and worries about inclusion and exclusion. The spiritual practices of the church become embodiments of the agenda of inclusion. Our dysfunction has reached into the very heart of the church's practices, so that looking to these practices to heal the church is a nonstarter. The problem simply breaks out all over again.

Nor can we appeal to the instrumentalities of episcopacy and oversight to take care of the situation. Episcopacy too has become hostage to the fortunes of inclusivism. Episcopacy has become systematically dysfunctional, unable to speak a

---

[16]Onora O'Neill, *A Question of Trust* (Cambridge: Cambridge University Press, 2002). Consider the following comment. "If the new methods and requirements supported and didn't obstruct the real purposes of each of these professions and institutions, the accountability revolution might achieve its aims. Unfortunately I think it often obstructs the proper aims of professional practice. Police procedures for preparing cases are so demanding that fewer cases can be prepared, and fewer criminals brought to court. Doctors speak of inroads that required record keeping makes into the time that they can spend finding out what is wrong with their patients and listening to their patients. Even children are not exempt from the new accountability: exams are more frequent and time for learning shrinks. In many parts of the public sector, complaint procedures are so burdensome that avoiding complaints, including ill-founded complaints, become the central institutional goal in its own right. We are heading toward defensive medicine, defensive teaching and defensive policing" (see ibid., pp. 49-50). We might now add "defensive ministry" and "defensive administration" to the list to make it representative of life in the church. O'Neill's little essay should be required reading for all leaders in the church.

word of healing precisely because trust has been eroded and alienation simmers below the surface.[17] In some circumstances the shepherds of the sheep have given up fleecing the sheep and taken to eating them alive when it suits them.

Nor can we appeal to the gospel, and that for four reasons.[18] First, the gospel is impotent because the gospel itself is now defined or characterized in terms of inclusion. Inclusivism is identified as either the essence of the gospel or as constitutive of the gospel. Second, the gospel is ineffective because the kind of power actually represented in the gospel by the cross and by the power of the Holy Spirit is de facto rejected in favor of the political power that has become the focus of attention and an addiction among us. We have taken to squabbling like the disciples of old on the road to Jerusalem about our seats in the kingdom, and we refuse to be dislodged from our priorities. Third, the gospel is null and void because the kind of transformative unity presented in Christ has been systematically undermined by the internal Balkanization of the faithful. We have a paranoiac distrust of any corporate decisions that do not represent the commitment to inclusivism. Fourth, the gospel fails because the kind of identity promised in the gospel and in baptism has been trumped by our biological and ethnic identities. We are first identified in terms of race, gender and ethnicity and only secondarily identified in terms of faith and baptism. Turning to the gospel has become another dead end.

The choice before us is stark. Wherever inclusivism has morphed from anthropocentrism into idolatry, we have two plain options. Either inclusivism, as we now know it, will die; or inclusivism, as we now know it, will kill us.

We may all hope for a better way ahead, but the first step to that goal is realism and skepticism all around. Even a small dose of sanctified cynicism may be in order. I recommend this medicine realizing that proponents of unconstrained inclusivism will be deeply upset by my analysis. Some of them know full well what they are doing; most do not. Hence they will be shocked at my narrative. I think that we should expect and understand this reaction. Most partisans of inclusivism operate from the best of motives; they genuinely believe that they are serving God; they are totally convinced that the cause of liberation requires them to act as they do; they may even agree (and then genuinely regret) that lines have been crossed that should not be crossed. However, what we have to face here is not the good intentions of agents; we have to deal with reality as it is.

---

[17]For an insightful analysis along these lines see Russell Reno, *In the Ruins of the Church* (Grand Rapids: Brazos, 2002).

[18]The same objections, *mutatis mutandis*, apply to appeals to Scripture.

In the meantime ordinary believers have to survive. What should they do when they find themselves immersed in a world where inclusivism is the primary commitment?[19]

Happily, of course, the world of inclusivism has fluid boundaries. It is not as if inclusivism rules as the reigning ideology everywhere or in every local church. Many local churches have never heard of inclusivism; it is in fact hard work to implement it across the board in the life of the church. I know of some local churches where inclusivism has been systematically imposed from the top down by self-assured and self-appointed hierarchies of power; in these cases the older members or the recalcitrant were simply driven out over time, and there was a complete turnover in the congregations. However, these cases are (I hope) exceptional. For the most part inclusivism works more at the level of intercongregational institutions; in Methodist terms it works at the connectional level. Moreover, even where inclusivism is the working ideology, it is not always easy to maintain it as the continuing or even inevitable commitment of any group. Inclusivism finds itself constantly overridden or challenged by competing allegiances; financial solvency, for example, is a powerful reminder of reality. This is one reason why its advocates keep watch for institutional backsliding and are alert to new openings to press their cause and remake the ethos of the church. So we should not exaggerate.[20]

Yet we still need to ask: what should ordinary believers do in these circumstances? One thing they must not do is to try and turn the clock back. We will never get beyond inclusivism to a better future until we recognize the initial problems it was meant to address and until we agree that it is crucial to rid the church of racism and patriarchy. Even if fixing the problems means putting up with the sins of inclusivists, even if we have to grin and bear the excesses of

---

[19]It is not easy to find the most felicitous way to frame the question before us. I spoke in an early draft of this paper I wrote here of the "faithful" rather than of "ordinary believers," and I meant by that those whose primary commitment is to the gospel. I have kept the designation of the "faithful" in the title because of its directness. However, as I have already noted, inclusivists aggressively insist that they too are committed to the gospel, so that language already cooks the books in advance. So, to be fair to the position I am criticizing, I have tried to find as neutral a way as possible to pursue my quarry. In doing so I note three points. First, it is inevitable in our present situation that we cannot find a neutral way to express the issue before us. Our dysfunction spills over into disputes about how best to ask our questions. Second, for me the issue is precisely one of faithfulness to the gospel, so that anything short of this will not be robust enough in content. Third, as should be clear by now, my concern is not the commitment to inclusivism, but to forms of inclusivism that become abusive and spiritually suffocating.

[20]There are days when I am tempted to believe that inclusivism has peaked. I observe that many are profoundly uneasy, even though they remain silent in public. However, reality readily makes it easy to overcome such temptation.

inclusivism, any church that is faithful to the gospel must come to terms with the core insights that drive the inclusivist agenda. Thus the ordinary believer should be patient, recognizing that righting past wrongs is painful and difficult. We simply have to bear the sins of the fathers as best we can; beyond that we must in mercy bind up the wounds of the fathers with sensitivity. As Winston Churchill once quipped: "When you are going through hell, keep going."[21] The moral and spiritual renewal of the church in this arena is inevitably a cross-generational operation. This is certainly true of all forms of renewal; hence we must be patient and long-suffering.[22] So patient endurance is surely the first order of business.

Second, it will not help to invite those who have "benefited" from inclusivism to move us beyond inclusivism. This is a tempting strategy in that it would forestall charges of backlash and backsliding. After all, if moves to change come from within those groups currently identified as victims and oppressed, then it will be more difficult to argue that it is covert racists and oppressors who fuel the move beyond inclusivism. If the champions and beneficiaries of inclusivism can take the lead in moving beyond inclusivism, then everyone benefits. However, the danger here is that we will be setting up genuine victims, who have already suffered enough, to be the targets of hard-line inclusivists. We have all seen this happen. Genuine feminists have been excoriated for false consciousness simply because they developed a critical disposition towards the favored forms and instrumentalities of feminism. No one wants to be accused of bad consciousness or to be labeled an Uncle Tom or an Oreo. We should not be parties to plans that set good people up for such targeting. In an ideal world, the best way forward would indeed be that the champions of inclusivism become its best critics, but to ask for this would impose a burden that is inappropriate. Any move to go beyond inclusivism on the part of genuine victims is a task of great danger and a work of supererogation; it is not a moral duty.

Third, if inclusivism has become spiritually suffocating, then the ordinary believer will have to take whatever steps they can to ensure their spiritual welfare. This is very common in much of contemporary Protestantism. To put the matter

---

[21]Quoted in Caitlin Flanagan, "How Serfdom Saved the Woman's Movement," *Atlantic Monthly*, March 2004, p. 114.

[22]I argue this case in "Staying the Course, On Unity, Division, and Renewal in The United Methodist Church," in *Ancient and Postmodern Christianity, Essays in Honor of Thomas C. Oden*, ed. Kenneth Tanner and Christopher Hall (Downers Grove, Ill.: InterVarsity Press, 2002), pp. 170-83. For my analysis of the bigger picture on renewal see *The Logic of Renewal* (Grand Rapids: Eerdmans, 2003).

in pastoral terms, when the sheep look up and are no longer fed, they simply wander off and find pastures wherever they can. When arrogant elites impose their pyrrhic, political victories on others, those imposed upon vote with their money and their feet. When inclusivism elbows out the great mercy of God and usurps the place of the cross in the gospel, ordinary believers readily slip away and find food for their souls elsewhere. It is easy to dismiss this as a form of ecclesial consumerism or of financial blackmail, but I think that this is a cynical, superficial and false reading of the situation. One of the great advantages of the separation of state and church is that denominations can no longer use coercion to impose their will on the faithful. Hence, there are hosts of ways to bypass those arenas of ecclesiastical life and practice that have become corrupt and idolatrous. The sheep are no longer confined to retreating into a world of personal piety, important as that measure is; they can readily wander off to greener pastures and be fed. Nor is it acceptable for the sheep to take to whining and complaining; they need to find their feet and go get food. In the limiting case, where things are hopelessly out of order, say, in one's local church, then one can simply leave and go elsewhere. In cases where there is a real danger to one's spiritual life, I would not hesitate to endorse such a strategy.

Fourth, the best antidote to abusive and self-serving forms of inclusivism is to reinstate the gospel at the core of the church's life. As I noted earlier, this is at present a tall order. The gospel itself is either neutralized or co-opted by the advocates of hard forms of inclusivism, so any appeal to the gospel simply reinforces the status quo. However, the point to observe here is that we are not trying to convert hardliners but to speak up in a different language and with a richer agenda in the life of the church. Because whole networks of leaders have gone astray does not mean that we have to go with them. Because wellmeaning ideologues have grabbed the microphone does not entail that all other means of communication are unplugged. Because suffocating and narrow moralists have bleated their way to the top does not mean that we have to follow them like sheep to the slaughter. Because hard-nosed strategists and their agents control critical committees does not mean that the rest of us should shut up and forget to vote our conscience. Indeed silence may well be a form of complicity. So ordinary believers should use every opportunity to change the subject and recover their nerve in the commitment to the gospel and the faith in which it dwells.

Inclusion arose as a legitimate effort to implement a glorious vision of equality that is embedded in the gospel; we can be grateful for those theologians, liberal, liberationist and otherwise, who drove home the inclusivist insight. It is now time to get to the news behind the news and work for a change of speech

and subject. It was Christ's cross and resurrection that won the victory over exclusion; it is the same cross and resurrection that will heal us of corruption and
idolatry carried out under the banner of inclusion. If contemporary inclusivists
cannot speak robustly in terms of the gospel, there is no reason the rest of us
should follow their lead. When it comes to our turn to speak, we can change the
subject and return to the first order discourse of the gospel. We can immerse
ourselves in the great themes of the gospel; we can drink afresh from the mercy
of God in the cross; we can ensure that the full faith of the church is tended to
and taught; we can lift up Christ like the serpent in the wilderness and watch
him draw all to himself; we can cry out for a fresh outpouring of the Holy Spirit
on the church; we can do all we can to ensure that the sacraments are duly administered; we can pray without ceasing for the comprehensive renewal of the
whole people of God. The sharp-edged Word of God is not intimidated by its
enemies; it is a healing Word of truth and salvation.

There is no recipe for how all this should be done. Clearly one point of entry
for change is the long-haul renewal in evangelism and the making of disciples
that is currently finding its way into the hard drive of United Methodism.[23] In
this instance, the sharing of the gospel as enacted by a rich band of multicultural and diverse witnesses would in itself provide a paradigm for change. In
this case inclusivism is wonderfully subordinated to the gospel in such a way
that the gospel becomes front and center in the practice of the church. The gospel supervenes beautifully in this instance on the practice of inclusivism.

Beyond this the ordinary believer will simply have to be versatile and creative in calling into question the corruption that we face. The strategies
adopted for change will have to match the context. In academic institutions it
will be possible to make the case that academic standards and virtue are at
stake when inclusivism is made the reigning orthodoxy. Indeed it is not difficult to spot cases of racism and matriarchy introduced under the banner of inclusivism that can be challenged head on for what they are, that is, gross forms
of injustice, preferment, nepotism or special treatment. Moreover, academic
communities that give up on intellectual virtue for the sake of inclusivism will
quickly find themselves mired in intellectual vice; in the end we must have
faith that intellectual virtue in the academy will win in any clash with the ideology of inclusivism and diversity.[24]

---

[23]To be sure, there are serious efforts to fend off this critical element in the renewal of the
church and to reduce renewal to the moral renovation of the tradition, but that is a topic for
another time and place.

[24]For the crucial place of intellectual virtue in education see my "Education, Social Transformation, and Intellectual Virtue," forthcoming.

In other arenas, say, in the election of bishops, we can argue that criteria of effectiveness and faithfulness are every bit as important as inclusivism; so success in elections cannot simply be reduced to skin color or to the presence or absence of certain biological organs. At present it is, of course, very difficult to overcome the quota system in place for committees, but in time we may find (and until then we can hope) that effective action that serves the good of the whole church, whoever carries it out and gets the credit, will be welcomed and fostered. We can allow our good deeds to give glory to God rather than to ourselves. I know of one instance where a General and Jurisdictional Conference delegation adopted a process of discernment that moved beyond our current ways of doing business together. This required creative and courageous leadership from the female heads (both clergy and lay) of the delegation, but the overall outcome for the group as a whole became in time the center of gravity of the work done together. It was a splendid moment of grace in the church.

It is grace in the end that will heal us of our anthropocentrism and idolatry. While the short-term prospects are grim, the long-term possibilities leave open the prospects of a new day. No doubt, when we get beyond inclusivism (and at present there is no end in sight), there will be other sins to repent of and new problems to be faced. "Sufficient unto the day are the troubles thereof," so we had better stick to the troubles we now face before we worry about the ones up ahead. The church is a moral and spiritual community that is constantly beset with its own failings and corruptions. The church is always a community of holiness in the making. The most difficult corruptions of all are those that stem from her own quest for perfection; it is especially troubling when the best becomes the enemy of the good and the pretext for evil. Yet within her bosom the church possesses the medicine for her many illnesses, and there is no reason to think that someone someday will not find the recipe we need to cure us of our current waywardness. Once the medicine begins to take effect, the grace of God now resisted will be the source of boundless healing; it is the gospel of our Lord and Savior, Jesus Christ, which alone can save us from our corruption and idolatry. We can surely hope that evangelicals will be assiduous in ensuring that this medicine is kept available for all who seek its healing.

8

"ABLE TO INSTRUCT ONE ANOTHER"
The Church as a Community of Moral Discourse

ALLEN VERHEY

It was no small compliment that Paul paid to the churches in Rome. They were, he said, "full of goodness, filled with all knowledge, and able to instruct one another" (Rom 15:14).

The commendation was, to be sure, also subtly a commandment.[1] When my mother used to say, "I am confident, Allen, that you are a well-behaved young man," I knew I had been not only praised but alerted to certain expectations. The Roman churches doubtlessly heard these words not only as praise but also as a vocation.[2] And it is the burden of this paper to claim that the continuing church is still—and is still called to be—a community of moral discourse and discernment.

---

[1] Paul had, in fact, just urged the Roman churches not to be conformed to the present evil age but to be transformed by the renewal of their mind so that they could discern the will of God (Rom 12:1-2). Although the NRSV translates it as a plural, "the renewing of your minds," the word is singular. It is a communal "mind" that is to be renewed.

[2] It was not just the Roman churches, it should be observed, who were commended as "able to instruct one another"—or called to the task of communal discernment. That commendation and calling were implicit in all of Paul's correspondence with the churches. Although Paul could write with apostolic authority (1 Cor 5:3-5), he seldom did. He rather "appealed" to the communal judgment of his readers (1 Cor 10:15; Philem 8-9). He used the language of polite request rather than the language of command, and he thus conveyed to the churches a sense of their ability and responsibility to be communities of moral discourse and discernment. Paul respected and nurtured the churches as communal contexts for moral deliberation and judgment. Moreover, this expectation that the churches could and would practice mutual admonition was not unique to Paul. The author of Hebrews, for example, exhorted his readers to "exhort one another" (Heb 3:13). The *Didache*, a second century manual for the churches, encouraged participation in the practice of mutual admonition: "Every day you should seek the company of saints to enjoy their refreshing conversation. You must not start a schism, but reconcile those at strife. 'Your judgments must be fair.' You must not play favorites when reproving transgressions. You must not be of two minds about your decision"

THE EARLY CHURCH AS A COMMUNITY OF MORAL DISCOURSE

The early churches were communities of moral discourse.[3] They talked together about what they should do or leave undone. When Christians met together in Rome—or in Corinth or in Antioch or in Jerusalem or elsewhere—they talked together about the choices they faced. They asked each other—and instructed each other—about their personal and communal responsibilities.

Their questions about personal responsibilities are frequently right on the surface of New Testament texts. They asked, for example, "What should I do about meat once offered to idols now offered to me?" (1 Cor 8:1) and "What should I do about sexual intercourse now that the ages have turned?" (1 Cor 7:1). It takes only a little imagination to penetrate the surface of such texts to the community's conversation about personal responsibilities. Questions about communal responsibilities are also there. They asked, for example, "What should *we* do about ordering our communities now that Gentiles are joining?" (Acts 15:5, 6) and, "What should *we* do about our relations with other communities, with the Roman Empire, for example, or with the poor in Jerusalem?" (Rom 13:1; 1 Cor 16:1). And beneath these questions, too, there were the conversations of the churches.

They were—and were to be—communities of moral discourse, "able to in-

---

(*Didache* 4.2-4; translated by Cyril C. Richardson in Cyril C. Richardson, ed., *Early Christian Fathers* [Philadelphia: Westminster Press, 1953]). And the *Epistle of Barnabas,* another second century text, urged its readers to "be good lawgivers to each other, remain faithful counselors to each other" (translated by Kirsopp Lake, in Kirsopp Lake, ed., *The Apostolic Fathers* [Cambridge, Mass.: Harvard University Press, 1952]). Indeed, Celsus, the learned opponent of the early Christian movement, evidently complaining about this practice of mutual admonition, poked fun at Christian communities that treated "stupid and uneducated yokels" as though they could learn and teach moral philosophy. And when Origen wrote his massive reply to the charges of Celsus, the Christian philosopher and theologian from Alexandria, accepted this particular charge—and delighted in it! (Origen, *Contra Celsum,* 6.1-2. See further Wayne A. Meeks, *The Origins of Christian Morality: The First Two Centuries* [New Haven: Yale University Press], pp. 102-3.)

[3]Concerning the church as a community of moral discourse, see especially the work of James Gustafson, "The Church: A Community of Moral Discourse," and "Two Requisites for the American Church: Moral Discourse and Institutional Power," in *The Church as Moral Decision Maker* (Philadelphia: Pilgrim, 1970), pp. 83-95 and 151-63, and *Treasure in Earthen Vessels* (New York: Harper & Brothers, 1961). On the ecclesial context for Christian ethics see especially Thomas Ogletree, "The Ecclesial Context of Christian Ethics," in *The Annual of the Society of Christian Ethics, 1984,* ed. Larry Rasmussen, pp. 1-17; James B. Nelson, *Moral Nexus: Ethics of Christian Identity and Community* (Philadelphia: Westminster Press, 1971); Stanley Hauerwas, *The Peaceable Kingdom* (Notre Dame, Ind.: University of Notre Dame Press, 1983), pp. 96-115; Yoder, *Peaceable Kingdom,* pp. 15-45; and Bruce C. Birch and Larry Rasmussen, *Bible and Ethics in the Christian Life,* rev. ed. (Minneapolis: Augsburg, 1989), pp. 17-34, 120-40.

struct one another," but it was not easy. Their vocation led them along a narrow path with temptations on either side. When personal choices had to be made, there was a temptation on the one side to deny or neglect the individual's responsibility, to surrender it to the group. The same Paul, however, who commended the Roman church as a community of moral discourse also insisted that "all be fully convinced in their own minds" (Rom 14:5) and observed that "each of us will be accountable to God" (Rom 14:12). The community of moral discourse was *not* a substitute for *personal* responsibility; instead, the community nurtured and respected the freedom and responsibility of each member.

There was, however, also a temptation on the other side, to treat personal choices as simply "private" matters, as no one else's business, as properly settled by the tastes and preferences of the free person, and therefore as outside the appropriate range of the community's discourse and mutual instruction. Personal choices remained personal, and individual responsibility was not surrendered to the group, but personal choices were made and individual responsibility was exercised *within* the community, *not* secretly and privately. The advice of Paul to the owner of Onesimus concerning what he should do about his runaway slave, for example, dealt with what was clearly (in the first century, at any rate) a very personal responsibility. The little letter we call Paul's letter to Philemon, however, was not a private letter;[4] it was addressed to the church (Philem 2). The personal choice concerning Onesimus was open to the review of the whole church—a church, it should be noted, which surely included other slaves. The personal decision was not private. They were "able to instruct one another" because personal responsibility was not denied but exercised within community.

When they faced decisions about the life of the community, there was a temptation on the one side to deny the community's responsibility for such decisions, to surrender it to a charismatic leader or to an ecclesiastical official. There must be leadership in any community, of course, and there was leadership in the early church. However, if the leaders circumvented or disregarded the moral discourse and mutual instruction of the Christian community, they subverted the community's vocation as a community "able to instruct one another." And if the church surrendered its responsibility to its leaders, she failed to honor her calling. Even while urging the Thessalonian church to "respect" her leaders and not to "despise the words of prophets," Paul insisted that they "test everything" (1 Thess 5:12, 20-21).

---

[4]See the illuminating study by Theo Preiss, "Life in Christ and Social Ethics in the Epistle to Philemon," in *Life in Christ* (London: SCM, 1957), pp. 32-42.

When the church faced decisions about the life of the community, there was a temptation on the other side, too. The church might surrender such choices not to a leader within the community but to some other and larger community. The church might regard such decisions as properly settled simply by the application of the generally accredited political wisdom of some broader community, some larger "public"—the conventional wisdom of life in the Greek city, the moral tradition of the polis, for example, or the generally accepted rules for life in the household. But when communal decisions were surrendered to another community, the vocation of the church to be a community of moral discourse was undercut, for there would be no call for a conversation about the identity and integrity of the particular community whose decision it was. The received political wisdom did function within the Christian communities, of course, but their communal decisions were not to be made on the basis of some other community's self-understanding. Their communal decisions were to be made in the name of the Lord whose people they were. They were "able to instruct one another" because communal responsibility was neither surrendered to the leadership nor given up to a different community.

THE EARLY CHURCH AS A COMMUNITY OF MORAL DELIBERATION

The early churches were communities of moral discourse by being communities of moral deliberation. It was as communities of moral deliberation that they were commended as "able to instruct one another." They not only discoursed; they deliberated. They talked together not only about *what* they ought to do but also about *why* they ought to do it. They asked *why* they ought to do one thing rather than another or something rather than nothing. The concrete advice of moral discourse led inevitably in these communities to the giving and hearing of reasons. Their moral discourse was not simply the exercise of rhetorical or social power; it involved deliberation, reason giving and reason hearing. Paul himself addressed the Corinthians as capable of deliberation, as "sensible," and invited them to "judge for yourselves what I say" (1 Cor 10:15).

It was as communities of moral deliberation that they found their way through the thicket of temptations that threatened their vocation to be "able to instruct one another." By their practice of giving and hearing reasons, they were able to honor personal responsibility without surrendering it to the group and to protect communal responsibility without surrendering it to the leadership. By their readiness to give reasons and to hear reasons they could resist the reduction of personal responsibility to secret and private preferences and the reduction of communal responsibility to the public standards of other communities. It was as communities of moral deliberation that they were commended as "able to instruct one another."

To be sure, a charismatic prophet in the community sometimes provided the answer to the question concerning what a person or the community should do. Such prophets evidently had the gift of knowing and making known in plain, intelligible speech the will of God for some concrete problem that the community or its members faced. Even so, the prophetic word had to be tested by the whole community in the light of the Christian tradition and confession (e.g., 1 Thess 5:20-21; 1 Jn 4:1-2). And that testing involved the church as a community of moral deliberation, giving and hearing reasons.

And to be sure, the official leadership of the community also sometimes provided the answer to the question concerning what a person or the community should do. But just as the charismatic advice required testing and deliberation, so did an official's pronouncements. There was no one in the community authorized to say, "Do as I say because I say it." Paul himself seldom invoked his own apostolic authority to put an end to the discourse of the churches; he rather "appealed" to his readers and to their deliberative judgment. He respected and honored the churches he addressed as communities of moral deliberation, as communities where reasons are given and heard, as communities where each must respect the other as a giver and hearer of reasons. Without that regard for one another they could not be communities of moral deliberation, and they would not have been "able to instruct one another."

Sometimes the reasons given were simply the moral commonplaces of a Jewish or Hellenistic culture, of the synagogue or the polis or the household. Sometimes the reasons involved an appeal to the law or the prophets or the writings, to the Scripture of the synagogue and the early church. Sometimes the reasons were simply what nature teaches (1 Cor 11:14-15) or what convention requires (1 Cor 11:16; 14:33). There was no wooden scheme for deliberation, no simple checklist for determining what should be done and what left undone, no fixed set of first principles to be applied deductively to questions of conduct. Reasons were given and heard in the community, but even the reasons had finally to be tested in the community—and defended or discarded or qualified by their coherence with the gospel. Exhortation was always "in Christ" (Phil 2:1), "in the Lord Jesus" (1 Thess 4:1), "by the meekness and gentleness of Christ" (2 Cor 10:1), "by the mercies of God" (Rom 12:1). This was more than pious rhetoric. Discourse and deliberation took place in this community in the service of their communal attempt to discern the shape and style of a life "worthy of the gospel of Christ" (Phil 1:27). Every judgment and every reason was to be tested and qualified by the truth that was not the possession of the church but its Lord. The church, like Paul, was to "take every thought captive to obey Christ" (2 Cor 10:5).

As moral discourse prompted moral deliberation, so moral deliberation in these communities required moral discernment, for the reasons themselves had to be tested by "the gospel of Christ." They not only asked what they should do (discourse) and about why they should do it (deliberation) but also about whether their choices and the reasons for them "fit" the gospel (discernment). It was as communities of moral discernment that they were commended as "able to instruct one another."

THE EARLY CHURCH AS A COMMUNITY OF MORAL DISCERNMENT

There is no theory of discernment in the New Testament,[5] and surely no recipe for it. Nevertheless, it is clear in the New Testament that discernment is neither simply a spontaneous intuition nor simply a deductive application of either philosophical principles or the prescriptions and prohibitions of Torah. Discernment, or the perception of what is fitting, is a complex human enterprise, involving different elements in different people in different communities in different proportions. Moral discernment in the community of Matthew, for example, almost certainly gave greater place and priority to the interpretation and application of the law of Moses than moral discernment in the community of Mark. And different people in any one community, say the Roman churches, had different strengths and weaknesses in discernment, different gifts and blind spots for the perception of what was fitting. Some were gifted with moral sensitivity; some with intellectual clarity; some with passion; some with reason; but each with their own experience. Some were blinded by fear; some were blinded by duty; the perception of each was abridged by investments in their culture or their class. As a community of moral discernment the church could capitalize on this variety of individual strengths and gifts and compensate for individual weaknesses and blind spots.

But more than that can and must be said, for communal discernment in the church was not just sharing the little moral wisdom each knew well and compensating for the abridgements (major or minor) of each one's moral vision.

---

[5]On discernment see James Gustafson, "Moral Discernment in the Christian Life," in *Norm and Context in Christian Life*, ed. Gene H. Outka and Paul Ramsey (New York: Charles Scribner's Sons, 1968), pp. 17-36; also Gustafson, *Ethics from a Theocentric Perspective: Vol. II: Ethics and Theology* (Chicago: University of Chicago Press, 1984), pp. 302-19. On Paul's "new discernment" see Allen Verhey, *The Great Reversal* (Grand Rapids: Eerdmans, 1984), pp. 106-13.

Communal discernment, or the perception of what is fitting, was always in the church to be the discernment of what is fitting to, or worthy of, *the gospel*. It was the gospel that made them a community, and it was the gospel, the "mercies of God," which called them to a discernment not conformed to this age, but transformed by the renewal of their mind (Rom 12:1-2). There were other assemblies and associations in the first century, of course, where there was moral discourse and deliberation, where there was talk together about what should be done and why. There were Jewish sects and Greek philosophical schools. There were synagogues and initiatory cults. There were voluntary associations or clubs. A first-century observer of a Christian community might easily have mistaken it initially for one or another of these associations.[6] But the church was *not* one or another of these associations. The church was a new and distinctive community by their common conviction that Jesus of Nazareth was the Christ, the anointed one of God, that he had made God known and disclosed the intentions of God with and for the world and that he had made humanity known and disclosed what human life could and should be like. The communal discernment of the church was a new and distinctive discernment because it finally transfigured questions of conduct and character into questions of the deeds and dispositions fitting to that gospel. As a community of moral discernment they tested all the reasons given in deliberation (including the appeals to Scripture!), against the story of Jesus of Nazareth. They transformed the question of what they should do into the question of how they might live the story they loved to tell.

And they did love to tell the story. They were a community of memory,[7] and it was always *as* a community of memory that they were *also* a community of moral discourse, deliberation and discernment.

THE EARLY CHURCH AS A COMMUNITY OF MEMORY

The early churches were communities of memory. Nowhere does the New Tes-

---

[6]See further the masterful work of Wayne Meeks, *The Moral World of the First Christians* (Philadelphia: Westminster Press, 1986), pp. 97-123.

[7]On the church as a community of memory see especially Gustafson, *Treasure in Earthen Vessels*, pp. 71-85, and Stanley Hauerwas, "The Moral Authority of Scripture: The Politics and Ethics of Remembering," in *A Community of Character* (Notre Dame, Ind.: University of Notre Dame Press, 1981), pp. 53-71. On memory in the New Testament see especially Nils A. Dahl, "Anamnesis: Memory and Commemoration in Early Christianity," in *Jesus in the Memory of the Early Church* (Minneapolis: Augsburg, 1976), pp. 11-29 (also pp. 167-75); Luke T. Johnson, *The Writings of the New Testament* (Philadelphia: Fortress, 1986), pp. 114-41; Allen Verhey, *Great Reversal*, pp. 34-61; and Richard J. Ginn, *The Present and the Past: A Study of Anamnesis* (Allison Park, Penn.: Pickwick, 1989).

tament pause to reflect on the nature of memory or its function in community. There is no more a theoretical account of memory than there is of discernment. But everywhere in the New Testament there is remembering.

The Gospels, for example, obviously proceed by way of remembrance.[8] They give literary expression to the oral tradition in which the church's memory of the words and deeds of Jesus was handed down. Hardly simply retrospective historical accounts, the Gospels nevertheless situated the lives of their readers in relation to the living Christ, the *present* Christ, by reminding them of Jesus.[9] They oriented their readers to a future in which the sovereignty of God and of this Christ would be unchallenged by re-membering Jesus. They nurtured and sustained communities of discern-ment by nurturing and sustaining the memory of the community. It is surely no literary accident that in Luke's Gospel the disciples at the empty tomb are instructed to "remember" (Lk 24:6-8) or that in John's Gospel it is said that the Paraclete, the promised Holy Spirit, will "bring to your re-membrance all that I said to you" (Jn 14:26; cf. 2:22, 12:16, 16:4). Each Gospel is a "remembrance," a literary commemoration of the crucified and risen Lord, shaping community, character and conduct into something worthy of the gospel.

In the Epistles, too, there is remembering. Paul explicitly says that he writes to the Romans "by way of reminder" (Rom 15:15; cf. also 2 Pet 3:1). The Epis-tles bear the tradition of the churches, and they ask their readers to remember it (1 Cor 15:1; Rev 3:3). From 1 Thessalonians,[10] which was very likely the first letter, to the later epistles' discourse (e.g., 2 Tim 2:8, 14; Jude 5; 2 Pet 1:12-13; 3:1), deliberation and discernment are evoked and sustained by the memory of Jesus. "Remember Jesus Christ, risen from the dead, descended from David, as preached in my gospel" (2 Tim 2:8) was not a call to preserve some historical data like an archivist; it was a call to preserve Christian identity and commu-nity and to sustain a common life worthy of the gospel.

The Epistles frequently remind their readers of the worship of the commu-

---

[8]One may object against the denotation of an ancient literary form which contained epi-sodes from the lives of famous men and against the connotation of a retrospective histor-ical account, but one must appreciate the continuity of the Gospels with the churches' memory of Jesus (cf. also Papias in Eusebius *Ecclesiastical History* 3.39 and, of course, Luke 1:1-4).

[9]The "remembered" Jesus is thus not to be identified with "the historical Jesus" sought by the Jesus Seminar. The "remembered" Jesus is not simply a figure out of the past whose life ended with his death but the risen Lord.

[10]E.g., 1 Thess 4:2; on the place of the tradition in 1 Thessalonians see Wayne Meeks, *Moral World of the First Christians*, pp. 125-30.

nity, and it is little wonder, for worship itself was remembrance. Hymns of the early church, themselves forms of remembrance and celebration, were remembered (e.g., Phil 2:6-11; Col 1:9-15) and used to nurture discernment of a way of life fitting to the convictions the church expressed in worship. Readers of the Epistles were frequently reminded of baptism (e.g., Rom 6:1-11; 1 Cor 1:12-16, 12:13; Gal 3:27-28; Eph 2:1-11; 1 Pet 3:21-22). Baptism in the name of Jesus and "into his death" was itself a remembrance—and not merely as an historical recollection—of the death and resurrection of Christ. Baptism established identity, initiated one into a community of common memory, and required fitting conduct. The Lord's Supper, too, was remembered, and the explicit instruction was that it be done "in remembrance" (Gk. *anamnēsis*) of Jesus the Christ (1 Cor 11:24-25; Lk 22:19). Again it will not do to construe this remembrance as merely historical recollection, as the preservation of historical data. In remembering that past, they owned the story of the suffering and death of a risen Lord as their own story. To eat the supper was to share, to participate (1 Cor 10:16; Gk. *koinōnia*), in the body of Christ. The memory of Jesus was constitutive of identity and community and decisive for discernment and deliberation. When the rich humiliated the poor, as they did in Corinth (1 Cor 11:22), when community was broken, as it was in Corinth, then "it is not the Lord's supper that you eat" (1 Cor 11:20), then the church eats the bread and drink the cup "in an unworthy manner" (1 Cor 11:27), then the meal is not truly "remembrance."

There may be no theory of memory, then, but there surely is remembering. Memory is crucial, and this much ought to be clear: In the New Testament memory is not simply a mental process of recollection, not just disinterested recall of objective historical data; memory is to own a particular history as one's own, to own a past and to own it as constitutive of identity and determinative for discernment. In the New Testament and in the church there is no identity apart from memory, and no community apart from common memory.

This usage of remembrance was hardly remarkable. Ordinary Greek was quite capable of analogous usage; the Greek term *anamnēsis* (Lk 22:19; 1 Cor 11:24-25) captures quite nicely the fact that memory is the antidote for amnesia and its attendant loss of identity. The New Testament and its churches, however, are especially indebted to the Hebrew Scriptures and to Jewish communities of faith for this usage of remembrance. The Hebrew Scriptures, too, are full of remembrance (Heb. *zakar*) and construe it as that which constitutes identity and determines dispositions and deeds. Again and again and yet again in the Old Testament God says to the people of Israel, "Remember." "Remember that you were slaves in Egypt" (Deut 5:15). "Remember the wonderful works the Lord has done" (Ps 105:5). "Remember . . ."

The greatest danger to their identity was forgetfulness, and the remedy for forgetfulness was usually a wonderful and lively story. "Take heed lest you forget" (Deut 8:11) was a summons to remember the stories your father and mother had told you about God and God's works of power and grace. "Remember the Lord your God" (Deut 8:18) was an invitation to tell those stories to your children and to your children's children. "We were slaves in Egypt and God rescued us from oppression by his powerful hand. Then in the wilderness we wandered and we wondered, hungry, thirsty, and anxious, and God gave us manna, enough for each, for none too much, for none too little." Story after story was told generation after generation. Sometimes the people very nearly forgot the stories—or forgot to tell them—and they very nearly lost their memory and their identity. But the remedy for forgetfulness was always to tell the old, old story—and a new generation would remember and own the story as their story and God as their God.[11]

The art of remembering always involved storytelling—and it always had the shape of obedience. To remember the Lord, to own the stories of God's glory, of God's works of power and grace, always meant among God's people to discern God's will and to do it. To remember God's rescue from Pharaoh's oppression took shape in obedience to a commandment not to oppress a hired hand or to cheat him out of a living (Lev 19:15). To remember God's gift of manna, enough for all to share, took shape in not piling up lands upon lands or riches upon riches and in leaving the edges of the field unharvested for the poor. To remember the stories was to let them form and inform character and community. To remember the stories was to live them, not just to recall them.[12]

---

[11]Notice, for example, in Deut 5:3 that to remember the covenant was to own it, to be identified by it, to have life shaped by it: "Not with our ancestors did the LORD make this covenant, but with us, who are all of us here alive today." Thanks to my colleague Barry Bandstra for calling attention to this passage.

[12]The remembered story provided the context for the legal traditions of Israel. The story provides, of course, the literary context. The story of Sinai is part of the larger story that moves from Abraham to slavery in Egypt to the exodus to the entry into the Promised Land. The story of Sinai comes after the exodus and before the entry into the Promised Land, and it is the story of Sinai where the collections of laws are gathered. The story of Sinai stretches from Lev 19 to Num 10. In that context diverse collections of laws are gathered. The story, moreover, provides the covenantal context for the legal stipulations. The suzerainty treaties of the ancient Near East began with the identification of the great king and a recital of the past history of the relationship of that king and his vassals before recounting the stipulations concerning loyalty to the suzerain and living peaceably with other vassals. And the covenantal literature of Israel follows the same pattern—as, for example, in the preface to the Decalogue, "I am the LORD your God, who brought you out to the land of Egypt, out of the house of slavery . . ." (Ex 20:2). The story, finally, provided the context for discernment

As it was with Israel, so it was with the church. They learned from the Hebrew Scriptures no theory of memory, but they learned to remember. Forgetfulness was still the greatest danger. The art of remembering still involved storytelling, and remembering still took the shape of discerning and doing the will of God. They were a community of discernment because they were a community of memory. They were "able to instruct one another" because they could remind one another of the story.

There were various contexts, of course, within which the church was a community of memory.[13] It is not my claim that the church was *only* a community of moral discourse; the church had other functions and intentions when it gathered in memory of Jesus. However, it *is* my claim that the community gathered in memory of Jesus, whatever else it was, was *also* a community of

---

in revising the laws of Israel. The Israelites could not simply create social legislation *ex nihilo*. Like us, they received traditions, but they set the received traditions in the context of the story, and the story nudged the legal traditions in the direction of something closer to what was fitting to the story. Perhaps the best illustration of this process is the variety of legal traditions concerning slavery. In the oldest biblical code, the Covenant Code of Ex 20:22–23:19, the received tradition may be presumed to be something like the Code of Hammurabi, but Israel's code, under the pressure of the story, is somewhat more generous with slaves (Ex 21:2-6). A later code, the Deuteronomic Code of Deut 4:44–28:44, revisits the received tradition, revising it into an instrument of reform. The law for the release of slaves in Deut 15:12-18 revisits the law of Ex 21:2-6 and revises it. It includes now an explicit reminder of the story: "Remember that you were a slave in the land of Egypt" (Deut 15:15). It is made more generous: "you shall not send him out empty-handed" (Deut 15:13). And it is expanded to include female slaves as well as male slaves (Deut 15:12, 17). And in the still later legal tradition, the Holiness Code of Lev 17–27, the law concerning slavery is revised again, made more fitting to the story, forbidding making a fellow Israelite a slave (Lev 25:39): "For they are my servants, whom I brought out of the land of Egypt; they shall not be sold as slaves are sold" (Lev 25:42). The laws are not given or received as a timeless code; they are open to reform and revision until the story is lived as well as told.

[13]They were a community of memory, for example, in the task of evangelism. But to announce that this Jesus is Lord and to invite others to share in that profession was always also to summon them to a revisioning of the whole of life with Christ at the right hand of God, to join in the communal task of discerning the shape and style of life fitting his Lordship. (On the connection of evangelism and Christian ethics see Richard Mouw, *Political Evangelism* [Grand Rapids: Eerdmans, 1973].)

They were a community of memory also, of course, in their services of worship. In preaching and prayer and hymn and sacrament they remembered Jesus and owned his story as their story, his life as their life, the "mind of Christ" as their mind (Phil 2:5, with reference to a hymn). In worship they owned an identity and a vision which evoked and sustained communal discernment of the deeds and dispositions which belonged to a life of service, a life of praise. (On the connection of worship and Christian ethics see James M. Gustafson "Spiritual Life and Moral Life," in *Theology and Christian Ethics* [Philadelphia: Pilgrim, 1974], pp. 161-76. On worship as a context for early Christian moral discernment and literary activity see C. D. Moule, *The Birth of the New Testament* [New York: Harper & Row, 1962], pp. 210-14.)

moral discourse, deliberation and discernment. In whatever way they remembered Jesus, the community also always bore a moral tradition that was never quite reducible to applying a code or trusting an intuition but always called forth discernment. In whatever way they remembered Jesus, the community formed character, nurtured certain dispositions, directed certain intentions, renewed minds and a common mind, and equipped a community for the vocation of being "able to instruct one another."

Because the remembered Jesus had been raised, because the ages had turned, communal discernment was *possible* in memory and hope. Because the remembered Jesus had not yet appeared in glory, because it was not yet the good future of God's unchallenged sovereignty, communal discernment was *necessary* to watchfulness. So Paul both commended the Roman churches and exhorted them (Rom 12:11-12). They were—and they were called to be—"full of goodness, filled with all knowledge, and able to instruct one another."

THE CONTINUING CHURCH

And the churches still are—and are still called to be—"full of goodness, filled with all knowledge, and able to instruct one another." Let us turn (finally) to the continuing church. Let it be admitted that such a commendation of the continuing church seems extravagant. Let the counterevidence of scandals and willful ignorance and bickering be acknowledged. But Paul's compliment must have seemed extravagant to the Romans, too. And there was more than a little evidence counter to Paul's commendation of the Roman churches, as well. Romantic notions of the early church may prompt an easy acceptance of Paul's commendation of the Roman churches while we presume that realism requires us to deny any such commendation of contemporary churches. It is easy—too easy—to say, "The Roman churches must have been wonderful communities. But that was the early church. My church is just not that gifted with knowledge and goodness, and we surely are not able to instruct one another." It is easy—but it is also wrong.

It is wrong, in the first place, because the Roman churches—or the Corinthian Christians, or any of the other early Christian communities—were made up of quite ordinary people. There was not a halo to be seen. There is no reason to think that moral discourse and mutual instruction came more naturally to those churches than it comes to contemporary churches. Can we really suppose that the Roman Christians had some "natural" readiness to be patient with the thoughts, words and deeds of others? Or, that they had a "natural" disposition to respect other members of their community as givers of reasons or as hearers of reasons? On the contrary, these Jewish and Gentile Christians in Rome did not even have a "natural" reason to regard themselves as members of the same community, and they had, therefore, no "natural" reason to care enough about each other to encourage or to admonish one another.

Indeed, what came "naturally" to these Roman Christians seems to have been accusations and epithets, suspicion and animosity. Jews had traditionally regarded Gentiles as idolaters and as "sinners"; Roman Gentiles had long regarded Jews as "superstitious"[14]; and that traditional animosity and suspicion evidently seemed "natural" to many of the Christians in Rome. Some Jewish Christians at Rome condemned the Gentiles as "sinners," and some Gentile Christians despised the Jews for their scruples about Sabbath and festivals and food. The "righteous" Jews called the Gentiles "sinners"; the Gentiles thought of themselves as "strong" and called the Jewish Christians "weak." The epithets, however, were only part of the problem. There were serious and substantive disagreements between Jewish Christians and Gentile Christians about the place of the law and about the meaning and scope of Christian freedom. These disagreements allowed Jewish Christians to use the Hebrew Scriptures like a weapon against Gentile "sinners" and Gentile Christians to flaunt their freedom in order to spite those Jewish legalists. Such moral differences— and the boasting and judging and enmity that surrounded them—may make one wonder not how I could make the claim that contemporary churches are *still* "full of goodness, filled with all knowledge, and able to instruct one another" but how Paul could have made that extravagant claim about the Roman Christians in the first place.

Paul's confidence was not founded on any "natural" saintliness of these Roman Christians. It was founded on the extravagant grace of God. It was founded on the gospel, "the power of God for salvation to everyone who has faith" (Rom 1:16), both Jew and Gentile. It was founded on what God had done in Christ to create such community and on what God had done in the Spirit to equip them for mutual instruction. Paul wrote "boldly" of that gospel. He reminded the *Jewish* Christians not only of the verdict of Scripture that "there is no one who is righteous" (Rom 3:10, citing Ps 14) but also of the gospel of God in which both Jew and Gentile are justified (Rom 3:21-26) and in which "there is no distinction" (Rom 3:22). There is no room in the gospel for boasting (Rom 3:27-31). There is no room in the gospel for condemnation (Rom 8:1). And he reminded the *Gentile* Christians of their baptism. They have died with Christ in his death to sin so that, as Christ was raised from the dead, they too "might

---

[14]See Robert L. Wilken, *The Christians as the Romans Saw Them* (New Haven: Yale University Press, 1984), pp. 50-67.

walk in newness of life" (Rom 6:4), so that they might be no longer sinners but "righteous" (Rom 6:1-23). There is no room in the gospel for the flaunting of one's freedom. He reminded them *all* that Christ had died for the "weak" and for "sinners" and for "enemies" (Rom 5:6-11) so that the "weak" might be "strong in faith," so that "sinners" might be "righteous," and enemies be reconciled both to God and to each other. He reminded them, in sum, that the gospel of God had made them a community, that they were members of "one body in Christ, and individually . . . members one of another" (Rom 12:5; cf. 1 Cor 12:27; Eph 4:25, 5:30). And having reminded them of the gospel of God, Paul invited them to the "obedience of faith." He called on them to "welcome one another" (Rom 15:7). And on the foundation of the gospel of God, he expressed his confidence that they were "able to instruct one another."

The second reason, therefore, that it is wrong to regard Paul's commendation of the Roman churches as inappropriate to the continuing churches is simply this: that the extravagant grace of God is still at work. God continues to create community and to equip the continuing churches for moral discourse.

The "knowledge" of the Roman churches was not simply a collation of what individual members knew that they knew; their "goodness" was not merely a sum of the little good individual members were proud of doing well. The Roman churches were full of "knowledge" and "goodness" because they remembered Jesus and shared in the knowledge and goodness of Christ. And because the continuing churches still remember Jesus, there continue to be reasons to commend them as "full of goodness, filled with all knowledge, and able to instruct one another." They are still able to be—and still called to be—communities of moral discourse and deliberation and discernment.

A CONTINUING TRADITION OF DISCOURSE, DELIBERATION AND DISCERNMENT

Paul's commendation may still seem extravagant. And acknowledging that the grace of God is the foundation of Paul's confidence may make it seem a commendation of God rather than a commendation of the Roman—or the continuing—churches. Permit me, therefore, to begin again with a more modest claim and to support it by calling attention to some very mundane features of the common lives of Christian community. The modest claim is this: Christian communities continue to be communities of moral discourse. Members of the churches still sometimes talk together about what they should do or leave undone.

The discourse can be quite informal. Conversations after worship, for example, are frequently about the prospects for a favorite team or about the prospects for a recent graduate, but I have overheard conversations that could prompt something like Paul's compliment. A father was sick and a mother had lost her job, and a conversation concerned how that family could be helped. A morning paper had a headline about homelessness in the city, and the conversation concerned how the congregation could respond. Such informal conversations are not all at church, of course. When they sit together at a block party there may be a conversation about whether and how to make a special effort to welcome some new (and different) neighbors. When they happen to meet in the market, they may talk about medical care for their aging parents or about parental care for their adolescent children. The discourse continues.

And it continues in more formal contexts, too, in contexts more intentionally committed to moral discourse. In a church's educational program, for example, there will be conversations about moral responsibilities. In one class there may be talk about choices that affect the air and the water that sustain life. In another class there may be a discussion of the violence in some distant part of the world, or of the violence in the church's neighborhood. A hospice nurse from the congregation may lead another class in reflection about decisions we need to make about our dying and our care for the dying. And in yet another class there may be a conversation about being young and single and sexual. The discourse continues.

And it continues in institutional settings. In a congregational meeting, for example, there may be a discussion of the funding for "benevolence," the fund to help the poor. In a committee for building expansion there may be a conversation about whether to take a loan from a bank that regularly refuses loans to minority businesses. In a committee to consider hiring someone to minister among them there may be talk about recognizing and utilizing the gifts of women. The lists could go on, of course, for the discourse goes on. The modest claim surely stands: Christian communities continue to be communities of moral discourse.

The discourse continues, but so do the temptations. With respect to personal choices it remains tempting to surrender personal responsibility to the group, to neglect or to disown one's own responsibility. In Western culture, however, it has become considerably more tempting to treat personal choices as purely "private" matters, as nobody else's business, as matters to be decided by the secret tastes and preferences of autonomous individuals. It is tempting, for example, to treat divorce as a purely "private" matter, as no business of the Christian community. The Christian tradition, however, contains convictions and practices about marriage that should make the community reticent to treat a personal decision by one of its members to divorce as a purely "private" choice. Moreover, Christian churches have reasons to think that a vision of autonomous selves, linked only by contract, is unable to give an adequate account of our common life—or of our marriages. If these things are so, then Christian communities may and must recognize that to treat personal decisions as purely "private" choices is a temptation, and they may and must resist temptation.

With respect to communal decisions, it is still tempting simply to surrender them to an ecclesiastical official, to some institutional leadership, but in our society it is still more tempting to treat communal choices as purely "public" matters to be decided by the generally accredited wisdom of some broader community. It is tempting, for example, for churches to make decisions about their investments simply on the basis of security and yield, the conventional wisdom about investments. But churches have some particular convictions that make them distinctive communities. They regard themselves as stewards, for example, and stewardship in Christian community entails more than getting top dollar; it means using our investments—and our borrowing and our buying and our selling, as well—in ways that honor God and serve God's cause. If churches are serious about being disciples of Christ and stewards of God's good gifts, therefore, they may recognize that to make communal decisions by the unqualified application of another community's standards—even if they are prudent and sensible standards—is a temptation. And they may and must resist temptation.

Churches are only able to resist these temptations when they continue to be not only communities of discourse but also communities of deliberation. There must be conversation not only about what should be done but also about *why* it should be done. It is critically important that members of Christian communities continue to give and to hear reasons. Giving voice to a rationale for a certain choice, and giving ear to it as well, is not, however, sufficient. Churches must also continue to test reasons by their coherence with the gospel, to defend or reject or qualify reasons by their congruity with the story of Christ. Churches must continue, that is to say, to be communities of discourse and deliberation by being communities of discernment and memory.

There are, after all, other communities in which there are conversations about what should be done and why. There are professional associations and labor unions, neighborhoods and political precincts, countries of which we are citizens, and many others. Each of these communities bears a tradition and forms character and, to some extent at least, influences the choices and decisions of its members. Indeed, for many of us participation in other communities is more determinative of our decisions than our membership in the church.[15] Nevertheless, churches can and sometimes do test and qualify these other traditions, call for the re-formation of character and conduct, and sustain discourse and deliberation in the service of discernment of a way of life "worthy of the gospel of Christ." The churches are not to be confused with any of the other associations. They continue to be distinctive communities of discourse and deliberation and discernment by remembering Jesus and by transforming questions of character and conduct into the question of how they may live the story they still love to tell.

Contemporary churches, then, continue to be—and to be called to be—communities of discourse, deliberation and discernment in memory of Jesus. They remember Jesus not simply as an object of historical recollection but as the living Lord who continues to abide with his continuing church and continues to call them to repentance and discipleship. Such remembrance still fills the church with goodness and knowledge and makes its members "able to instruct one another."

THE DANGER OF FORGETFULNESS IN MORAL DISCOURSE TODAY

Contemporary churches are not exempt from Paul's remarkable commendation of the Roman churches, or from its subtle vocation to be such communities. But it is not easy, and the greatest danger is still forgetfulness. In the context of moral differences, there are at least two ways in which the churches—and their ethicists—stand at particular risk of forgetfulness today: first, by their confidence in and enthusiasm for an impartial perspective, for universal rational principles, and second, by their confidence in and enthusiasm for certain partial and parochial values.

The danger of forgetfulness in moral Esperanto. The enthusiasm for an impartial perspective is not hard to understand. The moral pluralism of contemporary culture seems to require it. Christians can, of course, witness to their deepest convictions in a pluralist society, but they can hardly expect a non-Christian to find those Christian convictions persuasive grounds for doing something or for leaving something else undone. Therefore, many Christian ethicists have sought for moral principles which all persons do or can and should hold on the basis of reason alone, quite apart from their membership in particular communities with their specific moral traditions, and they have attempted to use those principles persuasively. To convince the non-

---

[15]James M. Gustafson, "Christian Ethics and Social Policy," in *Faith and Ethics: The Theology of H. R. Niebuhr*, ed. Paul Ramsey (New York: Harper & Row, 1957), p. 133.

Christian physician not to treat abortion as a morally trivial matter, to persuade a legislative body to protect the rights of the poor in the land, to argue before a corporation's Board of Directors that they should sacrifice some profit to protect against pollution from their factories—all such contexts for moral discourse seem to require not Christian conviction but pure and practical reason.

Theologically, the quest for an impartial perspective and for universal principles seems warranted by the conviction that the God who called a cosmos from chaos also established a certain moral order in the universe and wrote certain moral principles on human hearts (Rom 2:15). Philosophically, the quest for impartial reasons and universal principles has seemed not only permitted but also required. Kant's first formulation of the "categorical imperative," after all, was "Act only on that maxim whereby thou canst at the same time will that it should become a universal law."[16]

---

[16]Immanuel Kant, *Fundamental Principles of the Metaphysic of Morals* (*Grundlegung zur Metaphysik der Sitten*), trans. Thomas K. Abbott (New York: Liberal Arts Press, 1949), p. 30. Kant's project for morality, shared by many philosophers since, was to identify and to justify an impartial and rational principle for morality, a principle which *all* people can and must hold independently of their particular circumstances and conditions, independently of their particular communities and histories, quite apart from their specific loyalties and identities, quite apart from any particular narrative or story that they remember and from any putatively partial vision of human flourishing for which they hope. Kant's maxim would be more defensible if its minimal character were acknowledged—if he argued that maxims that cannot be universalized were immoral rather than that all maxims that can be universalized are duties. It is possible to universalize the maxim "Put your left shoe on first," but it is not a moral duty. The minimal character of Kant's imperatives is also manifest in that it does not rule out all immoral maxims. It is quite plausible that the rich fool of Luke could universalize the maxim on which he evidently acted: let each one look out for himself. Kant responds to this objection by saying that "many cases might occur in which one would have need of the love and sympathy of others" (p. 41). It is true that the rich fool later found himself inconsistently willing to abrogate that rule when he was in torment and needed a drop of water to cool his tongue, but one who is sure of his fortune and of his future universalizability will not establish the duty to be benevolent or prohibit self-centeredness. See William K. Frankena, *Ethics* (Englewood Cliffs, N.J.: Prentice-Hall, 1963), pp. 25-28. Many philosophers since Kant have identified the moral point of view with an impartial perspective. But because universalizability is a formal and empty principle, they have usually supplemented it with a principle taken to be required by it. Kant himself offered a second formulation of the categorical imperative: "So act as to treat humanity, whether in thine own person or in that of any other, in every case as an end withal, never as a means only" (*Fundamental Principles of the Metaphysic of Morals*, p. 46). That formulation has been critically important in public discourse in pluralist societies, for it insists upon respect for autonomy. Kant may have had a richer notion of "humanity" than many Kantians, but the richer notion was hard to sustain on purely rational grounds. At any rate, the principle has often been translated in pluralist societies into the universal principle of equal freedom, which assures people of the right to do as they please as long as it does not interfere with other people's equal right to do as they please.

The enthusiasm for an impartial perspective is not hard to understand, and the attempts at persuasion within a pluralistic society may not be given up. I do not say, and I do not mean, that an impartial perspective is morally unilluminating or that there are no universal principles knowable by reason. I do not claim that "the Enlightenment project" has altogether failed.[17] I hold no brief for a "theological veto" of natural morality,[18] not even within the church. For Christians to dismiss arguments based "on reason alone" strikes me as an *argumentum ad hominem* on the scale of an *argumentum ad*

The chief competitor to this general way of articulating a universal and rational principle has been utilitarianism, which requires all people to do whatever will bring the greatest good for the greatest number. The attraction of the good is universal, indeed analytical (since to call anything "good" is to say we are or should be attracted to it), and Bentham's dictum "everyone to count for one, nobody for more than one" preserves impartiality. The utilitarians have themselves argued about what is "good," and particularly about whether it is sufficient to say that pleasure or happiness is "good." John Stuart Mill already questioned Bentham's account of the pleasure principle, attempting to distinguish between "higher" and "lower" pleasures. "It is better to be a human being dissatisfied than a pig satisfied; better to be Socrates dissatisfied than a fool satisfied." See John Stuart Mill, *Utilitarianism*, in *Utilitarianism, Liberty, and Representative Government* (London: J. M. Dent & Sons, 1910; *Utilitarianism* was first published in 1863), p. 9. But it is hard to defend a richer notion of the good on the basis of reason alone. At any rate, the principle of utility has often been translated in pluralist societies into a universal principle of preference satisfaction: so act as to maximize the satisfaction of the preferences of the most people.

Many contemporary philosophers have challenged this "Enlightenment project" (especially noteworthy is Alasdair MacIntyre, *After Virtue* [Notre Dame, Ind.: University of Notre Dame Press, 1981]), this striving for a "Moral Esperanto," "an artificial moral language invented in the (unrealistic) hope that everyone will want to speak it" (Jeffrey Stout, *Ethics After Babel* [Boston: Beacon, 1988], p. 294). But the arguments most frequently made and credited in public discourse still seem to be that someone's freedom is being infringed on or that the pursuit of pleasure (or of satisfying preferences) is being hindered even though no one is being harmed. Evidently the public has not been persuaded which impartial principle is the *right* impartial principle, whether freedom or utility, but it has evidently been convinced that public discourse—including discourse in the church— should be limited and governed by impartial rational principles. And many Christian ethicists have evidently also been persuaded, for many speak and write more like followers of Kant or Mill than like disciples of Jesus. One might note, for example, how the Christian notion of love can sometimes be reduced to either a Kantian notion of respect for persons or a utilitarian notion of beneficence. (See Stanley Hauerwas, "Love's Not All You Need," in *Vision and Virtue*, pp. 111-26.)

[17]That "the Enlightenment project" has failed is MacIntyre's claim in *After Virtue*, pp. 35-39. The more modest claim would be that its successes have been minimal. In a conversation with a pluralist society we might do better as Christian ethicists to give up the pretentious attempt to construct what Stout calls "Moral Esperanto" and be satisfied to learn "Moral Pidgin."

[18]See Karl Barth *Church Dogmatics* 2/2, pp. 509-42; idem, "No!" in *Natural Theology: Comprising "Nature and Grace" by Professor Dr. Emil Brunner and the reply "No!" by Dr. Karl Barth* (London: Centenary, 1946), pp. 67-128.

humanum.[19] In the New Testament itself "natural morality" and moral commonplaces evidently enter into moral deliberation.

I do say, however, that the impartial perspective is not to be identified with the Christian perspective, that the impartial perspective can provide only a *minimal* account of the moral life, and that if its minimalism is not acknowledged, the church and its moral discourse will suffer forgetfulness.

The minimalism of the impartial perspective can be seen in the account it gives of relationships of covenant and community. The relationship of husband and wife for example—or of parent and child, or of pastor and parishioner, or simply of being "members one of another"—can from an impartial perspective only be construed as *contractual* relationships between autonomous individuals or as *instrumental* relationships to achieve some extrinsic good. The impartial perspective will not build or sustain or nurture *community*.

The minimalism of the impartial perspective can be seen in another way. It requires of people a certain alienation from themselves,[20] from the passions and loyalties that give them moral character and from the histories and community that give them moral identity, in order to adopt the impartial point of view. It is legitimate, indeed salutary, for people to attempt to see themselves as objectively as they can, as others see them. No one, however, can *live* that way, transcending their links with others in time and place, denying their mortal identity—at least, no one can live that way with integrity. The impartial perspective will not build or sustain or nurture *character*.

The minimalism of the impartial perspective can also be seen in its reticence to instruct anyone about values or, indeed, about what should be done. The standard of equal freedom prefers the question "who should decide?" to the question "what should be decided?"; and utilitarianism prefers to find procedures for satisfying the preferences of the greatest number while treating such preferences as matters of private taste. The impartial perspective by itself will not build or sustain or nurture moral *discourse* or deliberation or discernment, and it threatens to sunder the unity of life into a private realm of autonomy and preference and a public realm of impartiality.

The identification of Christian ethics with an impartial perspective and the failure to acknowledge the minimalism of such a perspective, then, threaten the ability of the church to form moral communities, to form moral character,

---

[19] An *argumentum ad hominem*, of course, is the fallacy that pretends to have discredited an argument by attacking the character of the person who made the argument. An *argumentum ad humanum* would be an argument that pretends to have discredited an argument by the observation that the person who made the argument is a human being.

[20] Hauerwas, *Peaceable Kingdom*, p. 18.

and to be a community of moral discourse, deliberation and discernment. The identification of Christian ethics with an impartial perspective and the failure to acknowledge the minimalism of such a perspective condemn the church—and her ethicists—to forgetfulness.

The danger of forgetfulness in parochialism. It is not just enthusiasm for an impartial perspective and universal principles that tempts us to forgetfulness and threatens the ability of members of the Christian community to instruct one another, however. So do parochialism and provincialism and chauvinism and any narrowness of vision or abridgment of perspective which may belong to particular communities as well as to individual members of the community. It is clear, I suppose, that whenever Christians identify or confuse the story of Jesus with "rags to riches" stories or stories of success through possibility thinking, they are in danger of forgetfulness. Surely, whenever they celebrate the story of America as the story that gives them identity and makes them a community in the church, they are at risk of forgetfulness. When the Lord's Supper is a place of happy division of denominations or happy segregation of races or happy separation of classes, then certainly the church is at risk of forgetfulness.

Christians also stand at risk of forgetfulness when any one good is made absolute, whether the sanctity of life, or the sanctity of truth, or any other genuine but partial good. They stand at risk of forgetfulness when they identify any one good with the cause of God and the triumph of that good with the reign of God.

I do not say, and I do not mean, that congregations of socially homogeneous people cannot be the church. I do not claim that the assimilation of particular loyalties and identities and histories and values and causes is forbidden to particular congregations in their particular times and places. Christians need not and should not dismiss the wisdom of particular cultures and histories from the reason-giving and reason-hearing of moral deliberation; the New Testament itself does not. And I do not say, and I do not mean, that the particular and partial goods sometimes identified with the cause of God are not *genuine* goods, that it is inappropriate to seek them, or that we may ever turn against them.

But I do say that the community that fails to acknowledge its parochialism is doomed to forgetfulness. I do say that when we encourage the churches to grow along socially homogeneous lines, we risk forgetfulness. And I do say that all the particular histories of persons in the church must be submissive to the story of Jesus, which gives the church identity and makes the church a community. All of our little certainties and all of our little virtues must be not only assimilated but also made submissive to Jesus, whose memory still fills the church with knowledge and goodness. All of our political and social and economic and national loyalties must be opened to question and criticism by our loyalty to Christ. All our genuine but partial goods must kneel before the one who is the way, the truth and the life, in whom the fullness of God and the fullness of good was pleased to dwell, and whose cosmic sovereignty we await. Then it will be the reign of *shalom*, even among the goods that all belong to God's intention, but here and now genuine goods can come into genuine conflict. Here and now *part* of what we know to be God's cause from the memory of Jesus can come into tragic conflict with another part of what we know to be God's cause from the same memory. Here and now watchfulness is required lest our defense of God's cause on one front leaves it open to attack on another. Watchfulness requires memory—and discourse with those who are different from us in the church.

We *need* those whom it is too much our impulse to shun and despise. Without them we stand at risk of an abridged perspective, at risk of confusing our particular ethnic, economic, professional or other tribal identities with our identity in Christ, at risk of identifying our particular but partial good with the reign of God, at risk of forgetfulness. It was not accidental that Paul commended the Roman churches, which included both Jewish and Gentile Christians. The Jewish Christians could remain Jewish Christians and the Gentile Christians could remain Gentile Christians, but they were nevertheless one in Christ and able to instruct one another. The very differences that made discourse difficult made it mutually instructive, too. They had to remember Jesus in whom there is "neither Jew nor Gentile." To be sure, Jews and Gentiles told the story somewhat differently, but it remained one story behind the different tellings.[21] And it was not incidental that the church to which Paul writes with advice to the master of the runaway slave, Onesimus, included slaves.

Even if, or especially if, a congregation is socially homogeneous, it needs to be in conversation with the heterogeneity of Christ's body, with *all* those who tell the story of Jesus and own it as their own. Without them and without the self-critical reflection, the repentance, nurtured by remembering Jesus in the context of the whole church, a church may nurture certain virtues, say, middle-class respectability or, more nobly, reverence for life, but it will not be the community which remembers Jesus and which, full of knowledge and goodness, is able to instruct

---

[21]The Gospels of Matthew and Mark may be taken as illustrative of this point. Mark, the earlier of the two, is written for a community of Gentile Christians; Matthew, for a largely Jewish Christian community. See Verhey, *The Great Reversal*, pp. 74-92.

one another in the great variety of goods and in the conflict of goods.

Such discourse will not always result in unanimity—and it need not. It may not—and often will not—resolve dilemmas or produce judgments which have the force of law in the Christian community. But it can—and sometimes does—bring conflicting interests, values and perspectives under the judgment and renewal of the one Christ whose story Christians celebrate. Mutual admonition and mutual accountability can encourage and help all Christians to bring every partial good, every political opinion, every social strategy, every economic goal and tactic, and every heritage captive to the Lord of the story.

A DIVERSITY OF GIFTS

The community that remembers the story of Jesus and would live it recognizes not only a variety of goods but also a variety of gifts. Discernment, or the perception of what is fitting to the story we love to tell, is not the task of the ethicist or the pastor alone. It is the task of the church in discourse. Christian ethics is not a substitute for that discourse. Discernment involves the diversity of gifts of the congregation—the gifts of wisdom and creativity, the gifts of indignation at injustice and sympathy with the suffering, the gifts of knowledge of people and places, the gifts of awareness of opportunities and obstructions, the gifts of technical knowledge and special skills—all enlightening the way to the particular and specific deeds that are worthy of the gospel in the place and times in which we live. Each gifted member of the church (and each member of the church *is* gifted) can only speak out of their own perspective and their own experience, but each is also willing to recognize the gifts of others, to listen to the reasons of others, and to see things differently because of the body of Christ.

There are various gifts, but it is also important to say that this diversity is a variety of *gifts*. Two things follow from this. The first is that there is no room for boasting in the community of discourse, neither by one member over against another, nor by the Christian community over against other communities. This language of "gift" should be enough to keep us from claiming moral superiority for Christians or for ourselves in comparison with other Christians. As Paul says, "If then you received it, why do you boast as if it were not a gift?" (1 Cor 4:6). If that is not enough to keep us from boasting, then we may need to be reminded also of the blemished history of the church, marred as it is by religious hatred, holy killings, pious self-righteousness and sanctified complacency with slavery and apartheid and the oppression of women and other injustices. When the church gathers for worship, it neither storms nor strolls into the presence of God; it always comes in repentance and confession;

it always longs to hear again the assurance of pardon. The gift of forgiveness permits no self-righteousness, but it does permit persons and communities to begin again to discern and to do God's will, and it does permit persons and communities to make the ambiguous choices courageously, confident of God's good gift of forgiveness.

Any Christian and any Christian community that remembers Jesus and remains alert to his call to repent and believe the gospel is unlikely to indulge in comparisons between their righteousness and the righteousness of their neighbors; in memory of Jesus such comparisons are unworthy and unfitting. A focus on the distinctiveness of the Christian life may very well contain a temptation to such comparisons and to such boasting. It should not surprise us—and it surely should not dismay us—if non-Christians make decisions similar to those Christians make or if they make them for some of the same reasons. The Christian community does not have a corner on moral truth. Indeed, it acknowledges that the Truth is not its possession but its Lord. It receives and celebrates (however imperfectly) the gifts the Lord gives to his church, including this one, that the Lord fills it with goodness and knowledge and enables mutual instruction. The church is *given* a particular identity to which it may and must be faithful. That gift does not provide a place for pride or room for sloth, but it still calls us to discernment.

The second thing that follows from the recognition of a variety of *gifts* is, well, gladness. "The disciples were glad when they saw the Lord" (Jn 20:20), and the church is still glad when it remembers him. The gospel is good news still, a story we may love to tell—and to live. A life worthy of the gospel—and a discernment worthy of the gospel—will be marked by a certain felicity. The gifts of God may be received with gratitude and joy, including the gifts for discourse and deliberation and discernment in the church. We may delight to be—to be gifted to be—"full of goodness, filled with all knowledge, and able to instruct one another." The choices, to be sure, are sometimes serious ones, and the task of discernment is sometimes sobering, but there is a joy that runs along our choices, a joy which enables us to make the hard choices and to bear the sufferings of the right choices without taking either them or ourselves too seriously. It is upon God—not upon us or our hard choices—that the good future of the world depends; we may be glad for that. And while we wait for that good future and watch for it, while we strive already to let its power be felt, if we must suffer a little for the right choices, then we only share in the suffering of Christ; and we may be glad for that as well. The gifts of God are demanding, but the demands of God are not burdensome but light with joy.

Paul's word to the Roman churches is a remarkable compliment and a demanding vocation, but it is also a commendation and a calling in which continuing churches may also delight. If we can recover this vision of the church, if we can receive with gratitude the gifts of God to the church for discourse and discernment, and if we can receive joyfully the demands upon us correlative to God's gifts, then perhaps the church will look less like an archaic museum piece to some of our contemporaries and more like a confident community that knows why it exists and why it acts, more like its Lord, whose story is its story, whose life is its life.[22]

---

[22]This paper draws heavily on Allen Verhey, *Remembering Jesus* (Grand Rapids: Eerdmans, 2002), pp. 14-48.

PART FOUR

THE CHURCH AS SACRAMENTAL COMMUNITY?

9

Beyond Theocracy and Individualism

The Significance of John Howard Yoder's Ecclesiology for Evangelicalism

CRAIG A. CARTER

Contemporary evangelicalism is often viewed as lacking an adequate ecclesiology. Critics from Catholic and Anglican traditions look suspiciously at the lack of accountability, carelessness about church order and the proliferation of new movements and offshoots of existing ones. They see no mechanism for safeguarding orthodoxy and no consciousness of standing in a specific tradition going back to the apostles. The growing array of evangelical denominations, independent churches and parachurch organizations is seen as giving late-capitalist consumer culture what it wants: designer religion. Individuals are free to pick and choose the elements of piety, doctrines, practices, rituals, level of involvement and ethical positions they want and discard the rest. The constantly evolving ethos of evangelical churches follows consumer trends in music and lifestyles. Participation is voluntary in the sense of being a matter of trivial preferences of autonomous individuals driven by nothing more than the satisfaction of felt needs. Over the past thirty years, many evangelicals, having come into contact with these criticisms of evangelicalism, have responded by taking the trail to Canterbury, or even on to Rome or Constantinople, in order to find a more adequate ecclesiology.[1]

According to Robert Webber, many evangelicals are attracted to the liturgical church because they are seeking a form of worship in which mystery has a

---

[1]See Robert Webber, *Evangelicals on the Canterbury Trail: Why Evangelicals Are Attracted to the Liturgical Church* (Waco, Tex.: Word, 1985).

place,[2] they appreciate the emphasis on sacramental reality,[3] they find Anglican worship to be more God-centered, Christ-centered and Scripture-centered,[4] and they desire a more holistic spirituality that embraces the whole church throughout history.[5] It is interesting to note, however, that Webber takes pains to deny that the choice to move into the Anglican tradition involves, for him, at least, any negative judgment on the evangelical tradition. Webber presents the Anglican option merely as a choice that is right for him. He says of the Baptist congregation of his parents: "I would never think of suggesting that these people become Anglican. Nor do I for one moment think my Anglican expression of the faith is a higher form of spirituality."[6] My question is, "why not?" After all, Webber describes the Anglican tradition as the fullness of the faith and evangelicalism as lacking extremely important aspects of ecclesiology. Yet his plea, in this book, seems to amount to "Please don't write me off and I promise I won't write you off." My difficulty with this approach is that it can easily be interpreted as merely extending the cafeteria menu to include the liturgical option, rather than as a radical challenge to modern individualism.

Late capitalist liberal democracy fosters individualism through consumerism, mass media, geographical mobility, high divorce rates and the breakdown of all intermediate social structures, including the family. The cult of therapy often functions to relieve guilt feelings in people who choose to put themselves and their own immediate happiness before fulfillment of their social duties. The resulting individualism makes the formation of countercultural, Christian communities extremely difficult. In the absence of determined moral and cultural resistance, Christians tend to be conformed to the world around them. The only real authority structure left in late modernity is the state. Individualism, therefore, comports well with theocracy in that there is a symbiosis between the autonomous individual and the state, which serves as the guardian of individual rights. In the absence of strong church communities that could serve as institutions of primary allegiance for Christians, Western Christians tend to identify their welfare with the nation-state that makes the pursuit of self-fulfillment possible. As Westerners (who happen also to be Christians), most evangelicals tend toward theocracy, even if that only means defending "Western values." So, ironically, modern Western individualism turns out to be closely linked with theocracy. Patriotic Christians are willing to die defending Western values, which

---

[2]Ibid., pp. 21-30.
[3]Ibid., pp. 43-56.
[4]Ibid., p. 41.
[5]Ibid., pp. 67-85.
[6]Ibid., p. 17.

they are incapable of distinguishing from Christian ones. The theocratic impulse animating evangelicals (and liberals, it must be said, as well) is not one in which the gospel is seriously being proposed as the basis for the whole of society; rather, it is one in which Christians conform their faith to the ideologies of late capitalist, liberal democratic nation states.

The acids of modern autonomous individualism have corroded Christian communities all over the Western world including Roman Catholic, Anglican and Magisterial Reformation traditions, as well as evangelical and free church traditions. Today in North America, the churches with liturgies and organs, collars and bishops, incense and prayer books may have a superficial appearance of being countercultural, but in reality many of these denominations are even further down the road toward consumer religion than free churches. The Anglican bishop of Vancouver recently has precipitated schism in order to implement his liberal beliefs within his diocese. In the interests of pandering to every individual's sexual preference, the church in this case has sought to be "inclusive" to the point of abandoning biblical morality. I would suggest that such churches have bought into the mentality of consumer religion every bit as much as the TV evangelists; they just offer a less vulgar (although still sentimentalized) product. If American evangelicals think of America as their church, Canadian Anglicans are committed to conforming to the secular political culture, which exalts the rights of autonomous individuals to self-fulfillment as the highest good. Evangelicals as well as nonevangelicals, and proponents of both low and high ecclesiologies alike, struggle with conformity to the world in the form of excessive, community-dissolving individualism and the theocratic temptation, which often accompanies it.

Given the reality of our present cultural situation, I have trouble seeing Webber's commendation of the Episcopal alternative as a solution to the problem of the church being conformed to the modern world of late-capitalist consumerism. Bruce Hindmarsh, in a recent paper, gets to the root of commitment to the consumer mentality when he argues,

> Early modern evangelicalism displayed an unprecedented . . . ecclesial consciousness that was characterized by an unparalleled subordination of church order to evangelical piety. The principle of unity among evangelicals was not typically spoken of as sacramental, nor did it have to do with authorized orders, forms or rites; the principle by which unity was discerned was evangelical piety itself.[7]

---

[7]Bruce Hindmarsh, "Is Evangelical Ecclesiology an Oxymoron? A Historical Perspective," in *Evangelical Ecclesiology: Reality or Illusion?* ed. John G. Stackhouse Jr. (Grand Rapids: Baker, 2003), p. 15.

When evangelical piety replaces the Word of God, mediated through preaching and sacraments, as what makes the church the church, then we have a serious problem. I grant that it is in some ways preferable that this piety should take the Christ-centered, evangelical form, as opposed to a generic human experience of the divine, which is often viewed by liberal Protestantism as the essence of faith. But no personal or generic human experience of Jesus Christ can ever adequately replace the living Lord Jesus Christ himself, mediated through preaching and sacraments, as the ground of unity in the church. When individual piety constitutes the basis of ecclesial unity, the individual is prior to the church in such a way that a cafeteria-style approach to Christianity is inevitable.

The excessive individualism of contemporary evangelicalism is also behind the tendency of evangelicals to embrace theocracy. What is intriguing about the rise of conservative Christian political action since the 1970s is how such an individualistic movement as evangelicalism could mount cohesive political action. But this anomaly disappears once one realizes that, for many American Christians, whether conservative or liberal, America functions as the church. Theocracy comes easily to those who believe that America is the city set on a hill, the successor to biblical Israel, and the means through which God is working to bring freedom to the world. From Walter Rauschenbush to Reinhold Niebuhr to Jerry Falwell, the basic view of America is the same; the differences are over what is wrong with America and how to fix it. That America should be the focus is not in dispute. Evangelicals will be susceptible to this kind of inadequate ecclesiology until they begin to take the church more seriously than the nation-state as their primary source of identity.

Given this background, I would like to suggest that evangelicals need to consider John Howard Yoder's ecclesiology for two reasons. First, he views individualism as a serious problem and counters it by making ecclesiology prior to individual piety. He offers an ecclesiology parallel to the traditional Roman Catholic position that there is no salvation outside the church insofar as he understands the church to be the embodiment of salvation. This poses a challenge to modern individualism at a far deeper level than merely advocating the liturgical church as one among several options. Secondly, Yoder also rejects theocracy and maintains a clear church-world distinction. His ecclesiology is able to move beyond individualism and theocracy because of his vision of the church as a covenanted community that bears witness to the triune God, who reveals himself decisively in Jesus Christ, and who is at work to redeem his whole creation.

YODER'S THREEFOLD TYPOLOGY OF ECCLESIOLOGY

In his article "A People in the World"[8] Yoder attempts to clarify the nature of what he calls the "believers' church vision." To do so, he uses a threefold typology, which analyzes three ecclesiological alternatives to Lutheranism in mid-sixteenth century central Europe.

First, Yoder points to those who seek to implement "the logic of theocratic humanism that Zwingli had borrowed from Erasmus, whereby the word of God, as spoken by the 'prophet' to the whole society brings about the renewing of that society according to the will of God."[9] This is the path of Zwingli himself, as well as the Reformed churches in Geneva, Heidelberg, the Netherlands and Scotland. It feeds into evangelicalism through Puritanism. In this vision, the renewal of church and society go hand in hand. Whether the church functions as an administrative department of the state, as with Bullinger or Erastus, or whether it is distinct as with Calvin and Knox, the same goal is in view: to ensure that the whole of society is ruled by those who take their cue from Scripture so that God may be glorified. In this approach, the locus of historical meaning is found in the movement of the whole of society as guided by the church. Yoder calls this type the "theocratic vision."[10]

Second, Yoder points to the spiritualizers, exemplified by Casper Schwenkfeld. They claimed to carry to its logical conclusion "the dismantling of externals and the search for the true inwardness of faith alone."[11] This emphasis has been part of Christianity in all centuries and feeds into evangelicalism through pietism and revivalism. Very often, as Yoder points out, those in this tradition contribute to social structures and do many good works, even while emphasizing that outward forms are insufficient without deep inward reality.[12] For this tradition, the locus of meaning shifts from society as a whole to the inner life of the individual.

Third, Yoder points to Anabaptism, as exemplified by Michael Stattler and Pilgrim Marpeck. Anabaptism was claiming to carry to its logical conclusion the restoration of original Christianity. The original Anabaptists in Zurich were colleagues of Zwingli's who wanted to press further with reforms, which both they and Zwingli believed to be biblical. Eventually they broke with Zwingli because of his reluctance to risk losing the support of the city council

---

[8]John Howard Yoder, "A People in the World," in *The Royal Priesthood: Essays Ecclesiological and Ecumenical*, ed. Michael G. Cartwright (Grand Rapids: Eerdmans, 1994), pp. 65-101.
[9]Ibid., p. 70.
[10]Ibid., p. 71.
[11]Ibid., p. 70.
[12]Ibid., p. 72.

by implementing too radical a reform program. The Anabaptists evangelized vigorously and established house churches in an ever-widening territory. They eventually developed into several families of denominations, including the Mennonites and the Hutterites.

As Yoder points out, it is interesting to note that each of these three types regarded the other two as having the same problem. From Zwingli's perspective, both the spiritualizers and the Anabaptists undermined Christian government. From Schwenkfeld's perspective, both the magisterial Reformers and the Anabaptists alike were too preoccupied with outward forms such as sacraments, ordination, church order, etc. From the Anabaptist perspective, both Zwingli and the spiritualizers denied the importance of proper church order. Schwenkfeld did not bother to challenge such things as the Mass or infant baptism because, for him, only spiritual reality mattered anyway. Zwingli could continue to let the Mass be celebrated long after he had come to the conclusion that it is theologically wrong because the true church is invisible and, therefore, the visible (imperfect) church can be reformed at whatever speed is compatible with the maintenance of public order. Yoder comments: "Thus both Schwenkfeld and Zwingli, in the name of a deeper spirituality, withstood the Anabaptist's call to bring into being a visible congregation of committed believers."[13]

Yoder's major ecclesiological thesis is that "the church is called to move beyond the oscillation between the theocratic and the spiritualist patterns, not to a compromise between the two or to a synthesis claiming like Hegel to 'assume' then both, but to what is genuinely a third option."[14] It is important to note at this point how his threefold typology allows us to see the believers' church type as something more than a vehicle for individualism and pietism.

The theocratic vision derives from the union of the Christian church and the Roman Empire, which took place during the third to fifth centuries after Christ. After the fateful separation of church and synagogue in the second century, the church grew to include perhaps ten percent of the population of the Roman Empire and increasingly distanced itself from its Jewish roots. In the final decade of the third century the last great wave of persecution occurred. In A.D. 313, Constantine's Edict of Milan extended toleration to Christianity and provided for the return of confiscated Christian property. Around A.D. 390 Emperor Theodosius closed the pagan temples and legally entrenched Christianity as the religion of the Empire. In A.D. 420 Augustine used the armed

---

[13]Ibid., p. 71.
[14]Ibid., p. 73.

might of Rome to help suppress the Donatists and the first persecution of Christians by Christians occurred. In A.D. 436 non-Christians were excluded from the army and a two-century long process was virtually complete; Christendom was born. For Yoder, the term "Constantinianism" does not merely refer to the actions of the historical man Constantine; it is actually a heresy named for a particular historical figure like Arianism or Pelagianism. Constantinianism is an ecclesiological heresy insofar as it erases the distinction between the church and the world, since the whole of society is now baptized. By failing to grant the world the freedom of unbelief, Constantinianism is inherently coercive. It is an eschatological heresy insofar as it erases the distinction between the current age and the kingdom of God by viewing this age in triumphalistic terms. But the tension created by pulling the kingdom back into history, ends up being resolved by means of a Platonic dualism in which the visible church is the mixed church of the wheat and the tares, while the true church is invisible. Yoder states:

> Previously Christians had known as a fact of experience that the church existed but had to believe against appearances that Christ ruled over the world. After Constantine one knew as a fact of experience that Christ was ruling over the world but had to believe against the evidence that there existed "a believing church." Thus the order of redemption was subordinated to that of preservation, and the Christian hope turned inside out.[15]

The Magisterial Reformers did not challenge Constantinianism in any fundamental sense. But, then again, neither did the spiritualizers. Only the Anabaptists challenged Constantinianism.

Yoder believes that we will have an adequate ecclesiology only once we have disavowed Constantinianism[16] and given up the theocratic vision. This is so for two reasons. First, the renunciation of the theocratic vision is necessary if we are going to develop an ecclesiology that understands the church as the locus of meaning in history. Yoder states: "From Genesis to Apocalypse, the meaning of history had been carried by the people of God as people, as community."[17] The rejection of Constantinianism is a necessary prerequisite to overcoming the problem of individualism because as long as the locus of meaning

---

[15]John Howard Yoder, "The Otherness of the Church," in *Royal Priesthood*, ed. Michael G. Cartwright (Grand Rapids: Eerdmans, 1994), p. 57.

[16]See his essay "The Disavowal of Constantine: An Alternative Perspective on Interfaith Dialogue," in *Royal Priesthood*, ed. Michael G. Cartwright (Grand Rapids: Eerdmans, 1994), pp. 242-61.

[17]John Howard Yoder, *The Priestly Kingdom: Social Ethics as Gospel* (Notre Dame, Ind.: University of Notre Dame Press, 1984), p. 138.

is society as a whole, the gathered community of believers will never be more than a dispensable aid to personal spirituality. Second, the renunciation of the theocratic vision is necessary if we are going to develop a noncoercive, disciplined community, which is ready for mission in the world. In a post-Constantinian ecclesiology, the dignity of the individual will be recognized in the fact that entrance into the church is voluntary and the tyranny of individualism will be prevented by the moral discipline of the freely covenanted community.

In order to be a sign of hope for the whole of creation, the church must be clearly distinct from the world and must be a community created by the Word of God and united by its faith in Jesus Christ. As Yoder points out, "[T]here can be no evangelistic call addressed to a person inviting him or her to enter into a new kind of fellowship and learning, if there is not such a body of persons, again distinct from the totality of society, to whom to come and from whom to learn."[18] What are the characteristics or marks of such a church?

YODER AND THE MARKS OF THE CHURCH

Yoder points out that the classic Reformation definition of the church as the place where the Word of God is properly preached and the sacraments are properly administered,[19] describes only the "superstructure" of the church and not the gathered congregation itself. The later addition of a third criterion, proper discipline, recognizes this omission but remains on an abstract level.

Yoder points out that two major leaders of the twentieth century ecumenical movement, Willem A. Visser't Hooft and Stephen Neill, found it necessary to move well beyond the Reformation criteria. Visser't Hooft identifies three key functions of the church: witness (*martyria*), service (*diakonia*), and communion or fellowship (*koinōnia*). While these might be seen as similar to the Reformation criteria, they are broader and less likely to be limited to clerical functions. They have to do with the church as a community of people in relationship to each other because of their relationship to God, and they imply a distinction between the church and the world. Neill suggests that three more marks need to be added to the traditional Reformation marks: "fire on earth" (missionary vitality), suffering and the mobility of the pilgrim. Once again, these marks refer to the body of believers, not just to the leadership. Yoder notes that Menno Simons added four marks of the church to the two listed by Luther: holy living, brotherly love, unreserved testimony and suffering.[20] Yo-

---

[18]Yoder, "A People in the World," p. 75.
[19]Ibid., pp. 75-76.
[20]Ibid., p. 77.

der expounds these marks and in so doing paints a picture of the believers' church ecclesiology he is advocating.

The church that is characterized by these marks will be one that is effective in its mission, says Yoder. But if these marks do not characterize the church, the mission will be compromised. Since these marks are incompatible with the Christendom situation and the Constantinian union of church and state, only a post-Constantinian ecclesiology will enable the church to carry out its evangelistic mission effectively.

In contrast to Yoder's believers' church ecclesiology stand two options, which define the spectrum for many Christians today. There is the "liberal" stance of the World Council of Churches in which the locus of meaning is the world as a whole. When Yoder wrote the essay "A People in the World" in the 1960s, the then-current slogans were "go where the action is" and "the secular city." We can easily update them to "the preferential option for the poor" and "eco-feminism," and note that the basic approach has not changed. The course of world history is where God is at work and the calling of the church is to try to catch up. On the other hand, there is the evangelical stance. There the locus of meaning is the individual soul. The success of the Christian mission is defined by the number of converted individuals who put their trust in Christ for what happens after death. Yoder argues that the predominant purpose of God, according to Scripture, is not to direct all of world history coercively to a certain end and it is not to make certain individuals whole, but it is to create a new covenant people which responds freely to God's call.[21] For Yoder,

> The political novelty that God brings into the world is a community of those who serve instead of ruling, who suffer instead of inflicting suffering, whose fellowship crosses social lines instead of reinforcing them. This new Christian community in which the walls are broken down not by human idealism or democratic legalism but by the work of Christ is not only a vehicle of the gospel or only a fruit of the gospel; it is the good news. It is not merely the agent of mission or the constituency of a mission agency. This is the mission.[22]

The believers' church ecclesiology is not a synthesis of the spiritualist and theocratic approaches. It is a genuinely third way, a unique ecclesiology. On the one hand, the church becomes the way of salvation. Yet, on the other hand, the primacy of the individual's free response to the preaching of the gospel is maintained.

For Yoder, the church does not have a "message" that is detachable from the

---

[21]Ibid., p. 91.
[22]Ibid.

congregation of believers united in faith because the gospel is not about isolated individuals, but rather about a witnessing community. God is not a solitary, unitary being, but rather a Trinity of persons relating to each other in love. Yoder's ecclesiology is trinitarian in the sense that only a loving community of disciples can bear an adequate witness to the Trinity. Individual hero-preachers cannot do it; only the congregation as a whole can do it. But can Yoder specify in more detail what it means for a community to be a Christian community? He can, and he does do so by means of his description of the practices of the Christian community in a little book called *Body Politics: Five Practices of the Christian Community Before the Watching World.*[23]

PRACTICING CHRISTIANITY: YODER'S DESCRIPTION OF CONGREGATIONAL LIFE

In this book, Yoder explicates the social-ethical meaning of certain social practices, which characterize the people of God. His focus is on binding and loosing, breaking bread together, baptism, the fullness of Christ (or charismatic body ministry), and the rule of Paul (or congregational dialogue as the means of decision making). He chooses, not without some hesitation, to retain the term *sacrament* to describe these practices.[24] The term is problematic for Yoder in two ways. First, it has certain superstitious and mechanical connotations, which have caused Baptists and Churches of Christ to substitute for it the term *ordinance.* Second, the term *sacrament* could be taken to mean an action done in the sacred sphere of worship that has no social or ethical meaning. Yoder is sensitive to the concerns about magic and cult and he wants to interpret these practices as social processes, not merely religious acts. Yet, he decides to retain the term *sacrament.* Why? The answer is intriguing. He says that these practices fit the traditional definition of sacraments in that they are events in which human action and divine action coincide.[25]

However, Yoder fundamentally challenges the traditional understanding of the category of sacrament by stretching its meaning in two ways. First, Yoder stretches the meaning from a ritual act done by the clergy to a social process enacted by the congregation as a whole. The five practices he discusses are practices of the congregation, not restricted to an ordained elite. Second, Yoder claims that these practices have meanings beyond the congregation for the

---

[23]John Howard Yoder, *Body Politics: Five Practices of the Christian Community Before the Watching World* (Nashville: Discipleship Resources, 1992).

[24]Yoder, *Body Politics*, p. 1.

[25]It is clear, however, that he would reject any theory of the sacraments that places them under the control of the church. Yoder believes that God acts through the sacraments sovereignly.

world. As Yoder sees it, liberating the control of the sacraments from the clergy and viewing them as practices of the people of God as a whole is the first step toward understanding their social-ethical relevance to the world as a whole.

For example, he discusses the economic implications of the breaking of bread and concludes that, when Jesus said, "When you do this, do it in my memory," he meant, "whenever you have your common meal."[26] Jesus was not calling his followers simply to perform a certain religious ritual in worship. That would perpetuate the religion/politics split that we often take for granted, but which Jesus, the Jewish prophet, could never have imagined. Rather, he intended that his disciples should live as a family in which those who are in need are cared for and supported by the community. We read in the Gospels that those who followed Jesus constituted a new social movement in which people left home, families and jobs to live communally. In Acts, the early church in Jerusalem practiced economic sharing. Connecting these two radical social movements were the resurrection appearances of the risen Lord Jesus Christ, nearly all of which focused on meals.

Is Yoder's account of social practices a "high church" or a "low church" account? It is hard to say. Consider binding and loosing. Jesus mandated the practice: "If your brother or sister sins, go and reprove that person when the two of you are alone. If he or she listens, you have won your brother or sister" (Mt 18:15). Also, God promises to be acting "in, with and under" this human activity so that "Whatever you bind on earth is bound in heaven" (Mt 18:18).[27] This, Yoder points out, is the language used by the Reformers to describe sacraments. Yoder wants us to understand the meaning of "binding and loosing" (which has also been known by Protestants as "church discipline" and by Roman Catholics as "the sacrament of penance") to be a sacrament. But he interprets "binding and loosing" as something done by members of the congregation to one another, not as an action that can only be done by an ordained minister. In some ways this is both a "high" and a "low" account of the sacraments.

The goal of binding and loosing is to deal with moral issues in such a way as to restore harmony and peace within the fellowship. The intention is to restore, not to punish and to serve the offender's well being by restoring him or her to the community.[28] Of course, this process is open to abuse, but Yoder argues that the worst abuses arise when membership in the Christian community is not voluntary, that is, when it is not a community to whose standards

---

[26]Yoder, *Body Politics*, p. 16.
[27]Ibid., p. 1.
[28]Ibid., p. 3.

and practices the members have committed themselves by means of a personal and free act.

The process of dialogue is viewed by Yoder as a means by which the community sometimes discovers the inadequacy of some of its rules. It involves a genuine effort to discern the true nature of the offense and to understand it in its fullest context. The possibility of progress in moral understanding through dialogue is assumed.[29] The concern is not for the reputation of the church or the upholding of abstract rules, but the wellbeing of the community, the quality of *koinonia*. The assumption is that conflict is socially useful because by dealing with it, we grow in our relationships to each other.[30] Conflict resolution, which today is becoming a major tool of resolving major social and ethnic strife on a global scale, and various forms of victim-offender reconciliation programs, are extensions of this basic practice of binding and loosing. Yoder concludes:

> To be human is to be in conflict, to offend and to be offended. To be human in the light of the gospel is to face conflict in redemptive dialogue. When we do that, it is God who does it. When we do that we demonstrate that to process conflict is not merely a palliative strategy for tolerable survival or psychic hygiene, but a mode of truth-finding and community-building. That is true in the gospel and it is true . . . in the world.[31]

The practice of truthful reconciliation of one to another is, not only a sacrament, but also the social shape of the church's witness to the world. For Yoder, this is an example of "social ethics as gospel."[32]

In discussing baptism, Yoder asserts that Christian baptism unites Jews and Gentiles into one new body, a new humanity.[33] Baptism was distorted by Constantinianism in that, after the fifth century, there was no one left to convert because the whole world had been declared Christian by imperial edict. Yoder comments: "That made baptism a celebration of birth, reinforcing in-group identity rather than a transcending of it. Then it was natural that a new theology had to be developed."[34] Yoder claims that what he terms a "sacramentalistic" understanding of baptism evolved, which involved the washing away of original sin mediated to the individual by a symbolic washing of water done by a priest. The breaking down of social barriers and the in-breaking of a new

---

[29]Ibid., p. 6.
[30]Ibid., p. 9.
[31]Ibid., p. 13.
[32]This is the subtitle of his book *The Priestly Kingdom*.
[33]Yoder, *Body Politics*, p. 30.
[34]Ibid., p. 31.

age disappeared from view. Yet Yoder also criticizes the Zwinglian view of baptism that reduces baptism to "an acted out message, which can be equally well translated into words."[35] Yoder states his own view as follows:

> [W]e might be able to resurrect what might be called a 'sacramental' . . . realism. In that understanding, just as we saw in an earlier chapter that breaking bread together is an economic act, so baptism is the formation of a new people whose newness and togetherness explicitly relativize prior stratifications and classification. Then we need no path, no line of argument, and no arbitrary statement . . . to get from there to inter-ethnic equality and reconciliation, either in the church or beyond.[36]

Yoder builds on this understanding of baptism to elucidate the mission of the church in contrast to evangelical and liberal understandings. For evangelicals, the mission of the church is usually defined as being to provide individuals, one at a time, with certain information and appeal to them to decide in favor of Jesus, a decision that is viewed as making the individual into a born-again believer. The church is understood to be a vehicle for supporting the mission and as a good method for nurturing the faith of the converted individuals. For liberals, mission is not the communication of one specific message, but rather, all kinds of involvement in the world that advances what God wants for the world. The church is called to discern movements of liberation and empowerment and to align itself with them. A third view of mission is that of the church growth movement. This approach sees the goal as the planting of viable congregations in every culture. So far, so good. But this movement tends to buy into the "homogeneous unit principle" and accept ethnic isolation and defensiveness if that will allow these congregations to grow faster. Most Christian missionary activity today operates on the basis of one of these three models.

It should be obvious, however, that Yoder's view of baptism means that the mission of the church cannot be reduced to any of these three models. For Yoder, the mission of the church and the social form of the church are the same thing and both are shaped by the community-creating, barrier-shattering practice of baptism. Yoder comments:

> The message of the church is that Christ has begun a new phase of world history. The primary characterization of that newness is that now within history there is a group of people whom it is not exaggerating to call a "new world" or a "new

---

[35]Ibid., p. 33.
[36]Ibid.

humanity." We know the new world has come because its formation breaches the previously followed boundaries that had been fixed by the orders of creation and providence.[37]

Egalitarianism has been promoted in the modern world by non-Christian social and intellectual movements such as the Enlightenment. But that happened, tragically, because the mainline Christian understanding of such matters pointed in the opposite direction. Yoder says: "Christian authorities claimed on the grounds of creation and providence that peoples, nations, and classes should stay apart, that men should rule over women, and that Europeans should rule the globe."[38] So it was left to the Enlightenment to champion the case for human equality. But, Yoder contends, "the New Testament has its own grounds for its own egalitarian witness, differently shaped from that of the Enlightenment, older and more deeply rooted, even though it has been lost and betrayed for centuries."[39]

The practice of what Yoder calls "the fullness of Christ" is based on Ephesians 4:11-13, in which Paul speaks of "a new mode of group relationships, in which every member of a body has a distinctly identifiable, divinely validated and empowered role."[40] In contrast to the near-universal tendency of the human race to single out the religious professional, who has direct contact with the divine and mediates it to the group, the New Testament makes ministry a function of the every member of the body. This Pauline vision, Yoder contends, has yet to be "consciously and consistently lived out."[41] He speaks of it as "the Reformation that has yet to happen."[42] Although elements of lay ministry have been present in many different renewal movements in church history, this vision of the congregation ministering to one another on the basis of gifts of the Spirit has yet to enliven the church as a whole. For Yoder, the ministry of all to all is really the ministry of the risen Lord Jesus working through the Holy Spirit.

The final practice discussed by Yoder is that of the rule of Paul, as found in 1 Corinthians 14.[43] There Paul tells his readers that the way the church should conduct its affairs is by means of congregational meetings in which everyone who is prompted by the Holy Spirit to speak, should be allowed to do so. The members of the church are to "weigh" what each person says and the body

---

[37]Ibid., p. 37.
[38]Ibid., p. 40.
[39]Ibid.
[40]Ibid., p. 47.
[41]Ibid., p. 57.
[42]Ibid., p. 59.
[43]For what follows, see *Body Politics*, pp. 61-70.

should move toward a unified judgment on the issue. Consensus is the goal. Acts 15 is an example of this process in action. The ecumenical councils of the early church arose out of this tradition. This vision has obvious implications for democracy and it is rooted in the conviction that the living Lord Jesus Christ is truly present in the meeting of believers and can guide and lead the congregation into unity if the congregation seeks him wholeheartedly.

CONCLUSION

The church practices discussed by Yoder embody the mission of the church to be "the new world on the way." As sacraments, they are events in which divine and human action coincide. It is not too much, therefore, to say that they form the shape of God's action in the world. God, by his Word, calls the church out of the world and forms it into the body of Jesus Christ as a witness to his grace. For Yoder, the spiritualist approach of adding personal depth and authenticity to the theocratic management of society does not add up to an adequate ec- clesiology. Only the believers' church vision of a covenanted fellowship of be- lievers in Jesus, who freely accept the discipline of discipleship, embodies the action of God in the world. Such a congregation will be characterized by holy living, brotherly love, unreserved testimony and suffering. Such a people, in order to carry out the essential mission of the church to be a witness to the grace of God in Jesus Christ, need not be perfect. It only need be visible and its very flaws will constitute an essential part of its witness, for it is a community of forgiveness, reconciliation and love, rather than a moral and spiritual elite attempting to rule over others. For this reason the gospel call to enter the church can be heard by those outside as truly good news.

Evangelicals need to grasp Yoder's point about the centrality of the visible, local church to God's redemptive work. We need to grasp the essential unity of the nature and mission of the church and the indispensability of the church for the preaching of the gospel. The gospel we preach is only a pale shadow of the New Testament message so long as it consists only of a call for individuals to do something inwardly or to take responsibility for managing society. To be the body of Christ is our calling and it is a high calling indeed.[44]

---

[44]I would like to thank my colleague at Tyndale Seminary, Dr. Jeffrey Greenman, for his help- ful comments on an earlier draft of this paper.

10

THE CHURCH AS "SACRAMENT"

GARY D. BADCOCK

Of all the churches in recent times, the Roman Catholic tradition above all has experienced a renewal in self-understanding. The dramatic developments in Roman ecclesiology can, of course, be spoken of in a number of ways. One of the more obvious "marks" of recent Roman ecclesiology, for example, has been a new openness to learn from and to collaborate with Christians of other traditions. Thus the hostile, narrow and quite intentionally anti-ecumenical spirit of Pius XI's *Mortalium Animos* (1928), in which the "subjects" of the See of Rome were forbidden from participating in the ecumenical meetings of "the dissidents," has been replaced by an altogether more accommodating attitude. For a great many ordinary Catholics, on the other hand, the really decisive shift that has come about is internal to the politics of the church, and involves a certain turn of attention from the ecclesiastical hierarchy to the life of the whole people of God. Thus a kind of willed concentration on the Church *of* and *for* the people is on many accounts the real hallmark of recent Roman ecclesiological self-understanding. The ministry of all the baptized, and indeed the "priesthood of all believers," have come explicitly to the fore. Though not all of this is especially well founded in the documents of the Second Vatican Council, this perception is very common among Catholics themselves, especially in the North American context, and accounts, no doubt, for much of the hostile sentiment one encounters among them toward the postconciliar claims of the hierarchy and the *magisterium*.

In fact, of course, the power of the hierarchy in general and of the *magisterium* in particular is firmly entrenched in the documents of Vatican II, so that it is difficult to see how the contemporary ideal of egalitarianism within Roman Catholicism can triumph in the long term, since there is so little in the way of a legal basis for it. I would like to suggest, therefore, that the more important shift in self-understanding to be seen in Roman ecclesiology appears at a very different point—and a far more interesting one theologically. The shift also merits a good deal more attention on the part of Christians from other traditions, including those of the evangelical world, than it has to date received. This is the idea found in the documents of Vatican II that the church is in itself sacramental—not simply in the sense that the church "contains" a variety of rites that are called sacraments, but that the church *itself* is to be understood and embraced as sacrament.

Let us first of all attempt to clarify the content of the Roman Catholic teaching on this point. The key document is the Vatican II "constitution on the Church," *Lumen Gentium* (1964). The language used is susceptible to a range of interpretations, and thus requires clarification. Though the church at one point is plainly identified as "the universal sacrament of salvation,"[1] the intention cannot be to speak of the church as sacramental in the same sense as baptism, the Eucharist, and the other five sacraments of the Catholic tradition. The church is not, in other words, sacrament number eight. Nor is the point that the church is a "sacramental" in the technical Roman sense that applies to vestments and the like. The key to what is meant, rather, is found where the idea is first announced, right at the beginning of *Lumen Gentium:*

> Christ is the Light of nations. Because this is so, this Sacred Synod gathered together in the Holy Spirit eagerly desires, by proclaiming the Gospel to every creature, to bring the light of Christ to all men, a light brightly visible on the countenance of the Church. Since the church is in Christ like a sacrament or as a sign and instrument both of a very closely knit union with God and of the unity of the whole human race, it desires now to unfold more fully to the faithful of the church and to the whole world its own inner nature and universal mission. (*Lumen Gentium*, 1)

The theme of the opening paragraphs of the document is the light of Christ that can be discerned in the life of the Church, insofar as it shines "on the countenance of the Church," and it is in this context that the church is defined as a sacrament, or sign and instrument, of union with God and of the unity of humanity. The usage here, however, is analogical: "the Church is in Christ like a sacrament (*Ecclesia sit in Christo veluti sacramentum*)." Thus an implicit distinction is made between the sacraments proper and the ecclesial "sacrament of salvation," for no good Catholic would ever say that the Eucharistic meal is "like a sacrament," whereas such language introduces the

---

[1] "Christ, having been lifted up from the earth has drawn all to Himself. Rising from the dead He sent His life-giving Spirit upon His disciples and through Him has established His Body which is the Church as the universal sacrament of salvation" (*Lumen Gentium*, 48).

doctrine of the church as sacrament in the documents of Vatican II.

In a helpful essay, Walter Kasper has written of the origins of this idea in the debates leading up to the Council.[2] Of special importance is the *"nouvelle théologie"* of and surrounding the great French Jesuit, Henri de Lubac, who sought to find a way beyond the sterile clericalism and triumphalism of the neo-scholastic tradition by means of a "rediscovery" of more venerable sources in Scripture and the Fathers. In Lubac's thought, the church is indeed the sacrament of Christ—so much so that, "strictly speaking, [the church] is nothing other than that, or at any rate, the rest is a superabundance."[3] Part of the point of this is that the church, the visible institution with all its trappings, is in and of itself nothing; in ecclesiology, rather, all depends upon Christ, and the relation established by grace between the church and Christ. Thus the church is not itself the object of faith; it is instead a medium by which Christ is made known and made available to the world.

This approach to ecclesiology within the *nouvelle théologie* of the middle decades of the twentieth century became very influential in European Catholic theology prior to Vatican II, and it was widely used as a way of avoiding the fossilized, and reactionary, orthodoxy of the time. Once the Council had been convened, it is not surprising that the idea very soon found its way into draft conciliar documents. It proved to be controversial, since all recognized that the doctrine of the church had never before been handled dogmatically under the technical heading of a sacrament, and a battle ensued over whether or not the term should indeed be used. In the end, the reforming movement won out, most likely because the phrase *"veluti sacramentum,"* which had wisely been inserted into the draft document by the German bishops, is what introduces the theme and so frames all other references to it.

Kasper makes one further point to which reference must be made. That is that the sense of "sacrament" underlying this new use of the word in an explicitly ecclesiological sense must be traced to the New Testament word *mystērion,* the word the Vulgate translated as *sacramentum,* but which in the Greek New Testament, of course, has wider and richer connotations. For in the New Testament, the "mystery" of the gospel is the very thing that confronts us in the summons to faith, repentance and obedience. A classic reference is 1 Timothy 3:16: "Beyond all question, the mystery of godliness is great: He appeared in a body, was vindicated by the Spirit, was seen by angels, was preached among

---

[2]Walter Kasper, "The Church as a Universal Sacrament of Salvation," in *Theology & Church,* trans. Margaret Kohl (London: SCM, 1989), pp. 111-28.
[3]Henri de Lubac, *The Splendor of the Church* (London: Sheed and Ward, 1956), p. 156.

the nations, was believed on in the world, was taken up in glory" (NIV).

Here "mystery" refers neither to what we do in baptism or Eucharist, nor to the church in and of itself—though it is significant that the preaching of Christ and his being believed on in the world (both of which ought to be comprehended in any ecclesiology) are included in the mystery itself. Fundamentally, however, the reference is to Jesus Christ as the incarnate Son of God and the Savior, who realizes in time God's eternal will to save. The *mystērion* is ultimately Christological.

It might be worthwhile to pause briefly at this juncture in order to observe that one of the great texts of the Protestant Reformation begins, at least, to make a similar point. In his 1520 treatise, *The Babylonian Captivity of the Church*, Martin Luther writes:

> To begin with, I must deny that there are seven sacraments, and, for the present maintain that there are but three: baptism, penance and the bread. . . . Yet, if I were to speak according to the usage of the Scriptures, I should have only one single sacrament, but with three sacramental signs.[4]

Luther's reference too is unmistakably Christological: the one sacrament is Jesus Christ, who for Luther (as for Rahner and Schillebeeckx in our own time) is something of a "primal sacrament," which the sacramental signs of the church merely represent. Luther did not, however, carry this line of thought much farther. As is well known, the Augustinian friar ultimately reverted to the standard Augustinian theory of the sacraments, arguing that the sacraments are "visible words," sensible instruments which, because authorized by the Word of God, become effectual means of grace in the life of faith.

But was Luther, and are we, right to abandon this line of thinking so quickly? Might it not be possible, after all, to ground the life of the church much more clearly than we tend to do in Christ as the "one single sacrament" of salvation? And if so, then is it possible for a biblical and evangelical doctrine of the church to draw upon these ideas in such a way as to embrace the notion of the church also as sacrament?

The answer to this, I wish to suggest, is "Yes"—though not, as we shall see, without considerable qualification. To begin with, there are significant historical and cultural problems that would need to be surmounted at this point, since questions of sacramental theology and practice are very jealously guarded by the various ecclesiastical institutions to which we belong, and

---

[4]Martin Luther, *The Babylonian Captivity of the Church*, in *Martin Luther's Basic Theological Writings*, ed. Timothy F. Lull (Minneapolis: Fortress, 1989), p. 274; *Luther's Works*, 36:11ff.

have long proven to be among the most divisive issues in Christianity. Our divisions run deep here, so much so that the fractures appear not only in relations between Roman Catholics and Protestants in general, but also in relations between Baptists and Methodists, or between Presbyterians and Lutherans. We not only practice differing sacramental polities, but we cherish and nurture these differences as matters of communal identity, perpetuating our divisions, for example, through a good deal of formal theological education. The latter seems often at this point to be an attempt to justify difference and division rather than to transcend it. Such problems have also been powerfully reinforced in the past decade by the advent of postmodernity on the theological landscape, for in postmodernity, difference is everything.

In face of such a depressing vision, it is comforting to note that the Bible is not only an inspired but also an inspiring book, challenging our complacencies and offering insight where nothing new seemed possible. In this case, reflection on use of the word *mystērion* or mystery is of special importance. For the *mystērion* in the full New Testament sense is concerned precisely with what surmounts human division, with what makes it theologically redundant, as it were, rather than with some puzzle that must be unraveled or some secret that we seek to know.

No full account of the New Testament use of *mystērion* can be provided within present constraints, of course, but such an account would have to include, for example, its Synoptic usage in connection with the parables (Mk 4 par.). In this connection, Jesus says to his disciples: "The [*mystērion*] of the kingdom of God has been given to you. But to those on the outside, everything is said in parables." (Mk 4:11 NIV). "Secret," which has become the conventional English translation in this text, simply does not do the word justice, but represents a considerable "undertranslation" of the Greek. Then there is the text from 1 Timothy already cited (1 Tim 3:16), in which the mystery of godliness is indeed great, since it embraces in one word the varied Christological "moments" of incarnation, resurrection, mission, and glorification. In Colossians 2:2-3, the "mystery of God" is flatly stated to be none other than Christ himself, "in whom are hidden all the treasures of wisdom and knowledge," while in Romans 16:25, the mystery is the purpose of God spoken through the prophets, that all nations might believe and obey.

This last Pauline theme is especially important for our purposes, and it is taken up more extensively in the epistle to the Ephesians. In Ephesians 1, first of all, we read of the *mystērion* of God's will, "to bring all things in heaven and on earth together under one head, even Christ" (Eph 1:9-10; the verb is *anakephalaiōsasthai*, "to recapitulate"). It is clear in Ephesians that the mystery has yet to be realized in its fullness, but nevertheless, the mystery is indeed at least proleptically realized in the church. Such realization of the eternal purpose of God in the church is a major theological theme of the epistle to the Ephesians. It appears again with special clarity in Ephesians 3, where in an "autobiographical" aside, Paul's apostleship is defined in relation to the "mystery of Christ" (Eph 3:4), which is that "through the gospel the Gentiles are heirs together with Israel, members together of one body, and sharers together in the promise in Christ Jesus" (Eph 3:6).

If a theological synthesis of the New Testament material were attempted, it might look something like this. In the concrete reality of Christ's person and work, the mystery of God's eternal will is both revealed and realized. To this mystery the church also belongs, for in the church, the saving work of God is brought to its natural fulfillment. Christ's work is completed, in other words, in the gathering of the church, for Christ's person and work is such as to create a space for others, so that he is not without those whom he calls to himself. Long ago God purposed to bring all things into unity with himself. To Abraham, he gave the promise of a blessing to all nations, and through the prophets, he made himself known as the God of all the earth. This he is now realizing in the creation of a people of God which includes Jew and Gentile in one body, who together have one head in the one Lord Jesus Christ. Thus the church is part of the mystery. It shares, derivatively but decisively, in the great *mystērion* of God's act of salvation.

Something of this, though to be sure by no means all of it, was present in the dogmatic statement quoted earlier from *Lumen Gentium*. Of course, in that document the idea of the unity of the church and of humanity itself in Christ is given a very particular Roman "twist," but the fact that such rich theological notes are sounded at all is significant and welcome. The sources are ultimately biblical. The theology in question also has the merit at least of surmounting the widespread tendency in much ecclesiology to downgrade the status of the church, as if it did not, after all, belong rightfully to the Christian confession, and to pretend that its affairs can be conducted in abstraction from the mystery of salvation. Thus a resource is given here by which perhaps we can rise above the pronounced tendency in almost all the churches to look inward rather than outward, to be obsessed with questions of appearance rather than with reality, and to behave as if the church were really, after all, merely "institutional."

What is at stake in the concept of the church as *mystērion*, or in a doctrine of the church as "in Christ like a sacrament," to quote again from Vatican II, is a very great matter indeed. Its implication is that the church in its inner nature, properly understood, is to be "a sign and instrument [of] union with God and of the unity of the whole human race." And if so, then the proper task of the church, its mission, must indeed be understood in its "universal" dimensions. Perhaps what is needed in response to this is first of all humility and honesty, humility and honesty sufficient to acknowledge the pettiness of so much of the church's life over against these great themes, and thus the extent to which the church can disappoint, and prove not so much the medium of the light of Christ as a massive obstacle to belief in God.

If it is true, therefore, that the doctrine of the church is at a deep level rooted in the *mysterion* of Jesus Christ, or that the church, whatever its faults, is called to be "in Christ" "like a sacrament or as a sign and instrument both of a very closely knit union with God and of the unity of the whole human race," then at this point we are brought face to face with a weighty matter indeed. Ultimately, the theological implication would be that the doctrine of the church is inseparable from the doctrine of Christ, so that ecclesiology must be held together with Christology. God in an act of sovereign grace chooses us for fellowship with himself, and with one another. Just as we are not who we are without Christ, then, so also Christ is not who he is without us.

A further major theological strand can be woven into the argument at this point, in order to flesh out and to provide substance to the case made. This is the central New Testament notion of the church as the "body of Christ." The significance of this idea for our theme is, of course, that the body of Christ is at the same time also what is offered to the church in the sacrament of Holy Communion. The very being of the church, therefore, can be intimately related to what happens in this sacrament of the Eucharist, so that here again, the church is associated closely with the concept of a sacrament. Taken together with the idea that the church is part of the *mysterion* of the gospel, such ideas have the potential to reinforce in a powerful way the theme of the church as sacramental.

A great deal depends, of course, on our use of the words "body of Christ." A major tendency in contemporary Western Christianity is to understand ecclesial "body of Christ" language as purely metaphorical. On one prominent view, body language is basically social in thrust, and refers to the varied roles played by individual believers in the life of the church as a whole. Like hands and feet, some have one work to do, while others have another. Often this claim is developed by those who wish to lay out grounds for an egalitarian ethos in the church, for as the apostle Paul teaches, even the seemingly weakest parts of the body have functions that are indispensable to the rest, so that we cannot live without each other. This view of the meaning of the ecclesial body of Christ is strongly defended by Avery Dulles who, in a hugely influential book, likened it in this respect to another "democratic" ecclesiological model, that of the "people of God":

> For many purposes the analogues of Body of Christ and People of God are virtually equivalent. Both of them are more democratic in tendency than . . . hierarchical models [of the Church]. They emphasize the immediate relationship of all believers to the Holy Spirit, who directs the whole Church.[5]

Unfortunately, the flaw in the egalitarian case is that the body image in social thought was in the ancient world and is still today in many societies a staple of political and social conservatism. To say that the weaker parts of the body have functions indispensable to the rest is to make a case, not for the equality of the parts, but rather for the indispensability of the weak, who need to be kept in their place for the good of the rest. As Dulles himself admits, the body analogy focuses attention "on the mutual service of the members toward one another and on the subordination of the particular good of any one group to that of the whole Body or People."[6] Though his intention here is undoubtedly to highlight the responsibility of the powerful—and thus of the clerical hierarchy—to the whole body, the implication could just as clearly be that the needs, say, of the whole people of God are best served when the good of women is subordinated to that of the whole body, and they are denied the dignity of clerical office. Body language cuts both ways.

At the other extreme stands the extraordinarily "realist" assertion that there is a strict identity between the literal body assumed by the Son of God in the womb of Mary, now risen and ascended into heaven, and the ecclesial body of Christ, the church. On some accounts, this identity also needs to be extended to include the Eucharistic body of Christ. There are various formulations of this thesis, from the argument for the idea that the church is an "extension of the incarnation" found in the theology of the French Jesuit, Emile Mersh and the English Anglican, Leslie Thornton, to the more Bultmannian variant advocated by, among others, John Robinson in his classic monograph, *The Body.*[7] Robinson went so far as to claim that the resurrection appearance of Christ to Saul (Paul) on the Road to Damascus was none other than a realization that Jesus was alive—in the community that Saul persecuted. The writer of Acts, in other words, got it right when he wrote of how Saul's vision of Jesus was accompanied by the revelation that in persecuting the church, he was in fact persecuting the risen, glorified One.

---

[5] Avery Dulles, *Models of the Church* (Garden City, N.Y.: Doubleday, 1974), p. 49.
[6] Ibid.
[7] John Robinson, *The Body* (London: SCM, 1952).

Even the American Lutheran Robert Jenson can be seen at times to approximate to such a view, though arguing on the basis of a different, very Lutheran appeal to the Christological doctrine of the *communicatio idiomatum*. According to Jenson, what Paul means when he speaks of the church as the body of Christ is that "the risen Christ as a complete living human person has a body and . . . the church is this body."[8] The argument turns in part upon debates in scholastic Lutheranism concerning the bodiliness of the post-resurrection Jesus, which in Lutheran orthodoxy was understood to share in the attributes of the divine nature of the Son of God. In debates concerning the manner of Christ's presence in the Eucharistic bread in particular, one of these attributes was especially stressed: ubiquity. According to scholastic Lutheran theory, the risen, ascended Christ is ubiquitous in his physical flesh by virtue of the *communicatio idiomatum*, and thus cannot be understood to be physically limited in heaven. Jenson argues that the risen body of Christ in its Christological sense (but by implication, in its ecclesiological and sacramental senses also) must be thoroughly reconceived. To "have" a body, he suggests, is to be available, to be a physical object available to others. In the church, Christ is available in our world, and in this sense, the church as the object in which the risen Christ is available to be found *is* the body of Christ.[9]

The implication of this would be that what happens in the Eucharist meal is of immense Christological and ecclesiological significance also. For here is concentrated at a point of infinite density the fact that in Christ, God gives himself through the material cosmos to the material cosmos. In the Eucharist, there is a continuing divine self-giving, which reveals the real core of the Christian gospel of God's love for a world which is through and through material, and which in Jenson's interpretation can brook no bifurcation into spiritual and inward versus merely material and outward. That the Word became flesh, and that the Word remains, postresurrection, flesh in the physical, fleshly being of the church is what grounds the Eucharistic meal, is what shines out through it, and is what ultimately wins the salvation of us creatures of flesh.

One further source of massive theological importance will serve to round out the picture: the great Swiss-German theologian, Karl Barth. For Barth too, in the massive ecclesiological sections of *Church Dogmatics* 4 in particular, also lays great stress upon the idea of the body of Christ in his approach to ecclesi-

---

[8]Robert W. Jenson, "The Church and the Sacraments," in *The Cambridge Companion to Christian Doctrine*, ed. Colin E. Gunton (Cambridge: Cambridge University Press, 1997), pp. 209-10.
[9]Robert W. Jenson, *Systematic Theology* (New York: Oxford University Press, 1997), 1:203-6.

ology, arguing that the church is not merely a *congregatio fidelium*, an assembly of the like-minded, but is ultimately nothing less than the risen Lord's "own earthly-historical form of existence."[10] The relation between the church and Christ is on this account not merely an external one, nor is the parallel between talk of the *body* of Jesus Christ himself, once for all assumed in the womb of Mary, and of the church as Christ's *body*, merely metaphorical. Barth insists in this matter that all docetism must be resisted, so that we allow ourselves to be confronted in our faith, in our theologies, in our practices and yes, even in our understanding of the church, that the earthly historical form of existence now enjoyed by the risen Lord is the one of which we are a part. This, Barth insists, *despite* all the evidence to the contrary in the pettiness, the fallibility, the pride, the sloth and the downright sinfulness of so much of what passes for the church of Jesus Christ.

What Barth does not say, of course, is that this is all there is to the risen Lord—which is, it seems to me, the error of Jenson. To put the point another way, there is nothing wrong with a Lutheran Christology that a good dose of Calvinism cannot cure, and this is, in a sense, the key to grasping Barth's point. Calvinism is, of course, characterized by a much stronger pneumatology than is Lutheranism, and this is something that has to be reckoned with from beginning to end in the theology of Karl Barth. That the church becomes the earthly-historical form of existence of the risen Lord in Barth's theology does not mean that at the resurrection, or the ascension, Jesus' flesh "passed over" into a new mode of physical presence, or bodily availability, called the *ecclesia*. What it means is, rather, that in the power of the Holy Spirit, the church receives the "impress" of the risen Lord, who has in the first instance made himself one with all humanity, and who brings this unity to fulfillment in the life of faith and obedience. Thus, it is not that Jesus has become the church, that he has no other body than this ecclesial body, but rather, that in the church there genuinely is this treasure of grace, present as in a clay pot by the power of the Spirit. No divinization of the earthly institution is in view, but its status as the people of God in Christ, genuinely reconciled in the flesh of Christ, certainly is. The point is related to Barth's doctrine of justification, for here, in our being Christ's very body, we see God's gracious act of reconciling the human creature to himself in Christ, recognized by faith and in our collective life of witness, worship and service in the power of the Holy Spirit.

The view that evangelicalism exists, in effect, without any real ecclesiology has become a commonplace observation in recent years, and it is not without

---

[10]Karl Barth *Church Dogmatics* 4/1, p. 643.

justification. I am not convinced, however, that the position is quite as bad as some suggest. Many evangelicals, after all, exist within the framework of wider institutional churches with reasonably settled and developed ecclesiologies, for example, of a Presbyterian or Anglican variety. In a manner of speaking, they exist "enhypostatically" in these larger ecclesial traditions. There are colleges to which they go to be educated that stand within the evangelical tradition; there are large publishing houses that support their witness. It cannot honestly be said that evangelicalism has no developed institutional framework for its life.

Individualism is another common accusation—an individualistic piety which focuses so excessively upon the dynamic of individual faith that the life of the Christian community is at best obscured and at worst occluded. Yet there is much in the evangelical world that militates against this view: the evangelical passion for small groups, for example, within which one's rough edges can be knocked off and one's life of faith and prayer nurtured; and a frequent willingness to attend public worship of one sort or another several times a *week* rather than perhaps once or twice a month are examples that leap instantly to mind. Individualism there may be, then, but it is not the only word to be used, and it might not be the really important one. So the question I want to pose in conclusion in the light of what I have argued is this: Is there more to evangelical ecclesiology than meets the eye, and if so, then how might it be possible to draw it out?

There is a striking passage at the beginning of Calvin's *Institutes*, book three, in which one of the great theologians of the Holy Spirit of all time speaks in the following terms:

> Until our minds become intent upon the Spirit, Christ, so to speak, lies idle because we coldly contemplate him as outside ourselves—indeed, far from us. We know, moreover, that he benefits only those whose "Head" he is, for whom he is "the first-born among brethren", and who, finally, "have put on him". This union alone ensures that, as far as we are concerned, he has not unprofitably come with the name of Savior. The same purpose is served by that sacred wedlock through which we are made flesh of his flesh and bone of his bone, and thus one with him. But he unites himself to us by the Spirit alone. By the grace and power of the same Spirit we are made his members, to keep us under himself and in turn to possess him.[11]

There are several interesting features in this account. One is that it appears immediately after the lengthy treatment of the person and work of Christ in

---

[11]John Calvin *Institutes of the Christian Religion* 3.1.3.

Institutes, book two. Calvin's point is clear: there is no adequate grasp of Christianity without an adequate grasp of the Holy Spirit, for without the Spirit, there is no union with Christ and no body with Christ as head—and this despite the sovereign grace of God in Jesus' incarnation, death and resurrection. But more important for our purposes is the clear implication that at the very heart of the church stands something that is *entirely* beyond the power of the church to control: the Pneumatological event by which we are made members of Christ's body, grasping him by faith.

Here in a nutshell we have a statement of what, surely, the evangelical tradition is all about: the personal encounter with and relationship to God. But it is false, I suggest, to think that this relationship is purely private. As we see from the active engagement with others in small groups, and as we see from the often formidable social, physical and financial apparatus that the evangelical movement in its many manifestations has produced *in order to sustain personal faith*, faith does not happen in a vacuum, but springs to life in specifically *ecclesial* contexts.

How might such ecclesial structures be better understood, or how might the implicit ecclesiology in operation here be brought more clearly to light for evangelicals? One possibility is that evangelicals take a leaf from the pages of other traditions at this point. First of all, there needs to be a recognition of the primal theological fact that the church is part of the *mystērion*, part of the gospel, rather than merely an accidental appendage that happens to be added to faith because we are social animals, or the like. It is not something theologically secondary, or derivative, but something theologically primary, and of the first importance. Such recognition ought not to be hard to encourage among evangelicals, because the theme is, after all, biblical.

Then, second, evangelicals in their thinking about Christology need to grasp the sense in which Jesus Christ the Son of God is not who he is without the church. In God's being as the one who freely loves the world, room is made for fellowship with the creature, and to this "moment" in the Christian understanding of God there must correspond an ecclesiological commitment to the church as something willed and chosen by God, rather than as a mere appendage to "other" things that constitute the gospel proper.

Finally, I wish to suggest that among the best ways of grasping the shape of this ecclesiology is through sustained reflection on the theme of the body of Christ, especially in its sacramental dimension. For the sacrament of the Lord's Table involves something far greater, deeper and richer than a private transaction between God and the soul. The Eucharistic meal is more than a badge by which we profess our faith, and even more than a means of grace. It is also in the wider Christian tradition one of the primary loci of ecclesiology. That is to say, in our theology and in our practice of the Eucharist, an understanding of the church is not only genuinely expressed, but also actually realized. In this ritual expression, in other words, there is hidden a rich theological resource that is, from the point of view of discursive theological formulation, quite inexhaustible. Like the sacraments themselves, insight here is available on a variety of levels, levels which are as accessible to the simple as to the wise. Augustine, for example, famously preached the theme to *children*.[12] Yet a theme announced to children is something that one could spend a lifetime of scholarship, prayer and service in fathoming. It is a shame that this fact, which is widely recognized in "catholic" Christianity, goes almost totally unnoticed among evangelicals.

The prospect of such an exploration will, of course, seem unfamiliar ground to many who tend often to be suspicious of, if not overtly hostile to, all that smacks of sacramental "superstition." This downplaying of the importance of the sacraments, however, is a great mistake, for not all that is sacramental is superstition, nor is it fair to claim that all who emphasize a sacramental expression in faith and worship have fallen away from the real nub of the faith. Is not the truth rather that this (highly prejudiced!) assumption is evidence of the extent to which the point is missed by evangelicals? In fact, evangelical Christians and churches have much to learn here. One clear gain to be made might be a recognition of the sense and of the extent to which an evangelical ecclesiological self-understanding of the church as the body of Christ would have to be thoroughly Pneumatological, just as also, one suspects, all evangelical understanding of the Eucharistic body of Christ is bound to be. Not least, actually pursuing this path that has been so fruitfully followed by other Christians would also bring home a realization that the way to a more adequate doctrine of the church among evangelicals cannot bypass the basic question of sacramental theology, as if all such business were irrelevant to the real task in hand. Unfortunately, one too often looks in vain for such a treatment in evangelical theology. As long as this remains the case, I suggest, one will find in it not only little interest in ecclesiology, but also little that is of genuine ecclesiological interest.

---

[12]Augustine *Sermon* 227, quoted by Gregory Dix, *The Shape of the Liturgy* (London: Dacre Press, 1945), p. 247.

11

SACRAMENTAL ECCLESIOLOGY

ELLEN T. CHARRY

I am increasingly realizing that a number of our ministerial students have no ecclesiology to speak of. For them, the church is a voluntary not-for-profit organization run like a local franchise. Like other organizations, the mission is to meet the needs of its target population in order to grow. Ministry means designing programs that address the widest array of tastes and needs as possible. Its watchword is hospitality, also known as inclusivity.

These students do not know what ecclesiology is, and would be suspicious of it if they did, because a theology of the church threatens the individualism that is the bedrock of this model, and the voluntarism of our students' identity. A theological understanding of the church is prior to the self-concept of the individual and that runs counter to the highly individualistic notion of selfhood that our students bring with them. It is not surprising that they resist ecclesiology, because it seeks to define its members rather than the other way round, now natural to us.

It is by no means insignificant that a book on evangelical ecclesiology would consider sacramental ecclesiology altogether, as it seems to fly in the face of the view that those who confess Jesus as Lord and are thereby justified by Christ's death through faith alone as the body of Christ make the church. This radical Reformation view reinforces the not-for-profit voluntary organizational model our students know, and so ecclesiology is quite difficult to teach.

To add sacraments into the mix complicates things even further. The fact that the section title for part four of this book is punctuated with a question mark tells all. I feel a bit like I am walking into a trap. I am deeply honored, but utterly unfit for the task assigned.

While from the perspective of the Great Church it is noteworthy that an evangelical community would entertain the prospect of sacramental ecclesiology, from another perspective, it is not that surprising. Since the 1940s the sacraments have been becoming the point around which divided churches have begun to reunify, de facto if not de jure. It is not to be forgotten that perhaps the most significant accomplishment of the Faith and Order movement of the twentieth century is the sacramental foundation of the church articulated in *Baptism, Eucharist, Ministry* (WCC, 1981). It directly addresses the tragic collapse of Protestant unity in 1529, around the doctrine of the real presence of Christ in the Eucharist, at the Colloquy of Marburg. It is ironically fitting that sacraments should now prove to be the point of Protestant rapprochement, and perhaps even beyond.

Considering sacramental ecclesiology is momentous because it is Christianity's great medicine for treating the tragic and dangerous fragmentation of our age. A fragmented world like ours needs to see how things connect, and a sacramental ecclesiology does that. To move forward along this line, however, requires laying down preoccupation with medieval ecclesiastical abuses that are not our own and focusing on the failures of our own time instead. A sacramental ecclesiology can do this because it discloses reality itself as theological, and the church as that means or locus whereby it is known and entered symbolically. It is an antidote to the foundation of our fragmentation—the incoherent and anti-theological ideal of the autonomous individual that is the only reality our students know.

A sacramental doctrine of the church holds that God's work in Israel and Christ, not an individual's decision for the church's faith, makes the church. This is difficult to act on because today, Christian confession is an identifying cultural marker. Because of this, it is more difficult to resist the radical Reformation view that the church is a community of true believers who constitute the church by virtue of their doctrinal agreement. This was not the ecclesiology of the magisterial Reformation—that God's work, not our faith or agreement on precise interpretation of particular doctrines, constitutes the church. Once we grasp that the church is prior to our faithfulness and even our understanding, we are moving toward a doctrine of the church than can address rather than reinforce individualism. One reason ecclesiology is so difficult for my students to grasp, I suspect, is that the more catechized among them place much weight on their intellectual ability to assent to precisely formulated doctrines. If doctrinal assent constitutes the church, it is not clear that the church exists apart from those who believe its faith. A sacramental ecclesiology offers another way.

PROCEDURE

Let us proceed in this enquiry into sacramental ecclesiology in a modified Thomist fashion of building blocks, to locate this discussion within some parameters by examining five questions: (1) Where is a sacramental ecclesiology located dogmatically? (2) What is ecclesiology? (3) What is the sacramental principle? (4) In what forms is the sacramental principle expressed? (5) What is sacramental ecclesiology?

SACRAMENTAL ECCLESIOLOGY AND DOGMATICS

I understand dogmatics to be the elaboration of Christian doctrine as set forth in the three articles of the Nicene Creed, each article of which identifies one of the three ways in which God is known. The Creed locates church and sacraments in the third article, that is, within the sphere of God as Holy Spirit. Placing church and baptism in the third article of the Creed was not simply because these things had to be got in somewhere and the end of the Creed was available, but because the holiness of God sanctifies those baptized into the death of Christ as members of his mystical body, the church. In this he is the Lord, the giver of life. The church's members are publicly sanctified by the Spirit and commissioned to take up the ministry of reconciliation accomplished by Christ's death. On this theology (2 Cor 5), the church is not an aggregate of individuals confessing the lordship of Christ, although confession of faith is essential for keeping its focus. Rather, the Spirit makes the church by sanctifying the bodies and continually vivifying the lives of those brought into her embrace through the symbolic power first of baptism and sustained in it by being fed of his body.

One powerful and little utilized ecclesiology lies in Ephesians 2. Its ecclesiology coheres with the reign of reconciliation created by the cross that baptism inducts us into and Eucharist sustains us in. The cross unified former enemies, putting to death the hostility that formerly separated them, and creating a newly commissioned people. Christ's death put hostility to death, reconciling Jews with Gentiles without their even knowing it. Baptism into that death of Christ is entrance into the death of hostility. It is the rite that enables each to affirm what has taken place on the cosmic plane.

This ecclesiology grounds a sacramental vision of the church. The institution is created by the reconciling work of God among enemies that does not ask them to consider it carefully and decide whether this set of beliefs and responsibilities is for them. Here God has acted decisively and given enemies access to the Father in one Spirit.

A sacramental ecclesiology is dogmatically located at the intersection of the Spirit with the cross of Christ and the sacrament of baptism. It is the point at which what are sometimes treated as separate doctrines are indissolubly linked. It is not our faithfulness that makes the church but the actions of God in Christ and the Spirit to which we much adjust ourselves. We do not ratify them; they identify us. The church is not a community of the doctrinally like-minded, but that community of persons whose identity, vision and mission are constituted as the redeeming and reconciling work of God in Israel and in Jesus Christ. Its members are grafted into that identity by the Holy Spirit and, by his power, are accountable to that identity, vision and mission in all that they are, all that they do and all that they have. This, I think, is the meaning of Deuteronomy 6:5, "You shall love the LORD your God with all your heart, and with all your soul, and with all your might."

ECCLESIOLOGY

Let us go back a step to ecclesiology itself. A doctrine of the church is a theo-logical interpretation of that institution called the *ecclesia* composed of those who are in Christ, or perhaps to put it a bit more sharply, those who have been taken into God's cosmic drama of salvation made known in the redemption of Israel from Egypt and in the cross of Christ. Paul is the first writer to think about and identify the church theologically. He refers to it variously as the body of Christ, or the body of which Christ is the head, or as God's field and building (1 Cor 3:9). It is clearly God's possession, a view with which Gospel parables that identify God as king or landlord concur, so it is not limited to Paul. Ephesians, which can be viewed as an ecclesiological treatise, also refers to the church as the household of God, as well as a building whose cornerstone is Christ (Eph 2:20). One of the more striking and audacious, even unnerving images, I think, is in 1 Corinthians 3:16-17, "Do you not know that you are God's temple and that God's Spirit dwells in you? If anyone destroys God's temple, God will destroy that person. For God's temple is holy, and you are that temple." Those who are in Christ are now God's house instead of the tem-ple in Jerusalem even while it is still operating! It is an outrageous thought.

The point of reviewing this list is that Paul and the evangelists used con-crete analogies and metaphors to convey to their listeners or readers that the church is God's property, his dwelling (even if the people own the land and the buildings). Theologically speaking, "the church" is an institution given a peculiarly honorable identity and high calling by virtue of her owner who sets the corporate culture into which members are acculturated. They have ful-filled the longing of Psalm 27:4:

One thing I asked of the LORD,
    that will I seek after:
to live in the house of the LORD

all the days of my life,
to behold the beauty of the LORD,
and to inquire in his temple.

My interest is not to commend one of these metaphors over others, although I think various ones have different advantages, but to draw out why my students do not grasp ecclesiology. They cannot appreciate the metaphors because they cannot distinguish between the church's belonging to us and its belonging to God. Their model of membership is based on human institutions like a health club where one pays dues or, perhaps if they are exceptionally sensible, democracy in which one supports the common good by paying taxes, obeying the law, voting and by God's grace, public service.

Becoming a member of the body of Christ, the household of God, the temple of God, is somewhat different from either the corporation or the democratic state. The point of the corporation is to produce goods and services that we are willing to pay for. The point of the state is to protect and defend the nation. In both of these, the consumer and the citizen get what they pay for: durable and consumable goods, services, highways, police departments, armed forces, a judiciary, etc. The marketplace waxes and wanes by the behavior of its patrons; the democratic state represents its citizens in making laws and policies for the good of the whole. In both cases, the member of the health club and the citizen act from positions of strength, holding the power of the wallet in the first case, and the power of the vote in the other.

Theologically speaking, the church is quite different, although it might not look all that different to the innocent eye. Although it has rules and procedures of polity and legislative bodies that often appear to function like corporations or the state, we do not make these decisions as we would as if we were members of a board of trustees of a corporation. The church is not responsible to us in quite the way the corporation and democratic state are in providing goods, services and physical protections. The church is God's institution; it makes us, we do not make it. God has designs on us through the church and we should come to it knowing that. He wants us in a way different from the way the corporation and the state want us. The former wants our money and loyalty to their products. The latter wants our loyalty too, so that we internalize the rule of law that contributes to a safe and peaceable society. But God wants us differently: he wants to enter us, that is, to take us over spiritually and that in baptism.

Church members may have difficulty understanding this because for them I suspect the church may function like the health club or the state in that they see it as dispensing services that they need. I come to church, assent to these beliefs, and I get to take salvation home with me. Further, we all make ourselves, perhaps over and over, and are to resist being made by anything else as an infringement of our dignity and freedom. To tell someone that they have been captured for God by the death of God incarnate and taken into the life of God in baptism runs quite counter to our modern energies that are far more proactive. Just imagine what it would be to introduce yourself in a group of folks at a meeting or cocktail party by saying, "I am the temple of the Holy Spirit." I recall being arrested when entering the cathedral in New Orleans. There was a poster on the wall with the figure of a man pointing his finger at me and it read, "You are the body of Christ." Oh! I said to myself. Now while this can be interpreted individualistically, if membership is through baptism I think the danger may be checked, at least with a symbolic understanding of baptism.

Of course, Western ecclesiology went through many incarnations after the New Testament, most of which need not detain us here. However, I would like to make one comment that is germane to this discussion that may be of interest to this particular company. The medieval church was identified in terms of its leadership rather than in terms of the whole body. An unfortunate consequence of this was that the variety and concreteness of the biblical metaphors and images was lost. When they challenged medieval ecclesiology, the magisterial Reformers did not return to New Testament metaphors for the most part, but defined the church in terms of specific practices, mostly functions to be carried out by the ordained. Luther identified seven notes or marks. Calvin stressed two, defining the church as that place where the word is preached and the sacraments duly administered. Discipline was also important to him. In short, the ecclesiological shift from the medieval to Protestant ecclesiology was from functionaries to functions.

While this point is probably familiar, it bears repeating for two reasons. First, the concrete images of and metaphors for God and the church—God as landowner, owner of the vineyard—offered by Scripture did not guide ecclesiological thinking until Vatican II. Second, there is something a bit misleading in Calvin's way of defining the church as two or three functions, for it separates and appears to set Word and sacrament over against one another. Such a separation, however, is quite unnecessary where the sacraments are duly administered, because proper liturgical celebration is always both Word and sacrament by virtue of the liturgy. Especially since the liturgical renewal movement that arose throughout the churches in the wake of Vatican II, the fullness of salvation history is proclaimed at every sacramental celebration, sometimes, I suspect, even more aptly than the preacher of the day may express it.

This is, in my judgment, the importance of *Baptism, Eucharist, Ministry.* One of the more significant contributions of a full liturgical setting for the sacraments is the proclamation of the doctrine of the Trinity that is the reality into which we are baptized and that creates the church.

(As an aside: Sadly, this doctrine has been quite lost to the laity, and has now been abolished in most sacramental liturgies written after 1983 in favor of first-person unitarianism. We now have God, Christ and the Spirit, in order to avoid the word Father.)

The advantage that the biblical images and metaphors have over defining the church as functionaries or functions has been brought forward by the ecclesiologies of Vatican II. The people of God image emerged in Pope Paul VI's dogmatic constitution on the church, *Lumen Gentium* (Paul 4, 1964). It notes, paraphrasing Saints Cyprian, Augustine and John Damascene that "the Church has been seen as 'a people made one with the unity of the Father, the Son and the Holy Spirit' " (1:4). One advantage of concrete metaphors for the church is that they engage the claims laid on us by God imaginatively. In this they stretch our self-understanding.

THE SACRAMENTAL PRINCIPLE

Having offered some thoughts on what the church is and is not, we may turn to the next element needed for developing a sacramental ecclesiology: the sacramental principle. It is difficult to ignore the sacramental principle because it is deep within Christian confession. It is born of the incarnation, the claim that God's presence with us, his self-revelation, is as one of us. The sacramental principle is extrapolated from the confession that God became a human being. It is that material things reveal and bring divine grace to us. It overcomes the divide between heaven and earth, spirit and matter. God descends to humanness and carries humanness to godness. St. Augustine explains the reason for God's humanization. It is to persuade us how much God loved us in order to give us the courage to reach up to him, and become partakers of his divinity.[1]

This has been a most contentious issue in Christian theology, especially among those anxious to maintain a strong divide between creature and Creator in order to protect our humility. I think the difference between Augustine's view and the later Western view rests on a judgment about what we need from God. It is a psychological judgment as to whether, as Augustine put it, we need encouragement from God or whether, as perhaps Calvin thought, we need a deep lesson in humility. My own view is that some of us need one

---

[1]St. Augustine *De Trinitate* 4.1.2.

more than the other depending on our temperament or perhaps one at one time and the other at another time, depending on our circumstance, and that it is difficult and perhaps unwise to make one judgment for everyone all the time. Do we need the courage to reach up or do we need to be brought low in order to turn to God? In truth, the difficult choice need not be made, for courage and humility work hand in hand.

The sacramental principle says that God comes to us sensuously in the incarnation.

> He dealt with us in such a way that we could progress rather in his strength; he arranged it so that the power of charity would be brought to perfection in the weakness of humility. This is the meaning of the psalm where it says, "O God, you are setting apart a voluntary rain for your inheritance, and it has been weakened; but you have perfected it" (Ps 68:9). What he means by voluntary rain is nothing other than grace, which is not paid out as earned but given gratis; that is why it is called grace. He was not obliged to give it because we deserved it; he gave it voluntarily because he wished to. Knowing this we will put no trust in ourselves.[2]

God's power and love are visible (the pillars of cloud and fire), tangible (doubting Thomas touching Jesus' wounds), edible (manna in the wilderness), audible (thunder and lightning at Sinai) and fragrant (Jacob smelling Esau's garments as the smell of a field that God has blessed, or 2 Esdras's paraphrase of the fourth day of creation [6:44]).

The sacramental principle then is that God's grace and judgment come to us through matter because we more readily grasp things sensuously than conceptually. It would not be appropriate to contrast the sacramental principle with the conceptual principle of Christian theology. Theology formulates doctrinal propositions from Scripture and tradition. On this view, we confess propositions, like "Jesus is Lord," or "Christ is the medicine of the world," or "God is one substance in three persons," or "Jesus Christ is one person with two natures." Pitting doctrine against sacraments is, I think, both unnecessary and detrimental to piety and to theology for it suggests a division between experience and cognition that is arbitrary and unrealistic. There was a time when modernity hoped that we could isolate the mind and the judgments about truth that it could make, but that time is now past. Cognition and sensation, ideas and experience work together and different people are differently able in this regard. Augustine's point is more readily brought into play for the sake of understanding divine grace than is cognition.

---

[2]Ibid., pp. 153-54.

Concepts are not formed in a space into which only ideas may enter—even Kant realized that—but are shaped by what we know, and that is structured through sensuous as well as cognitive experience. So, the sacramental principle is that God appeals to the mind through our senses, as the psalmist has it:

O taste and see that the LORD is good;
    happy are those who take refuge in him. (Ps 34:8)

The order is important here. We can only take refuge in that which looks and tastes good. God must seduce us.

This discussion is meant to underline one advantage of the sacramental principle. It applies to those whose intellectual grasp of the rites and liturgies of the church is both strong and weak. Just as music and art speak in ways that words may not and need not enter, sacramental action and liturgical gesture have the ability to bind us into the body of Christ experientially. That is why sacramental churches will serve communion to the mentally retarded and young children. God can be tasted without words.

Now I presume that what is at issue among the communions is not the sacramental principle itself, for contesting that would be to contest the incarnation itself, and none of the groups I have mentioned does that. The issue now, it seems to me, is not so much the question of the real presence, as it was then, but rather how wide a swath the path of divine grace takes and what it accomplishes. The more catholic the tradition the wider and more powerful the swath divine grace takes.

The fact that late medieval religion appealed to sight, touch and taste infuriated the Reformers because it did not stress understanding. They wanted articulate religion, not a sense of the sacred around which one can regulate one's life. All revolutions have those who go to the extreme. Here it was Zwingli who completely separated internal from external influence.[3] The sacraments, for example, have no meaning in and of themselves, but only articulate faith effectuates them. This thinking quite contradicts the theology of Ephesians 2.

One can appreciate the objection to the absence of adequate catechesis in the medieval church, but that, it seems to me, does not legitimate locating the efficacy of the sacraments in the individual rather than in the Holy Spirit. Here we make a case for softening the Zwinglian view in favor of St. Thomas

---

[3]P. Stephens, "Zwingli's Sacramental Views," in *Prophet, Pastor, Protestant: The Work of Huldrych Zwingli After 500 Years*, ed. E. J. Furcha and H. Wayne Pipkin (Allison Park, Penn.: Pickwick, 1984), pp. 155-69.

Aquinas's view of the sacraments. Let us begin with some simple examples and then move to theological ones.

As my children turned three years old I taught them to brush their teeth. We did it together every morning and every night for about five years. By the time they were eight they began doing it on their own, both because it had become ritualized and because they had, by then, been to the dentist enough times to connect brushing with hygiene. Behavioral patterns and understanding go hand in hand.

When one of our daughters was in junior high, my husband went up to her room one evening and helped her order and clean up her room, to teach her that an ordered life is an ordered mind. An ordered life orders the mind. What began as an imposed chore slowly became an act of self-care. The external was internalized. The ego-alien became ego-syntonic. Practicing a musical instrument, a sport, or any craft or skill is the same. What begin as small exercises that are difficult to accomplish because they require so much attention become second-nature as they are internalized. It is not that they become meaningless rote activities, but that a certain degree of accomplishment enables the details to take care of themselves and artistry begins to emerge. The move is from careful attention to freedom. The self forms by mastering skills. Although genetic endowment helps, it does not suffice. People are not born but become artists, athletes, musicians, scholars, craftsmen and so forth. It is the same with being a Christian.

Pharisaic piety is the original pattern. It works from outside in. As a child, I said my prayers with my parents every night. After a while, I did not need them. It is a piety that works from outside in, and then comes out again. The Pharisees, now recognized as Orthodox Jews, wash their hands whenever they eat. My mother taught me that one too, and I still do it. But she did not teach me to recite the blessing that Orthodox Jews say when they wash before eating. Too bad—it would have sanctified my hands for the activity I was about to undertake. All this is to say that outward and visible forms perform inward and invisible work that later may well become visible again in a different form. Now let us turn to Christian liturgical gesture.

St. Basil the Great of Caesarea was the first I am aware of who discussed the importance of liturgical gesture, posture and movement, particularly. In his treatise "On the Holy Spirit" he explains what kneeling and then rising to a standing position at prayer and crossing oneself accomplish in the formation of the self. Liturgical gestures—like their secular counterparts, shaking hands, saluting the flag or swearing an oath—use movement to embed in us not only an attitude of awe and respect for worship, but important things about God and his doings with us. The gestures enact theological teaching. He did not write this apologetically, as I must now, because it never occurred to anyone then that liturgical movement, posture and gesture were inferior ways of learning of God than was hearing. The gestures themselves shape what we understand and who we are. It is in this sense that symbols lead us into the reality they represent. Of course, one must pay attention to what one is doing, but I do not think that Christians have ever disagreed over that.

Here we will continue to follow St. Thomas in his understanding of sacrament. It is quite broad. According to him, sacraments are signs of a sacred reality that sanctifies persons.[4] Working through those who had come before him, notably St. Augustine and Hugh of St. Victor, Thomas taught that the sacraments are more than a remedy for sin. They symbolize the incarnate Word; the sign itself makes the reality real to us.

Recently, much has been made of the distinction between sign and symbol, sign being too weak a word for a culture that uses signage to direct us to the nearest motel and restaurant off the highway. Symbols remain more powerful for us than do signs. For example, at graduation we process in academic regalia. At the airport we distinguish gate agents from pilots and flight attendants by the pins, epaulets and uniforms they wear, as we do doctors and nurses from orderlies and housekeepers. When I see a police officer I instinctively look at my speed.

Symbols present authority while signs point the way to a goal. Symbols do not point to something else, but bear the power or authority of the office and encompass us within its reach. Because of this, sacraments are now often referred to as symbols rather than signs. This may not have been a needed distinction in St. Thomas's day, but I think it is in ours.

I will add a further note on the importance of symbols. It is not only the officer's badge that gives me pause; it is also his badge that gives (or certainly should give) him pause. Once he has gone through the necessary testing and training and is publicly and formally sworn in as a keeper of the peace, the status conferred on him will affect him as well as me. Unfortunately, this authority may have a negative effect, as we see in cases of police brutality, but, when mature persons hold this office, the effect of being bestowed this sacred trust for public peace and safety should lift them to their best. He is not really the same person after being sworn in that he was before. Vows do that. By symbolizing the authority of the office, public ceremonies with oaths and

---

[4]St. Thomas Aquinas, ST 3a: q. 60, in *The Sacraments: Summa Theologiae* 3a. 60-65, Blackfriars, vol. 56.

vows bestow power. So it is with sacraments. By them we participate in the reality they carry with them. We become the field, the building, the temple of the Holy Spirit.

Perhaps you are involved with personnel matters at work. Hiring is an unusually difficult task, not only because we cannot possibly know enough about a candidate to make a well-informed judgment, but also because we do not know what the power of an office will do to the candidate. We speak of people rising to the occasion, for example. The grace of God is like that too; it raises us to itself, ennobling us with its dignity and beauty once, of course, we begin to grasp it. Life-long catechesis/Christian learning is of especial importance because we are able to grasp the wisdom and beauty of God and articulate it differently at different ages and under different circumstances throughout life.

I will offer one final example of the power of symbols from secular life: the courtroom. It is highly stylized and therefore all the more powerful. In the courtroom, one knows everyone's role in the drama by where they are sitting, and in the case of the judge, what he or she is wearing. The agents all have an identity by virtue of their training, office or indictment to carry out justice and protect the public. Some gestures and words are ancient, reminding all participants of the seriousness of the proceedings that pursue a sacred and necessary, if sometimes unpleasant, task on behalf of all.

All too often, Christians think of salvation as a private possession or personal prize that they gleefully stroke and protect, rather than a way of life in community. God's life with Israel and Jesus Christ is a public and communal story that is never private though it may be quite personal. In honoring the identity and calling given by the sacred reality, the sacraments symbolize that public and communal identity that we receive as (perhaps unwilling) participants in God's redemption of the cosmos. There is a difference between the baptized and the non-baptized. They belong to and live in different worlds, and are under different authority.

I, along with many others, have been suggesting that symbol may better capture Thomas's import than does the word sign. If so, we may say then that sacraments are liturgical enactments that symbolize a sacred reality. Further, he taught that sacraments sanctify those who receive them. They do this, I think, by separating or designating individuals for certain responsibility, work or office for which they are particularly equipped or are being prepared. Liturgical enactment establishes the office, status, responsibility or calling that sets these individuals apart from others. That is, sanctity or holiness is not a behavior goal that one struggles to maintain, as John Bunyan's pilgrim, Christian, thought, by enduring in the trust that God loves rather than spurns me. Rather it is an ontological status or identity bestowed by God in an ecclesial context.

FORMS OF SACRAMENTAL EXPRESSION

The fourth parameter for discussing sacramental ecclesiology treats various forms in which the sacramental principle is expressed. Here we mention three: (1) sacraments that induct us into and confirm us in the work of God in Israel and Christ—baptism, chrismation, confirmation and Eucharist; (2) sacraments that carry that identity forward in the church and world by dedicating our bodies and our efforts to special ministries, or rededicating these to God's work in Israel and Christ after or in the face of some threatened disruption—footwashing, ordination, marriage, reconciliation, anointing; and (3) blessings that consecrate places for our just and proper use—consecration of a home, a building.

(We might think of these three types of sacrament the way we think of orders in the church. My church has bishops, priests, deacons and laity. Other churches have presbyters, elders and laity, or elders, deacons and laity. Whatever the case, any church that ordains will have something comparable.)

In a sacramental ensemble of initiatory rites, God sets us into the drama of salvation and we are sanctified, made ready for the tasks ahead as members of the body of Christ. Baptism, chrismation and confirmation induct people into the redemption of Israel and the death and resurrection of Christ, setting them in the church as the foundation of the Christian life. These ceremonies define and identify them like any swearing in ceremony. Baptismal rites sanctify in this objective sense. They do not confirm previously cultivated piety, but call for it. Sacred washing creates the church by placing us in the midst of the redeeming work of God in Israel and his reconciling work in Christ. Sacred eating at the Lord's Table carries forward the dedicatory work of baptism, reinforcing its cultivation throughout life. It strengthens and, where needed, realigns the church as a body whose identity is in the work of God.

Now let us turn to those sacraments that dedicate our bodies to special ministries or rededicate us to God's work in Israel and Christ after or in the face of some disruption—footwashing, ordination, marriage, reconciliation, anointing. I mention footwashing first because it is the great neglected sacrament of the church, yet one of the most clarifying. What could focus attention more on the Christian calling to service than washing another's feet and kissing them, as a confession of who we are? No words need be spoken. Actions speak louder.

I will pause over ordination only to suggest that it may be a subcategory of the dedication to service encompassed in footwashing. Christian marriage is not only service but also a consecration of the body to special purpose. By being consecrated to one another in sacred trust, husband and wife are dedicating themselves to the wellbeing of society as well.

Sadly, reconciliation has dropped away, despite the Roman Church representing it in communal formats. This is unfortunate, for today many people who may have lost touch with their baptismal identity are reclaiming it and returning to the church where they receive proper guidance in their various Christian ministries in the world. These moments of being found and led back into the church by God's grace deserve the opportunity for public authorization and rededication.

Among this group of sacraments, perhaps anointing is the one that is currently being most revived. It enacts God's embrace of suffering. Rites for healing both from illness and psychological trauma are proliferating. They encase suffering in the mantle of divine compassion and care and enable the church to embrace the sufferer. Sacraments of healing may more often encourage than set apart, as do other sacramental practices. Here, people who may have been set apart by accident or circumstance are being woven back into the body of Christ to reclaim their own noble identity at the proper time through ecclesial embrace.

Finally, we consider blessings. These may authorize or consecrate places and spaces for Christian use, like a home, a church building, or a space set aside for a special ministry. Or, they may sanctify important or difficult moments in life. Some of these might be annual rededication to one's baptism or marriage on the appropriate date, the blessing of children as they begin school or at graduation, the anniversary of a particular ministry, or other life transitions that reaffirm our life under divine authority.

SACRAMENTAL ECCLESIOLOGY

Now we come to the fifth question. What is a sacramental ecclesiology? A sacramental ecclesiology is the teaching that the church—that body whose identity, vision and mission are constituted by its participation in the work of God in Israel and Jesus Christ—is enacted and symbolized through the sacraments. It claims not only that the church is the field, building, temple or household of God, but also that it is so by virtue of symbolic participation in that work. The church is created by God's work in Israel and in Christ and his holiness sanctifies those who participate in that drama liturgically and sacramentally. Her members are accountable to the church's identity, vision, mission and ministry. A sacramental ecclesiology is broad, for it follows St. Augustine's insistence that the church is a mixed multitude of the pious and the impious, a school for sinners, not a club of the saved, as Rowan Greer often put it. Luther and Calvin, of course, followed Augustine. In short, a sacramental ecclesiology means that the church is that community comprised of those who are sanctified into the drama of God by virtue of sacramental grace effectuated by the holiness of God himself, rather than anything of their own doing.

Now, you may well ask, what is the place for faith, and what is the role of preaching? Sacramental ecclesiology sends the message, "come as you are," but it does not invite anyone to stay as they are, for formation is transformation, even if incrementally so. God is patient with the church, sometimes too patient for my taste. This is a vision of the church in which God often works with us slowly and gently rather than through a dramatic moment of illumination, although perhaps often, both are more at play than entrenched camps like to admit.

Having been engrafted into the drama of salvation, the sacred reality that sacraments symbolize must take up residence in the church's members. Faith is a gift of divine grace. It cannot be forced. Two people may experience the same upbringing, either Christian or non-Christian, and one will become a faithful disciple and the other not. The ability to be taken with this story and this identity into which one has been put—forcibly in the case of captured infants—cannot be commanded, only commended for consideration. That is where preaching and teaching come to the fore. They help those whose spiritual identity has been aroused by grace to understand who they are and be challenged to struggle with and live into that identity and calling.

Further, although the church opens her arms to everyone, not everything is appropriate there. Her members must be socialized and acculturated into those practices, beliefs and behaviors that are apposite, and encouraged to resist or desist from those that are not. That is another of the important functions of preaching and teaching, verbal forms of proclamation that, like repeatable sacraments, reinforce and rebind the community around its center: the reign of reconciliation rather than conquest.

Still, in a sacramental ecclesiology, preaching and teaching are not the point, but are necessary guides for figuring how together we live who we have been made by God. To put a sharp point on the difference between a faith ecclesiology and a sacramental one, we might suggest that a faith-based theology stands on justification by faith in the mercy of God known to Israel and in Christ, while a sacramental theology stands on justification by the work of God in Israel and Christ symbolized through ceremonial reenactment. Of course, preaching and teaching are important in either case.

CONCLUSION

A sacramental ecclesiology is the idea that the body of Christ is that community of persons whose identity, vision and mission are constituted by being made part of the community created by the redeeming and reconciling work of God in Israel and in Jesus Christ. Her members are grafted into that symbolic identity by the Holy Spirit in baptism and, by being sealed as Christ's own forever, are co-opted into that identity, vision and mission in all that they are, all that they do, and all that they have. The baptized do not create their own identity because they are under orders to be faithful to the one they have from God. Their belonging is not a matter of choice but of willingness to accept and grow into who they are by God's grace. Perhaps it is only after all of this that the meaning of Deuteronomy 6:5 as a confession of gratitude comes into focus: "you shall love the Lord your God with all your heart, with all your soul, and with all your might."

PART FIVE

LOCATING THE
CHURCH CULTURALLY

12

THE CHURCH AS SOCIAL THEORY
A Reformed Engagement with Radical Orthodoxy

JAMES K. A. SMITH

Currents in contemporary ecclesiology have increasingly thematized the church as polis (Hauerwas, Hütter, Long, et al.). A refined, critical version of the church-as-polis model has been offered by "Radical Orthodoxy" as articulated in the work of John Milbank, Graham Ward, William Cavanaugh and Daniel Bell. Are there resources for an evangelical ecclesiology to be found in Radical Orthodoxy? Can evangelicals be radically orthodox? Can we be anything *but?*[1]

THE CHURCH AS SOCIAL THEORY: RADICAL ORTHODOXY'S ECCLESIOLOGY

A Christian sociology. As Stanley Hauerwas has claimed, "The church does not *have* a social ethic; the church *is* a social ethic."[2] Milbank's claim echoes this sentiment: the church does not *have* a social theory; it *is* a social theory.[3]

---

[1]Some material previously appeared in *Introducing Radical Orthodoxy: Mapping a Post-Secular Theology* (Grand Rapids: Baker Academic, 2004), reproduced here with the kind permission of the publisher.

[2]Stanley Hauerwas, *The Peaceable Kingdom: A Primer in Christian Ethics* (Notre Dame, Ind.: University of Notre Dame Press, 1983), p. 99. The question of the relationship between Hauerwas and Radical Orthodoxy is an important one. When Ward or Pickstock discusses theologians who they see as operating within the same "sensibility," Hauerwas is always on the list. In addition, some of the authors in the Radical Orthodoxy series were students of Hauerwas (Bell, Hanby, Long) and we'll find their voice prevalent in the discussions of ecclesiology.

[3]John Milbank, *Theology and Social Theory* (Oxford: Blackwell, 1990), p. 380 (henceforth abbreviated as *TST*). And correlatively, "*all* theology has to reconceive itself as a kind of 'Christian sociology': that is to say, as the explication of a socio-linguistic practice" (p. 381). This bears affinity to Lindbeck's "postliberal" account of theology (in *Nature of Doctrine*).

To put this otherwise: Christian social theory is "first and foremost an *ec-clesiology*."[4] But in order to understand these claims, we need to get a handle on what Milbank means by a "sociology" or a "social theory." Clearly it is not a merely empirical description of social organization; rather (somewhat in the vein of Marx and the Frankfurt school[5]) what is being offered is a *normative* or a priori account of human relationality within communities. But what is needed for a normative social theory is a normative account of human nature and the nature of human relationships—what we might call a "philosophical anthropology."[6] Here Milbank's critique of secular sociology echoes the critique of Herman Dooyeweerd articulated a generation earlier. Dooyeweerd also emphasized that the "descriptions" of social structures offered by social science must presuppose a "theoretical view of the totality of human social relationships."[7] And like Milbank, Dooyeweerd argues that such a theory will always already be rooted in theological commitments; thus every social theory will be, at root, *confessional*.[8] So Radical Orthodoxy begins by putting that on the table: a Christian social theory begins from a sense of the normative vocation of the human community and the way in which that (creational) vocation is renewed in the life and practice of the church.

Redeeming community: The church as polis. Thus Radical Orthodoxy offers a story about human society and community in terms of creation, Fall and redemption.[9] As Cavanaugh recounts it, "Humankind was created for communion"[10]; in other words, with creation there is a kind of "natural

---

[4]This, of course, raises an important question: if a Christian sociology is really an *ecclesiology*, then what does a Christian social theory have to say about *other* societies? As Milbank says here, the church's account of society—that is, of authentic human community—is "only an account of other human societies to the extent that the Church defines itself, in its practice, as in continuity and discontinuity with these societies" (*Theology and Social Theory*, p. 380). But if one responds that, as a result, a Christian sociology cannot give "a universal 'rational' account of the 'social' character of all societies," Milbank's response is simple: this is because no such sociology is possible on any grounds (pp. 380-81).

[5]See Rolf Wiggershaus, *The Frankfurt School* (Cambridge, Mass.: MIT Press, 1994) for a discussion of their self-understanding regarding the normative or prescriptive nature of social theory.

[6]Sociologist Christian Smith has unapologetically taken up such a project in his recent work, *Moral, Believing Animals: Human Personhood and Culture* (Oxford: Oxford University Press, 2003).

[7]Herman Dooyeweerd, *A Christian Theory of Social Institutions*, trans. Magnus Verbrugge, ed. John Witte Jr. (La Jolla, Calif.: Herman Dooyeweerd Foundation, 1986), pp. 33, 38.

[8]Ibid., pp. 45-58.

[9]William Cavanaugh, "The City," in *Radical Orthodoxy: A New Theology* (London: Routledge, 1998), p. 182.

[10]Cavanaugh, "City," p. 182.

unity"[11] of the human race grounded in the *imago Dei*—which grounds both humanity's participation in God and one another.[12] The disruption of this unity and communion is occasioned by the Fall, beginning with Adam's attempt to blame Eve for sin, and spilling over into the murderous narratives of Gen 3—11. So contrary to the modern secular narratives of Hobbes or Machiavelli, humanity is not *originally* at war as part of some kind of "natural" opposition between individuals; rather, this is a postlapsarian condition. In fact, Cavanaugh suggests, "the effect of sin is the very creation of individuals as such, that is, the creation of an ontological distinction between individual and group."[13] Redemption of sociality, then, means the restoration of original unity or communion. This happens "through participation in Christ's Body" and only in Christ's body[14] insofar as it is "in Christ Jesus" that peace and reconciliation are effected (Eph 2:13-18). So the *ekklēsia* is the site of renewed creational community, albeit an eschatological anticipation. In Augustinian terms, the true commonwealth—and hence communion—is located not in the empire, but the *ecclesia*.[15] Here we locate one of the reasons that Ward and Pickstock suggest a substantial constructive agreement between Radical Orthodoxy and the theological project of Hauerwas. While there will be points of disagreement, I think it is both justified and helpful to see Hauerwas's project as allied with Radical Orthodoxy's account of the church as *polis*—and to see both as a constructive way forward to Christian thought and practice.

It is this account of human community which undergirds Radical Ortho-

---

[11]The notion of "unity" will give some pause (particularly for those inspired by Derrida and Levinas), seeming to suggest a kind of hegemony or totalizing imposition of "sameness." But this is not the case: the "unity" here is one of *communal difference*—recalling that the "analogical worldview" (Ward) is the only one really able to conceive of differences *in nonoppositional relation*. The unity is one of *koinonia*, which is the community of those who are different.

[12]Cavanaugh, "City," p. 184. Cavanaugh cites Lubac who sums up patristic anthropology: "For the divine image does not differ from one individual to another: in all it is the same image. The same mysterious participation in God which causes the soul to exist effects at one and the same time the unity of spirits among themselves" (p. 183).

[13]Cavanaugh, "City," p. 184.

[14]As we will see below, then, the question will be: *where* do we find or participate in Christ's body? Ward's account of the diffusion of Christ's body, as well as Milbank's most recent comments on the church, seem to make Christ's body co-extensive with humanity. Cavanaugh hints in that direction as well: "The salvation of individuals is only through Christ's salvation of the whole of humanity" ("City," p. 184). Below I'll suggest that a more persistent Augustinian picture will link the body of Christ to election. (For all my reservations about Kuyper's ecclesiology, he is more of an Augustinian in this respect than Radical Orthodoxy.)

[15]Cavanaugh, "City," p. 185.

doxy's critique of secular modernity, and the state in particular.[16] In other words, the Fall is the advent of social atomism and individualism, and the modern state, working with a pseudo-soteriology, attempts to effect "peace" but ends up with only a parody of the *ecclesia* insofar as it attempts to construct a "community" *without* calling into question the supposed "naturalness" of individualistic opposition and *without* the redemption effected in Christ. Rather, the modern state[17] attempts to effect peace—now understood negatively, as merely the absence of conflict or the undoing of the *bellum omnis contra omnem*—by contract; the "new Adam" that will save us is not the Son, but Leviathan.[18] It is in this sense that Radical Orthodoxy sees the state as a quasi- or pseudo-ecclesia, and sees the *ecclesia* as the only authentic *polis*. Here Radical Orthodoxy clearly echoes the Hauerwasian understanding of the church as an alternative polity and "holy nation." As Hauerwas puts it, "The church therefore is a polity like any other, but it is also *unlike* any other insofar as it is formed by a people who have no reason to fear the truth." Because the church is called as its own polis and nation, Christians "are at home in no nation."[19] The church, then, is not an organization that can fit within the "civil society" of the nation-state or regnant polis precisely because it is an *alternative* polis that calls into question the aims of the state—whether ancient or modern. "The church," Hauerwas remarks, "does not exist to provide an ethos for democracy or any other form of social organization, but stands as a political alternative to every nation, witnessing to the kind of social life possible for those that have been formed by the story of Christ."[20] The church as a community—both

---

[16]For more on this, see James K. A. Smith, *Introducing Radical Orthodoxy: Mapping a Post-Secular Theology* (Grand Rapids: Baker Academic, 2004), chap. 4.

[17]Though it would seem that this is not the case for *just* the modern state. As Peter J. Leithart comments, "Aristotle's *Politics* begins with the claim that 'every state is an association (*koinonia*)'" and that "the city (*polis*) is the highest kind of *koinonia*, a political *koinonia*" (*Against Christianity* [Moscow, Idaho: Canon, 2003], p. 25). He goes on to note the way in which the Church forms an alternative *koinōnia* (Acts 2): "Paul did not attempt to find a place for the Church in the nooks and crannies of the Greco-Roman *polis*. The Church was not an addition, but an alternative to, the *koinonia* of the *polis*" (pp. 26-27). The difference between ancient and modern is the difference between city-state and nation-state. But both, it seems, have the characteristic of quasi-ecclesiality (in which the ultimate telos of humanity and human community is *immanentized*).

[18]Cavanaugh, "City," p. 188. The results of such a salvation are minimal: "Beginning with an anthropology of formally equal individuals guided by no common ends, the best the state can hope to do is to keep these individuals from interfering with each other's rights" (*Radical Orthodoxy*, p. 193).

[19]Hauerwas, *Peaceable Kingdom*, p. 102.

[20]Stanley Hauerwas, "Reforming Christian Social Ethics: Ten Theses," in *The Hauerwas Reader*, ed. John Berkman and Michael Cartwright (Durham, N.C.: Duke University Press, 2001),

a polis and *koinōnia*—is constituted differently precisely because it is animated by the Holy Spirit and has as its telos and aim friendship with God and neighbor. Authentic relations of charity and love are possible within this community because it *alone* is the community in which "the love of God is shed abroad in our hearts through the Holy Spirit which is given to us" (Rom 5:5). So what distinguishes the community which is the body of Christ is not only its redirection to humanity's proper telos, but also the regeneration of the heart which makes redirection toward and pursuit of this telos possible.

This is precisely why the church is a *sacramental* community, for this redirection is not only a question of salvation but sanctification: it is not an event but the fruit of discipleship. Worship *is* political precisely because it forms us otherwise—renewing our creational vocation.[21] The Eucharist, for instance, is both a political (i.e., polis-related) reality which "undercuts the primacy of contract and exchange in modern social relations"[22] as well as a means of grace which nourishes the community (and individuals within the community) to pursue its proper telos and enact authentic sociality.[23] The Eucharist also "transgresses national boundaries and redefines who our fellow-citizens are," reminding us that we are primarily citizens of a global polis who pledge allegiance to Christ, not the nation-state that we currently inhabit.[24] The central point is that the constitution of this community in which authentic sociality is renewed is not the mere product of "Christian"[25] thinking or principles, but the embodied *practice* of the church where Word and sacrament are means of grace for the alternative formation that is the neces-

---

pp. 114-15. For an oblique justification of my overlapping of Hauerwas and Radical Orthodoxy on these points, see William Cavanaugh's wonderful introduction to the *Hauerwas Reader*, "Stan the Man: A Thoroughly Biased Account of a Completely Unobjective Person," pp. 17-32.

[21]For Augustine, a true "commonwealth" or *res publica* is only possible where there is *true worship* (see *City of God* 19.11-28). My thanks to Robert Dodaro for discussions on this point.

[22]Cavanaugh, "City," p. 195.

[23]From a Reformed perspective, this would require that we abandon Kuyper's flattened, unsacramental ecclesiology and recover instead Calvin's robust, sacramental ecclesiology, including his doctrine of "real presence." For an account which attempts to restore a certain co-centrality to the table in Reformed worship, see Keith A. Mathison, *Given for You: Reclaiming Calvin's Doctrine of the Lord's Supper* (Phillipsburg, N.J.: Presbyterian & Reformed, 2002).

[24]Quoted passage from Cavanaugh, "City," p. 194. This undergirds one of Hauerwas's basic arguments for Christian pacifism: if my fundamental allegiance is to Christ, and my fundamental citizenship is as a member of his Body, then how could I participate in actions which—in the service of the interests of the nation-state—would require me to kill a brother or sister in Christ who currently inhabits a different nation-state?

[25]Leithart well articulates all the problems with the abstraction of "Christianity" apart from the concrete, incarnate embodiment of the church (*Against Christianity*, pp. 13-40).

sary condition for this community of love to take shape as a colony of the "heavenly commonwealth [*politeuma*[26]]" whose Lord is not Caesar but Christ (Phil 3:20).

The Christian community, then, is a unique polis which is demarcated by (1) a distinct narrative that is recounted in distinct practices; (2) a different telos which is transcendent to the contemporary order; and (3) the common presence of the Spirit at work amongst its members through Word and sacrament. As such, it stands in contrast to every other polis insofar as no other shares its narrative (the Scriptures) nor is any other the site for the Spirit's regenerative, sacramental and sanctifying presence.

EROTIC SUBJECTS: A POSTMODERN AUGUSTINIANISM

The Augustinian axiom noted above points to a central theme in Radical Orthodoxy's understanding of community and human nature: against rationalist reductions of the self to a *rational animal*, and against rule-oriented ethical accounts of the self as an *autonomous subject*, Radical Orthodoxy recaptures the Augustinian vision of the creature as a *desiring agent*. As creatures defined by *love*, we are fundamentally characterized by a desire, an erotic pull toward the Creator—and because this desire can *only* find its proper target in the Creator, its misdirection toward anything else (such as a mere aspect of creation) generates only anxiety and restlessness.[27] Selfhood, then, is *intentional*. The primary intentional relation of the self to its world is not theoretical reflection (Husserl) or pragmatic concern (Heidegger), but rather *love* (Augustine). As ek-static, the self is defined by its *love*, its *eros*; thus Radical Orthodoxy's conception of the self calls into question the reductionist accounts of the self of-

---

[26]See N. T. Wright, "Paul's Gospel and Caesar's Empire," in *Paul and Politics: Essays in Honor of Krister Stendahl*, ed. Richard A. Horsley (Harrisburg, Penn.: Trinity Press International, 2000), pp. 173-81. As Leithart points out, many English translations fail to convey the political nature of Paul's call to the Philippians to live as a community of friends who are citizens of a different empire. In particular, Paul's exhortation to conduct themselves as citizens (*politeuo*, Phil 1:27) is often unrendered, thus missing the link with Phil 3:20 and the general sense in which Paul is calling them to constitute an alternative polis: "The Philippians, so proud of being Roman citizens and so protective of Roman custom, needed to learn to live as citizens of a different commonwealth that placed new demands on its citizens" (Leithart, *Against Christianity*, p. 28). The translation to a context of American empire seems clear enough.

[27]This is the focus of Augustine's narrative from books two through five of the *Confessions*, where he seeks to illustrate the frustrations of a misdirected desire—or better, an idolatrous desire which substitutes alternatives to the Creator. I have analyzed this in more detail in my "Confessions of an Existentialist: Reading Augustine After Heidegger," *New Blackfriars* 82 (2001): 273-82 (part 1), 335-47 (part 2), and *Speech and Theology*, chap. 4.

fered by rationalism, liberalism and capitalism.[28] Describing this desire-structure as "the doxological self," Hanby rightly describes it as one which the self "cannot escape, but can only pervert."[29]

Daniel Bell expounds the way in which Bernard of Clairvaux developed this account of the human person as desiring subject who "thirsts" for God (Ps 63:1). For Bernard, desire is a basic movement of being human and therefore should not be construed in negative terms (as it was by the Stoics, or even Buddhism); rather, desire is a gift of God engendered by God's own desire: "Human desire is nothing less than a mirror of the positive, creative desire of God."[30] As such, human desire is not the result of a lack or privation, but rather plentitude and excess—a positive movement toward God. Because such desire is constitutive of creaturehood in its original goodness, "Bernard speaks of human desire continuing in heaven."[31] So despite historical tendencies to equate desire *as such* with sin and fallenness, for Bernard desire is a creational good. However, this does not prevent Bernard from giving an account of fallen desire; rather, invoking a framework analogous to Augustine's *ordo amoris*, Bernard is able to describe corrupted desire precisely as the misdirection of this good creational structure.[32] Bernard articulates this by distinguishing between the "image" of God and the "likeness" of God: "The 'image' was deemed a reference to a fundamental ontological reality, in Bernard's case, desire. The 'likeness,' in turn, was equated with an ethical orientation, with the direction of this desire in harmony with God. Hence when Bernard asserts that humanity lost its likeness, he is saying that human desire is no longer in harmony with the desire from whence it came."[33] The Fall is not the occasion for the *advent* of desire, but rather the distortion and misdirection of the creational structure of desire: or as Bell puts it, the problem is ethical, not ontological: "Desire remains positive, productive. Only now it finds joy in the wrong productions; it takes pleasure in the wrong goods."[34] Redemption, then, is precisely the reor-

---

[28]I have further explored this Augustinian account of the self in *Speech and Theology*, chap. 4. For a more systematic philosophical anthropology ordered around this center of love, see James H. Olthuis, *The Beautiful Risk* (Grand Rapids: Zondervan, 2001).

[29]Cavanaugh, "City," p. 115. In *Augustine and Modernity*, Hanby goes on to show the way in which Augustine's conception of the self in terms of desire informs his critique of Stoicism (which he takes to be proto-modern) [pp. 93-94].

[30]Bell, *Liberation Theology After the End of History*, p. 90.

[31]Ibid.

[32]This echoes the Reformational framework of structure/direction articulated in Albert Wolters, *Creation Regained*. Cf. also H. Dooyeweerd, *In the Twilight of Western Thought* (Philadelphia: Presbyterian & Reformed, 1960), pp. 129-30.

[33]Bell, *Liberation Theology After the End of History*, pp. 90-91.

[34]Ibid., p. 91.

dering of desire to its creational aim by the Word who came to heal desire. And as Ward concludes, authentic (and properly directed) *eros* is also communal: Christian desire is never a private, Kierkegaardian-like love affair with the absolute, but always an embodied desiring for the Creator which, as in the Trinity, always already involves a third: the Other. Thus Ward can reconfigure the *ecclesia* as an "erotic community."[35]

The burden of this postmodern Augustinian understanding of the self in terms of desire is, then, to unveil the radically different ways in which desire is *formed* in modernity and postmodernity—and the function of the church as the site of a proper and *counter*-formation. In other words, the erotic *structure* of the creature can take different directions, and these different *intentions* are the products of the formation of desire by particular stories, narrated by particular communities, and enacted by particular disciplines. Radical Orthodoxy is very much concerned to analyze the specific forms of desire produced by different communities and articulate the antithesis between these and the church as the site for authentic *eros*. It is these analyses to which we now turn.

TECHNOLOGIES OF DESIRE: CHURCH, STATE, MARKET

While trumpeting the "end of history" and the triumph of liberal, free-market democracy, Francis Fukuyama conceded the Augustinian axiom above insofar as he suggested that the globalization of liberal democracy and the free market confirmed it as the regime that best "satisfies the most basic human longings."[36] By assuming that humans have basic or fundamental desires, Fukuyama also confirmed that capitalism and liberal democracy are not just instrumental goods, but rather set themselves up as *ultimate* goods—as systems and institutions which would purport to satisfy humanity's most basic desires. But of course, if one begins with Augustine with the assumption that humanity's most basic desire is *for God*, then any regime which would pretend to fulfill such a desire could only be an idol—not merely an "economic theory" or a political framework subservient to God, but a rival god. As such, the relationship between Christianity (or better, the body of Christ) and these politico-economic regimes cannot be one of simply rapprochement or accommodation. Insofar as these regimes ultimately seek to

---

[35]Graham Ward, *Cities of God*, Radical Orthodoxy Series (London: Routledge, 2000), pp. 152-81.

[36]Francis Fukuyama, "Reflections on *The End of History*, Five Years Later," in *After History? Francis Fukuyama and His Critics*, ed. Timothy Burns (Lanham, Md.: Rowman & Littlefield, 1994), p. 241, cited in Bell, *Liberation Theology*, p. 1.

satisfy "the most basic human longings," they set themselves up in contest with the God of Jesus Christ, who also claims to and offers to satisfy these most basic human desires. The Christian, therefore, must critically consider whether it is possible to serve both.

Daniel Bell's brilliant analysis refines this contestation even further, along two levels. First, he forces us to reconsider, today, what is the most important "competitor" of Christ and his body, the church. From the first century and into modernity, if the church has been aware of competing allegiances, it has been especially suspicious of the *state*—particularly in its *imperial* form—as that which most threatens the authentic polis which is the church. Thus the early *ecclesia* unfolded in the shadow of a politically constituted empire, and both the church and the empire recognized that the gospel of Christ subverts the empire's claims to monopolize allegiance (cf. Acts 16).[37] Through modernity, this political regime crystallized in the form of the nation-state, but still demanded the same kind of total, or at least, ultimate allegiance that trumped others.[38] (Anything like a "Patriot Act" can broach no compromise.) In this respect, one could see Yoder's and Hauerwas's analyses largely working within a paradigm where the state is the looming idol that the church is most tempted to worship. But Bell suggests that this is a dated, and therefore somewhat impotent, mode of analysis and critique, for in a globalized world it is no longer states that wield imperialist power, but rather capitalism and the market.[39] While there is obviously a link between this globalized market and North Atlantic nation states, especially the United States, the new empire is capitalism as a global, transnational phenomenon—an empire of which states are only colonies.[40] This is also why he criticizes liberation theology for continuing to think that "statecraft"[41] is the means for securing

---

[37]Cf. N. T. Wright, "Paul's Gospel and Caesar's Empire."

[38]Cavanaugh, "City," p. 183.

[39]Bell's consideration of this "new empire" echoes the analyses of Hardt and Negri's *Empire*.

[40]This contention regarding the trumping of the state by the market does not mitigate the critiques of Yoder, Hauerwas and others insofar as states *serve* capitalism and remain a primary mode of formation. The reason for this deep coalescence is due to the fundamental link between liberalism and capitalism (see Long, *Divine Economy*, pp. 10-12); therefore Hauerwas's critique still holds insofar as liberalism is now a "worldview" which is imbedded in transnational capitalism, not just nation-states.

[41]Bell defines "statecraft" as that (modern) conception of politics "that holds that the realm where persons come together in a polity, in a politics, is rightly overseen by and finds its highest expression in the state; it is the investiture of the state with sovereign authority over the socius and, consequently, privileging the state as the fulcrum of social and political change" (*Liberation Theology*, p. 13). Milbank takes this notion of *sovereignty* to be central to the modern nation-state and that which was most threatened by the attacks of 9/11 (Milbank, "Sovereignty, Empire, Capital, and Terror," pp. 63-69).

peace and justice. For what can states really do in the face of the transnational phenomenon of the market—particularly when states are servants *of*
this market? Following Deleuze and Guattari, Bell considers the way in
which capitalism has unleashed a "deterritorializing" power that now ex-
ceeds that of the state and overwhelms it—as a kind of invention that Doctor
Frankenstein can no longer control. Thus the state can no longer play the reg-
ulative role it once did. Capitalism, then, is the new empire to which the gospel must be opposed precisely because it demands an allegiance which rivals
our allegiance to Christ.

   Second, Bell refines the analysis by specifically considering this tension and
clash in terms of *desire*, or more specifically what he calls, in Foucauldian
terms, "technologies of desire."[42] By this he means to indicate the fairly classical notion that selfhood (and community) is the product of formation, and formation is the product of a regime of disciplines and practices. Disciplines are
aimed at forming certain *kinds* of persons whose aim or *intentio* is a particular
telos[43] (or "vision of the Good").[44] Cashing this out in the Augustinian terms
above, discipline is aimed at the formation of desire—and desire, it will be re-
called, constitutes the heart of the self. It is in these terms that we are able to
understand that "the conflict between capitalism and Christianity is nothing
less than a clash of opposing technologies of desire,"[45] for each is trying to
form very different people for very different ends. In particular, capitalism is
a technology of desire that *de*forms creational desire, misdirecting it to an idol-

---

[42]For my own critical appropriation of Foucault for thinking about Christian discipleship,
see my *Demythologizing Postmodernism: Critical Direction for the Emerging Church* (forthcoming), chap. 4.

[43]On this score, the case of the "state" is ambiguous. On the one hand, the modern liberal
state is too vacuous to offer a substantive vision of the good. As Milbank suggests, "The
modern secular state rests on no substantive values. It lacks full legitimacy even of the
sort that Saint Paul ascribed to the 'powers that be,' because it exists mainly to uphold the
market system, which is an ordering of a substantively anarchic (and therefore not divinely appointed in Saint Paul's sense) competition between wills to power" ("Sovereignty," p. 64). On the other hand, its very liberalism *is* a particular vision of the good
which it holds exclusively. It is in this sense that we must appreciate the way that liberalism is a worldview, and therefore fundamentally religious (or theological)—and therefore
a gospel competing with the Gospel of the Crucified. John Owen is helpfully forthright in
describing liberalism in these terms: "Liberalism is first a worldview, a set of fundamental
categories through which individuals understand themselves and the world. It thus
shapes individuals' conceptions of their identities and interests by telling them of what
human nature and the good consist." See John Owen IV, *Liberal Peace, Liberal War* (Ithaca,
N.Y.: Cornell University Press, 1997), p. 19.

[44]In this respect, Bell's neologism "technologies of desire" describes the notion of disciplinary
formation at the heart of both Foucault's and Hauerwas's ethics.

[45]Bell, *Liberation Theology*, p. 2.

atrous telos (viz., consumption, accumulation and disposal of material goods as the primary mode for securing happiness).[46] When even the church has become co-opted by the regnant capitalist technologies of desire—as its consumerization of religious fetishes confirms—what possibilities could remain for the *healing* of desire?

By considering capitalism as a (globalized) technology of desire, Bell means to unveil its theological (albeit idolatrous) freight. Far from being merely a "neutral" mode for economic distribution, capitalism is a particular religious (and imperial) vision of "basic human longings" (Fukuyama) or desires. Capitalism, then, is not merely an instrument or tool which can be put to work as a servant of other substantive construals of the good; rather, it proposes its own account of the telos to which human desire ought to be aimed (consumption and accumulation). This alternative telos can only be seen as a rival god and therefore an idol which must be resisted by those who would follow the crucified.[47]

Why, then, has the church failed to resist capitalist discipline—or even worse, how did the church come to *serve* capitalist discipline? Again, this stems from the fact that the church and individual Christians have bought secular economics' myth of religious neutrality; in other words, the church believed economists when they pronounced the "facts" of economic reality which turned out to confirm capitalism's picture of the world. By granting the very notion of a secular, autonomous temporal realm, the church left it to supposedly "secular reason" to describe the "realities" of economic organization. But what was being purveyed under the banner of science and facts

---

[46]Long is particularly interested to deconstruct the way economics undertakes this project under the guise of a neutral, scientific account of "the facts" (accepting Weber's fact/value distinction). But Long doesn't buy it: "While it appears to give us merely the facts, it gives us much more. It invites us to construe our lives, primarily our lives as family members, in terms of the activities of producers and consumers" (*Divine Economy*, p. 4).

[47]Here we must note an important qualification: some might hear this radical, trenchant critique of capitalism as a rather naive, and very *un*-Reformed banishment of economics as inherently sinful. But this is not the case at all. In fact, such a response naively and unimaginatively assumes that economic distribution could *only* be capitalist. Within a Reformed rubric, I would affirm that the sphere of commerce, exchange and distribution of goods is indeed a good structure of creation. But capitalism is a particular direction in which that good structure has been taken—and more specifically, it is a *mis*direction of creational norms for commerce, exchange and distribution. To reject capitalism as basically idolatrous is not naively to reject the realm of economic and commercial vocation. But it does require redirecting our practices in this sphere (as seen in the early church's mode of distribution and exchange). My thanks to Bill Dyrness for pushing me on this point.

was, in fact, an idolatrous theology; admitting the trojan horse of secular economic theory into the church was at the same time an admission of a false
religion which seductively offers an account of the telos of human desire
which is deeply antithetical to the message of the cross.

Having unveiled the ultimately theological or confessional nature of capitalism and thus pointing to the dangers of its secular liturgies and modes of
discipline (in advertising, for instance), the constructive aspect of Bell's project
is to consider the way in which Christianity offers a different technology of desire—a technology which actually *heals* desire and offers a "therapy" for distorted desire. In this sense, Christianity is "a therapy, a way of life that releases
desire from its bondage, that cures the madness so that desire may once again
flow as it was created to do."[48] Given the transnational "megapolis" of capitalism—and hence its deterritorialized means of discipline in which states are
merely municipalities for its administration of its technology of desire—the
only way in which capitalist technologies of desire can be resisted is by an alternative polis, itself transnational, which is not simply another subsector of
the state or "civil society" (which is itself a subsector of capitalism).[49] Where
could we find such a site? This alternative polis, for Bell, is located in the *ecclesia*, the universal and catholic body of Christ. Hence, "[i]f Christians are to resist capitalism, if Christianity is to heal desire, the modern differentiation of
life, with its separation of politics and religion, must be refused."[50] In other
words, if we accept the modern compartmentalization of life into "sacred" and
"secular" realms (which map onto the "private" and "public" distinction), and
if we concede the shape of economics and politics to the secular, public realm,
then we are, in fact, serving other gods either without knowing it, or without
sensing a tension between that and our confession of faith in Christ. We will
end up spending our workweek making cakes for the queen of heaven and
spending our weekends with Yahweh (Jer 7:16-19)—without seeing the way in
which our service to the queen of heaven is forming us into queen-of-heaven
kinds of people. Thus Bell not only calls into question the sacred-secular, pri-
vate-public distinctions of modernity; he also calls into question the apolitical
understandings of the church which have dominated modern theology and

---

[48]Ibid., p. 3.
[49]This is one reason why I think Miroslav Volf's critique of Bell is somewhat mistargeted on
this score. Volf takes Bell to task for proposing the Church as "an alternative to the state"
(Volf, "*Liberation Theology After the End of History*: An Exchange," *Modern Theology* 19 [2003]:
263). But this is not really Bell's claim. The problem here is capitalism, which is *transnational*; entities operating at the "level" of the state will be insufficient to resist its deterrito-
rialization.
[50]Bell, *Liberation Theology*, p. 71.

practice. Like Hauerwas, Bell asserts that the church does not *have* a politics; it *is* a politics. The means for securing justice and resisting capitalist discipline, then, is not "statecraft," but rather *being* the church as the site for an alternative (creational, and therefore proper) technology of desire. This requires "Christianity's reassertion in the material realm as the true politics. Christianity is the true politics, the true polity, over against the agony of capitalist discipline, in the Augustinian sense that the church embodies the true form of human social, political, and economic organization because its order is one of liturgy, or worship of the triune God."[51] So "the Christian *mythos* finds its political correlate, not in the state—even one ordered toward the common good—but in the Church as the exemplary form of human community."[52] The only technology of desire that can properly resist capitalist discipline is one that is directed to the creational telos of humanity: the triune God. Insofar as such a redirection of desire requires regeneration of the desiring heart and the continued sanctification of the desiring agent, and insofar as the site for such regeneration and sanctification of desire is the sacramental worship community, then resistance to capitalist discipline can only happen in the *ecclesia*.[53] It is the very material practices of baptism, Eucharist, prayer and catechesis which transform the self and heal desire.[54] Sacramental worship will be the primary site for the reformation of human desire which, in a capitalist world, can only be a subversive, countercultural gesture.[55]

---

[51]Ibid., p. 4.

[52]Ibid., p. 72.

[53]This is where Miroslav Volf lodges one of his major complaints with Bell's argument. Volf criticizes "the absence—or rather insufficient presence—of the Holy Spirit in Bell's technology of desire. In other words, the church with its practices has absorbed the Holy Spirit" (Volf, "Exchange," p. 265). As he reiterates it in his response to Bell's response, Volf's "free church" line comes to the fore when he emphasizes "the *internal* work of the Spirit" which is not necessarily connected to the Church: "It is *God* who opens the hearts to the Gospel, *God* who kills the old self and makes alive the new, *God* who comes to dwell in the soul—and all the self-binding of God to the means of grace notwithstanding, God does all this when and where God wants, with no strict correlation between external means of grace ('technologies') and their internal effect" (Volf, "Against a Pretentious Church: A Rejoinder to Bell's Response," *Modern Theology* 19 [2003]: 283). But this just seems to be a reiteration of a "Protestant principle" that feeds into the minimalist ecclesiologies of evangelicalism—as well as that of Kuyper. I would affirm, with Calvin, the correlation of the means of grace with the advent of grace, even while agreeing with Volf regarding the necessity of "subjective appropriation" (Volf, "Exchange," p. 266).

[54]Bell, *Liberation Theology,* pp. 85-86.

[55]Bell's project raises a nexus of important questions that I cannot sufficiently address here. In particular, further reflection is needed on the relationship between change in *agents* and change in *structures*—or, in other words, the role of the Great Commission with respect to

CONCLUSION: REFORMING RADICAL ORTHODOXY AND RADICALIZING REFORMED ECCLESIOLOGY

From a Reformed perspective, particularly in the heritage of Kuyper and Dooyeweerd (less so in the sacerdotal tradition of Calvin's Geneva), one of the most disconcerting aspects of Radical Orthodoxy's account of cultural engagement is its attribution of this work of cultural redemption to the church *as such*, and its suggestion that the state and church are, fundamentally, competitors—one polis versus another. If Leviathan swallowed the church, the Reformed tradition would worry that Bell's "more substantive ecclesiology" signals a church which threatens to ingest the state. In the orthodox Kuyperian picture of social institutions, the state and the church are distinct spheres—and for Dooyeweerd, at least, these spheres are constitutive of creation as created.[56] If the state is creational, *and* the church is creational, then their distinction must be essential (even if their differentiation is only unfolded in history). In that case, where Radical Orthodoxy tends to see a relation of competition between the church and the state (competing for the task of specifying the telos of human community), the Reformational tradition would see two legitimately distinct spheres of social organization and community. Is there a way to account for the difference?

I would suggest a couple of points to consider. First, I do think there is a tendency in Radical Orthodoxy to conflate and confuse a particular *direction* of the state with the *structure* of the state as such. As we saw in Bell's discussion of desire, it is important to distinguish between the creational structure and the postlapsarian direction in which that structure can and has been taken. In this

---

the Cultural Mandate. Having been extricated from a fundamentalist and revivalist fixation on "evangelism" as the only agent of social change, evangelical theology has finally come to appreciate the necessary requirements of *structural* change. However, there is a tendency within the Reformed tradition to think *structural* change is a necessary *and sufficient* condition for the advent of justice. But are we perhaps in a place where we can once again, tentatively, think about the role of the conversion of individual agents as a necessary condition? In other words, have we made sin *only* structural? Bell (*Liberation Theology,* pp. 177-78) seems to keep both aspects in helpful tension. I think the same is true in Miroslav Volf, *Exclusion and Embrace* (Nashville: Abingdon, 1996), pp. 20-22 and *passim.* I hope to return to these questions in later research.

[56]There is a tendency within the tradition, stemming from Kuyper, to see the advent of the state with the Fall, such that the "restraining" work of the state is needed only *after* the advent of sin which disorders creation (see Kuyper, *Calvinism*, pp. 79-81). In this sense, Kuyper's framework might be more amenable to something like Cavanaugh's or Bell's claims. For Dooyeweerd, however, the state is a "natural" or "creational" social institution, as is the church (see *A Christian Theory of Social Institutions*, pp. 86-93). Here he simply echoes the Augustinian and Reformed tradition which sees the church as instituted with Adam.

respect, the Reformational tradition would affirm Radical Orthodoxy's critique of the state as a quasi-ecclesia and pseudo-soteriological institution precisely by seeing such a version of the state as a disordering of creational structures, where the state has assumed the role of the church, and thus both confused distinct aspects of creation as well as falsely specifying the end to which humanity is called. But unlike Radical Orthodoxy, the Reformational tradition—because it recognizes this distinction between creation structure and postlapsarian direction—would point to the possibility of constituting the state otherwise. The state, *as state*, could be properly ordered toward the Creator *without* the state becoming the *ecclesia*. However, in the picture I have given so far, it seems that the church is a remedial site for the renewal of authentic community, and as such, after the eschaton and securing of this renewal, it would seem that the church would wither away and what we would have is a universal human community—a polis?—properly oriented to God (a "holy nation"). This then would raise questions about Dooyeweerd's contention that the church and state are essential creational spheres; for, if that is the case, how do they persist in the eschaton? In this respect, Kuyper's account of the state as a postlapsarian phenomenon[57] would seem to require an eschatological correlate in which the "need" for the state is erased in the eschaton and only the church would perdure. This linkage of the state to the Fall, in Kuyper, resonates with the picture painted by Cavanaugh and Bell. Where they differ, however, is with respect to the preeschatological relationships between the two institutions. It seems to me that one could take a Kuyperian—though not Dooyeweerdian—logic concerning the state in the direction of Radical Orthodoxy, recognizing a kind of essential fallenness about the state. But even this would require a revision of Kuyper's positive posture toward the state as an institution. A third way might be found in a new appropriation of the work of Klaas Schilder.[58]

---

[57]It almost seems that, for Kuyper, the church is a kind of quasi-redemptive structure even though it is not a *creational* structure included in the pronouncement of goodness in Genesis 1:31.

[58]This is a direction for future research, spurred by Richard Mouw's suggestions in "Klaas Schilder as Public Theologian," *Calvin Theological Journal* 38, no. 2 (2003): 281-98. Mouw suggests a certain overlap between Schilder's Reformed version and the Anabaptist vision of Hauerwas, with some important differences. For instance, while Schilder advocated a kind of "abstinence" with respect to sociopolitical engagement, "it is not because he is convinced that a larger cultural program is illegitimate as such, but rather it is because of his gloomy assessment of the historical circumstances in which he finds himself" (p. 292). This might be a way of saying that I disagree with Radical Orthodoxy's conflation of structure and direction with respect to the state, but given the current configuration of the state, I think we should perhaps posture ourselves as if the structure itself were flawed.

Second, I do think that Radical Orthodoxy's account of the church as the only true polis is persuasive precisely because it begins, in a way, with a more robust account of the Fall and the way in which alternative social communities are fundamentally *mis*directed and operate on the basis of a fundamentally flawed anthropology (and ontology). In this sense, I think Radical Orthodoxy could be an occasion for the Reformed tradition to reconsider and reappropriate both its sense of antithesis[59] and more consistently think through its theology of election and regeneration. If authentic community is only possible where there is love, and love is only properly shed abroad in our hearts by the Spirit's indwelling presence (Rom 5:5), and the Spirit only indwells the redeemed (i.e., the elect), then authentic community is only possible in the company of the redeemed[60]—the renewed polis that is the church. If that is the case, then Reformed confidence in the possibilities of just communities or social structures must be revisited in light of the Reformed tradition's own Augustinian theology. In this respect, I think the Reformed account should be revised in the direction of Radical Orthodoxy.[61]

---

[59]Of course, this will require rethinking the notion of "common grace" as bequeathed to us by Kuyper and appropriated in quite disturbing ways in contemporary Reformed thought. In this sense, in my future research I hope to take up the line of thought suggested by Klaas Schilder, *Christ and Culture*, trans. G. van Rongen and W. Helder (Winnipeg, Man.: Premier Printing, 1977), perhaps answering Richard Mouw's call for an "American 'translator-interpreter' " of Schilder's thought for the contemporary context. See Mouw, "Klaas Schilder," p. 288. (Hopefully a Canadian can fit the bill.)

[60]One can find evidence for this logic in Dooyeweerd when, speaking of the possibility of authentic communion between fellow human beings, he claims: "A real inner meeting presupposes real self-knowledge and can only occur in the central religious sphere of our relation with our fellow-man" (*In the Twilight*, pp. 125-26). If, as Dooyeweerd goes on to argue, "real self-knowledge" is only possible on the basis of "the Word-revelation of God operating in the heart, in the religious center of our existence by the power of the Holy Spirit" (ibid., p. 126), then it would seem that authentic sociality is only possible in the community of the Spirit (the church).

[61]In *Introducing Radical Orthodoxy*, chap. 7, I go on to unpack a criticism of Ward and Milbank for blurring the boundaries between church and world.

13

THE DESIRE OF THE CHURCH

WILLIE JAMES JENNINGS

The church reveals the miracle of our redemption. Yet there is a basic question that must be answered in order to appreciate this miracle: What is the social character of that redemption? In its multiple ways the Christian tradition teaches us that we have been redeemed from the distortions of creation. This essay focuses on two crucial distortions of creation, the implications of which have not been fully recognized in our ecclesiologies. These distortions are of sight and desire within the social formation and performance of gender. Any theological account of the church that will be truly responsive to the current situation of Christianity in the Western world and that will meaningfully engage contemporary visions of relationships, life and desire must address the problem of the visual in modernity.

Many of our current discussions about ecclesiology move back and forth between two important sets of concerns. On the one hand, there is renewed interest in determining exactly what is meant by claiming the church as the locus of salvation. Whether by locus we envision a new polis, or a new politic, or new strategies of public engagement, or a rehearsal of aspects of a redeemed creation, the concern here is the precise delineation of the relation of the divine with the human and the trinitarian character of our participation in the life and work of God. On the other hand, there is also great interest in the sacramental character of church life and practice. Here we find vital conversations about the formation of Christian identity through a constellation of sacramental practices that might challenge some of the significant deformations of our lives in the world. These conversations are also alerting us to the profound dangers of a divided church and renewing interest in serious theological engagement with ecumenism.

However, both these sets of ecclesiological concerns will foster short-sighted conversations as long as those conversations are allowed to bypass the

crucial theological problem of life in community—how men and women see
each other in a fallen world. This is indeed an ancient problem. Yet in our contemporary situation this ancient problem presses on us with new force. This
essay outlines the new force of this ancient problem and in so doing seeks to
underscore the great need to grasp an ecclesiology that reorients visual life
and gender relations.

Henri Nouwen writes, "Just as we are responsible for what we eat, so we
are responsible for what we see."[1]

Naomi Wolf, in her famous and thought-provoking book *The Beauty Myth*,
suggests that the anti-woman bias of the Judeo-Christian tradition played a
central role in forming what she calls the cult of beauty that damages the lives
of women. Genesis 2:21-23 exposes for Wolf the logic of this cult.

> And the LORD God caused a deep sleep to fall upon Adam, and he slept; and he
> took one of his ribs. (KJV)

This is all of the text Wolf quotes because she grasps, she believes, the interpretative direction of the text. She states,

> Western women absorb from those verses the sense that their bodies are second-
> rate, an afterthought: Though God made Adam from clay, in his own image, Eve
> is an expendable rib. God breathed life directly into Adam's nostrils, inspiring his
> body with divinity; but Eve's body is twice removed from the Maker's hand, im-
> perfect matter born of matter. Genesis explains why it is women who often need
> to offer their bodies to any male *gaze* that will legitimize them. "Beauty" now
> gives the female body the legitimacy that God withheld.[2] (emphasis added)

I focus on Wolf's reading of the creation story's male and female not as an
example of imprecise or bad exegesis of biblical texts. Nor do I draw attention
to it as an example of a secular mind revealing modernity's ignorance before a
religious tradition. I do so because Wolf's account of the creation story, as well
as her entire book, deserves our attention—both capture a sense of tragedy in
the way men and women look at each other and their world. (Later I will return to a more extensive consideration of this tragic way of seeing discerned
in Wolf's *The Beauty Myth*.) At this point, I want to commend Wolf for putting
her finger on something in the text that our churches and theologians tend to
miss: the relation of God to our gaze. Or to put this in the form of a question—

---

[1] *Behold the Beauty of the Lord: Praying with Icons* (Notre Dame, Ind.: Ave Maria Press, 1987), p.
12.
[2] Naomi Wolf, *The Beauty Myth: How Images of Beauty Are Used Against Women* (New York: Harper Collins, 1991), p. 93.

What does divine presence have to do with the way we see one another and our world?

At the close of the passage above, Wolf states, " 'Beauty' now gives the female body the legitimacy that God withheld." Biblical scholars should strenuously object to this statement. "The text does not say or infer that," they should say. However, I contend that Wolf sees something important. But she is looking at a reflection and not the actual thing itself. In order to see correctly what Wolf is seeing incorrectly, we need to examine two moments in the creation story of humanity female and male. Christians of most, if not all, ecclesial traditions know these two moments: first, the moment of deception and self-deception found in Genesis 3:1-6 (especially Gen 3:6), and second, the moment of loss in Genesis 3:8-13. However, these moments are not often read together closely enough to illumine their implications for our lives. Interpreted together, these passages help us see the deep connections among sight, desire and community.

THE FORMATION OF THE UNHOLY ICON

In the winter semester of 1932-1933 at the University of Berlin, Dietrich Bonhoeffer read to his students in his class on "Creation and Sin" his theological interpretation of Genesis 2:23-25. "This at last is bone of my bones, flesh of my flesh." This text, Bonhoeffer said, reveals the church in its original form.[3] This is not a new idea in Bonhoeffer. He draws on ancient Christian sensibilities that saw in this passage a holism and unity intended by God. Human community and world were to be one reality in communion with God. Indeed this is what God desired, what God called good. This is church not defined through a history of sin and redemption, of human distinctions (that is, of Israel, of church or world), and not even of eschatological hope, but church defined as humanity communing with God in the world of God's creation and divine desire. Only in the context of this divine intentionality can we begin to feel the ramifications of humanity's moment of deception and self-deception, humanity's fall.

> Now the serpent was more crafty than any other wild animal that the LORD God had made. He said to the woman, "Did God say, 'You shall not eat from any tree

---

[3]Bonhoeffer, *Creation and Fall: A Theological Exposition of Genesis 1–3*, vol. 3, Dietrich Bonhoeffer Works (Minneapolis: Fortress, 1997). "By the creation of the other person freedom and creatureliness are bound together in love. That is why the other person is once again grace to the first person, just as the prohibition against eating from the tree of knowledge was grace. In this common bearing of the limit by the first two persons in community, the character of this community as the church is authenticated" (p. 99).

in the garden'?" The woman said to the serpent, "We may eat of the fruit of the trees in the garden; but God said, 'You shall not eat of the fruit of the tree that is in the middle of the garden, nor shall you touch it, or you shall die.' " But the serpent said to the woman, "You will not die." (Gen 3:1-4)

We know the story of the crafty serpent, but we must remember that the serpent's words create the conditions for deception. Bonhoeffer suggests the serpent's words introduce the religious question, "Did God say?"[4] The religious question introduces God to humanity in a new way. God is no longer speaking, confronting humanity. Through the question (which grammatically positions God as a third-person singular), God becomes visible only as a question. The serpent submerges God's actions and intentions into questions. What emerges is a God repositioned as one in need of clarification and truthful discernment.

God knows that on the day that you eat from it, your eyes will be opened and you will become like gods, knowing good and evil. (Gen 3:5)[5]

What also emerges is a new focus for humanity, the tree. The serpent reintroduces God and proposes another point to organize humanity's self-reflection, the tree of knowledge of good and evil. Before we move further into this moment we must rehearse an ancient theological idea slightly alluded to earlier. God creates not out of necessity but, in a sense, out of desire. Desire is all around us—it is woven into our very being. We are not merely desiring machines (as Gilles Deleuze suggested);[6] we are formed and shaped in desire. God and the creation are not bound in the same reality of desire, but desire has its source (its roots) in the triune life of God. The desire that is all around us is a creaturely reality. The creaturely reality of desire echoes God's willingness to call us into existence through love. Desire is the reality that should call us to God and to one another.

However, in this moment of deception and self-deception desire becomes distorted in the process of disobedience. We must not forget the work of the serpent: his words create the condition for this moment. His words work in tandem with the tree. His words offer up the tree in a new way. The tree becomes an unholy icon.

---

[4]Bonhoeffer, *Creation and Fall*, pp. 103-10.
[5]Everett Fox, *The Five Books of Moses: A New Translation with Introductions, Commentary, and Notes* (New York: Schocken, 1995), p. 21.
[6]Gilles Deleuze and Félix Guattari, *Anti-Oedipus: Capitalism and Schizophrenia* (Minneapolis: University of Minnesota Press, 1983). "Everywhere *it* is machines—real ones, not figurative ones: machines driving other machines, machines being driven by other machines, with all the necessary couplings and connections," p. 1.

> So when the woman saw that the tree was good for food, and that it was a delight to the eyes, and that the tree was to be desired to make one wise, she took of its fruit and ate; and she also gave some to her husband, who was with her, and he ate. (Gen 3:6)

The words of the serpent have done their work in humanity. "You shall be like gods." The words of the serpent invite humanity to a journey of transcendence—to transcend the word of God and become gods. Humanity as male and female is turned away from God, listening to the serpent. Male and female no longer look at one another preparing for communion with God. Their focus is on the tree, the unholy icon. The tree of knowledge comes *between* male and female. Their focus turns sight and desire against humanity. The tree is a delight to the eyes and it is to be desired. Our sight is turned against us. We desire what we should not and we consume that which will destroy us. The tree is indeed icon, unholy icon because to look on it is to begin the journey of disobedience. This formation of the unholy icon illumines the moment of self-deception and it also helps us narrate the moment of loss. The unholy icon distorts humanity's sight.

Humanity's turning toward the tree (and consuming the fruit) means that we will see God in a different way—not as the one that confronts us, encounters us as the context of our knowledge (of God and ourselves). God becomes the one absent from our desire and whom we await in fear. Equally tragic, humanity male and female lose their sense of unity, of oneness. This loss of their sense of one-flesh pivots on a distortion of sight; they have turned from God and looked toward the abyss of nothingness concealed by the tree. Their bodies now have the abyss of nothingness as their backdrop. Nakedness, once the signature that announces the beginning of communion, but now refracted through the unholy icon, witnesses only fragility, vulnerability and death.

> Then the eyes of both were opened, and they knew that they were naked; and they sewed fig leaves together and made loincloths for themselves. They heard the sound of the LORD God walking in the garden at the time of the evening breeze, and the man and his wife hid themselves from the presence of the LORD God among the trees of the garden. But the LORD God called to the man, and said to him, "Where are you?" He said, "I heard the sound of you in the garden, and I was afraid, because I was naked; and I hid myself." He said, "Who told you that you were naked? Have you eaten from the tree of which I commanded you not to eat?" (Gen 3:7-11)

Humanity disrupts the divine trajectory by turning toward the tree. God comes to walk with humanity; the life of communion, of one flesh, is ready to begin. But its very beginning is also its ending in sin. God comes to walk with humanity and humanity hides from God. God must call out to those who should not be hidden. God must seek those whom God should not have to find. God's question, the first question to us in sin is simple but powerful, "Where are you?" This is the essential context for interpreting life in community, life as humanity. God must seek out those created for communion. God must seek those who interrupted the trajectory of life.

They hide their bodies from God. God's voice, rather than calling them to communion, repels them; it brings fear to humanity in sin. This hiddenness of body is also the closure of God's word of interpretation for the body, God's word to us of how to understand our bodies. Humanity says to God, "I hid because I was naked." I did not want you to see me like this. God's response in the story again shakes our foundations, "Who told you that you were naked?" Are we indeed able to interpret our own bodies, our own condition as creatures? Communion was to be the context for seeing our bodies, for knowing them, understanding them, indeed living as bodies with God. But we ended a journey before it began. We hid from God and in that hiding we turned from the one who would enable us to see our bodies rightly. In a sense, we closed off sight of our bodies and this closure is in the very act of seeing that "I am naked." We see but we cannot see.

Distorted sight and consumption mark the beginning of sin's journey. Yet as Phyllis Trible reminds us in her classic book *God and the Rhetoric of Sexuality*, "Oppositions within one flesh have appeared at the turning point of disobedience."[7] We disrupted divine desire. We disrupted God's walk with us. Within this terrible reality we find the disruption between male and female.

> He said, "Who told you that you were naked? Have you eaten from the tree of which I commanded you not to eat?" The man said, "The woman whom you gave to be with me, she gave me fruit from the tree, and I ate." Then the LORD God said to the woman, "What is this that you have done?" The woman said, "The serpent tricked me, and I ate." (Gen 3:11-13)

The relationship male and female is no longer seen as the realization of our humanity. The relationship will not be seen as life-giving and life-sustaining. Rather the relationship will be a constant struggle, navigating relations of power. The moment of loss affects sight, that is, it affects our seeing, knowing

---

[7]Phyllis Trible, *God and the Rhetoric of Sexuality* (Philadelphia: Fortress, 1978), p. 113.

and understanding. It is indeed the beginning of an epistemological crisis, not first of the individual, but of male and female in relationship. Here is where I suggest we have not held the moment of self-deception and the moment of loss close enough to gather the implications for our lives.

THE GENDERED SOCIAL STRUCTURE OF SIN: WE DO NOT SEE EACH OTHER

Sin is a reality of the human condition. Few among us would find the credibility of that statement a stumbling block on the journey of faith. Yet we often look past a crucial arena in which this condition plays itself out. Sin is the disruption of communion that deeply affects the formation of persons, and not just any communion but the communion of male and female. This is what has been ignored in our discussions of sin. Sin is indeed social, but we have not reckoned with the gendered social structure of sin. At the intersection of encounter between male and female with God, at the very point that our identity as human beings is formed, there is an epistemological crisis. We do not see each other. More specifically, we do not see ourselves in each other. We only see each other as bodies for use. Fundamentally, sin as condition means that men and women have never entered into the kind of relationships that truly allow them to see themselves in each other and to become "one flesh" beyond categories of use-value.

What would life be like if the world (the social world of life, language games and labor) were built by men and women in conversation and communion with one another and with God? What would life be like if the personhood of each individual was shaped by the "full voice" of men and women in conversation? We rarely ask these questions because we cannot imagine their importance. But these questions point to one of the fundamental sites of sin, the formation of gender roles that define men and women without encounter with one another and communion with God. My point is not the importance of gender definition. It is the importance of communion. We live in gendered worlds built upon the isolation of men from women and women from men and both from God. Our sinful condition manifests the deepest hubris: we do not believe we need each other to know ourselves, to understand ourselves, to see ourselves. Without a gendered epistemological subordination and reorientation to one another we cannot handle desire.

Desire is of the body and it is good. Yet what is the consequence for our body when desire is turned against us? Desire fractures and it fragments. First, it fractures the communion that constitutes humanity. The unholy icon came between male and female; thus distorted desire (and distorted sight) remains

THE COMMUNITY OF THE WORD

between male and female. This is distorted desire for everything, including one another's bodies. To desire another is not the point of distortion. The point of distortion is the looking beyond, looking through the creaturely other to achieve self-gratification (self-knowledge) and in so doing to constitute an isolated self ("the tree was to be desired to make one wise"). And second, distorted desire fragments. It separates us from one another in our desiring. Our desiring facilitated by the unholy icon becomes private, isolated hunger. Desire is no longer bound to the community of male and female with God. It is my desire. I am left alone with a reality intended for communion and community, a reality I cannot bear alone. Desire was never meant to be carried alone. Desire is of the body and it is good, but its goodness was intended for communal interpretation and expression.

IMAGINING DESIRE: THE ICON AND RELATIONSHIP

The unholy icon facilitates distorted private desire and distorted sight of one another. In light of this suggestion, let us return to Naomi Wolf's text *The Beauty Myth* to consider more carefully her thesis that beauty has become a socially constructed prison for women. Wolf's argument is more far-reaching than saying that women are judged by their outward appearance or that there are demeaning and derogatory images of women in popular culture. Wolf discerns that something has gone terribly wrong with our gaze. Wolf recognizes that there is something horrible standing between men and women: the idealized beautiful woman.

Idealized beautiful women do not just stand between men and women. More horrible yet, idealized beautiful women enter us, separating us from each other and from our bodies. They also separate women from their own bodies. These idealized beautiful women are not idealized primarily in thought but through the practices of capitalist societies and consumer culture. These idealized bodies are distorted, deformed, refashioned to establish an ever-changing yet ever-constant posture for consumption. The beauty pornography, as Wolf calls it, of consumer culture needs to keep men from forming deep bonds with any one woman and to keep women dissatisfied with themselves. This is done by placing a built-in obsolescence in the beauty object itself because she (that object) must, like all objects of consumption, be disposable or changeable.[8]

Changeable and disposable—beauty pornography begets beauty sadomasochism. Wolf brilliantly narrates the ways idealized beautiful images help chil-

---

[8]Wolf, *The Beauty Myth*, p. 144.

dren interpret their bodies.[9] These idealized images guide sexual expression, gender demonstration and interpersonal interaction. Having worked their way into our relationships and our bodies, we often feel powerless against the inertia of the beauty myth's blinding gaze. Wolf states:

> So the beauty myth sets it up this way: A high rating as an art object is the most valuable tribute a woman can exact from her lover. If he appreciates her face and body because it is hers, that is next to worthless. The myth contrives to make women offend men by scrutinizing honest appreciation when they give it; it can make men offend women merely by giving them honest appreciation. It can manage to contaminate the sentence "You're beautiful" which is next to "I love you" in expressing a bond of regard between a woman and a man.[10]

Through her analysis Wolf wanders into "the garden of our familiar" (to play with that phrase coined by Alice Walker). She wanders near the tree of knowledge unaware of what she is about to touch. Yet her analysis needs to be augmented by the insights of two social theorists, Jean Baudrillard and Zygmunt Bauman. With Baudrillard and Bauman we gain a greater sense of the ways relationships are facilitated by images. Indeed, with them we can understand that the image is always "in between."

Jean Baudrillard, in his pivotal text *Simulacra and Simulation*, grasps the power of image formation in a far more comprehensive manner than Wolf.[11] Baudrillard's subtle but powerful insight is that in our era the referent (of anything) is inconsequential. But Baudrillard isn't engaging in antirealist preaching. In our time, copies, images (the *simulacra* as he calls them) are everything. We have been drawn into the processes of simulation via ubiquitous media. We have walked away from the need to socially connect "the real" to its representation. Baudrillard is not saying that we no longer care about the truth; rather we trust that truth may be known and disseminated through simula-

---

[9]Ibid., p. 156. "Each woman has to learn for herself, from nowhere, how to feel sexual (though she learns constantly how to look sexual). She is given no counterculture of female lust looking outward, no description of the intricate, curious *presence* of her genital sensations or the way they continually enrich her body's knowledge. Left to herself in the dark, she has very little choice: she must absorb the dominant culture's fantasies as her own." Wolf's account here is worth pondering because it captures a sense of the isolation created by desire constructed outside the female body and then imposed upon the body. However, her account begs the question whether anyone (male or female) can in fact "look outward" without succumbing to distorted desire.

[10]Ibid., p. 171.

[11]Jean Baudrillard, *Simulacra and Simulation* (Ann Arbor: University of Michigan Press, 1994). See Douglas Kellner, *Jean Baudrillard: From Marxism to Postmodernism and Beyond* (Stanford, Calif.: Stanford University Press, 1989).

tion. We trust that the real may be re-presented to us in a variety of ways. What often goes unarticulated for us, by us, are the linkages of these various ways of simulation. The commercial, the movie, the television show, the radio interview, the book, art and news, comedy and tragedy, all these showings do work for us. They tightly weave together imagination with representation. Imagination and representation have always worked together. But with simulation the imagining is done for us (taken from us), and thus everything is renarrated on our behalf. Historical events are renarrated, destroyed and remade in a way that neutralizes their meaning and energy. So, for example, the Civil War happened like a football game happened like violence is happening. All are real because all are simulated. Baudrillard contends that the social is being lost in simulation. We are losing our ability to see ourselves as actually connected to one another as real bodies in space and time. A sense of connection, Baudrillard believes, should lead us to act out of concern for one another.

What keeps us from seeing and knowing our connection to one another is in fact the constant simulation of the masses—the masses in joy, the masses in hatred doing violence, the masses protesting. We react to the spectacle of the masses by watching, that is, consuming the masses. This first action of consumption (watching) often exhausts any subsequent social action. In all this the image of the social thwarts the social. Baudrillard helps us realize what is at stake in the workings of images: *Images are the inescapable facilitators of relationships.* Baudrillard's insight is not new; indeed he rehearses in a different way our turning to the unholy icon to facilitate the forming of images that mutilate relationships. Moving from Baudrillard's thought to Bauman's insights, we gain deeper consideration of the relation of desire to image.

Zygmunt Bauman, sociologist and cultural sage, helps us understand the ways that desire in consumer society again and again reframes what is natural. Bauman suggests in *Society Under Siege* that consumer society brings us into a cycle of consumption that intends to hide our bodies from death.[12] The result of every advertisement, of every little drama known as a commercial, is to say to us, "This will save you from death by saving you from the little deaths that lead to the end. If you don't buy this product then discomfort, frustration, shame, pain, sickness, danger, violence, loss of love, isolation, or even death will be the result." Yet, as Bauman theorizes, focusing on needs was only the launching pad for desire (in modernity); indeed the point of the cycle is to articulate desire as the foundation of our lives, the ground of being. *Desiring is what keeps us from death.* Herein lies the genius of capitalist consumer society:

---

[12]Zygmunt Bauman, *Society Under Siege* (Cambridge: Polity, 2002).

it has tapped into our fear of death. Yet there is more than "need" here with desire—more than mere survival. "The survival at stake is not that of the consumer's body or social identity, but of the desire itself; that desire which makes the consumer—the consuming desire of consuming."[13]

Bauman, who is not a theologian, makes a clearly theological point. Desire (in modernity) long ago walked away from its connection to our needs for survival. Bauman quotes Harvie Ferguson:

> Desire links consumption to self-expression, and to notions of taste and discrimination. The individual expresses himself or herself through their possessions. But in advanced capitalist society, committed to the continuing expansion of production, this is a very limiting psychological framework which ultimately gives way to a quite different psychic "economy". The wish replaces desire as the motivating force of consumption.[14]

Bauman understands that ever-expanding production in modernity's capitalist societies needs a wider arena in which to expand consumption. So desire tied to need "cannot keep pace,"[15] but desire tied to dream, to fantasy, to wish-fulfillment opens to the limitlessness of our existence. Bauman is exactly right; however, desire is not being supplemented. Rather this is an instance of desire's all encompassing reality: desire is not simply of the body. The body is in desire. Desiring is bound to seeing, to taking in what is before us—to the receptivity that is the creature. This is why the iconic is fundamental to the creature.

We create images to facilitate our desiring. Remember the commandment to Israel: You shall not make for yourself an idol (Ex 20:4), but remember it in a different way. The command against idol-making comes immediately after the introduction of the God of Israel to God's people and the introduction of this God as their deliverer. Immediately, they are told that idol production must end. Idols are creaturely forms that fix our looking on the creature. The idol can take multiple forms (whatever we imagine) but the point is the same: the idol coordinates the network of worldly desire—the desire of the flesh, the desire of the eyes and the pride in riches (1 Jn 2:16). The idol turns us inward: it turns our dreams and fantasies inward toward the creature.

Image-making and desiring are bound together. Image-making is the expression of our desiring. We consume and we create images. We create while consuming. For humanity in sin, idol production is inevitable. Idols facilitate our worldly desiring. Idol production is the result of our dream and fantasy

---

[13]*Society Under Siege*, p. 184.
[14]Ibid., p. 185.
[15]Ibid.

life turned toward the creature. But we must hold the horror of idol production together with our distorted relationships male and female. The one is bound to the other. Idols come into existence in the space created by our turning away from one another as men and women as well as our turning away from God. Idols live between us, facilitating distorted desire and distorting relationship.

THE HOLY ICON AND RELATIONSHIPS

The only way to stop idol production is to return to the unholy icon and reverse its horrible trajectory. But what is an icon? Only now can we begin to understand that an icon is a point of focus that facilitates desire and guides relationships male and female. An icon nurtures our seeing and knowing. By its words the serpent invited humanity male and female to turn their focus away from God to a point that would distort them and begin their journey of disobedience. The only way to reverse this journey of disobedience is to establish a new point of focus. Into humanity comes the holy icon. The life of Jesus overcomes the fracture and fragment of desire. From the beginning of his life with us, Jesus is the holy icon who comes *between* male and female to replace (and reverse) the powerful affects of the unholy icon. Jesus is from the beginning *in-between*. Remember Joseph and Mary.

> Now the birth of Jesus the Messiah took place in this way. When his mother Mary had been engaged to Joseph, but before they lived together, she was found to be with child from the Holy Spirit. Her husband Joseph, being a righteous man and unwilling to expose her to public disgrace, planned to dismiss her quietly. But just when he had resolved to do this, an angel of the Lord appeared to him in a dream and said, "Joseph, son of David, do not be afraid to take Mary as your wife, for the child conceived in her is from the Holy Spirit. She will bear a son, and you are to name him Jesus, for he will save his people from their sins." All this took place to fulfill what had been spoken by the Lord through the prophet: "Look, the virgin shall conceive and bear a son, and they shall name him Emmanuel," which means, "God is with us." When Joseph awoke from sleep, he did as the angel of the Lord commanded him; he took her as his wife, but had no marital relations with her until she had borne a son; and he named him Jesus. (Mt 1:18-25)

Mary and Joseph must allow the holy icon to be between them. Together they must share this "shame" with only a dream and a vision to defend their decision. This is the first disruption of human community trapped in distorted desire. Mary and Joseph claim that this child is the desire of God and not first their own desire. The reordering of desire is the overturning of shame and its power in sin. Mary and Joseph cannot hide. They must witness this miracle of new life. Here they must bear in their own bodies the space between what is and what ought to be. What is (the way of sin in the world) has been broken open, and what ought to be (the way of salvation) has been placed in human flesh.

The communion with God and with one another, male and female has begun afresh. Joseph, like the first Adam, awakes from his sleep and obeys the divine command. He will confess that Mary is bone of his bone, flesh of his flesh. Yet between them is the deliverance that all men and women need, the reordering of desire. The reordering of desire begins in the body of Jesus. He will live out in a body just like ours (with its wayward desires) the will of his Father enabled by the Spirit of God. His body will become the new icon that reorders our desire. We can truly be like God by drawing near his body.

The image of God (*imago Dei*) is a matter of desire. The life of the Son of God with his Father in the Spirit may be appropriately expressed in words of creaturely desire. "This is my Son, the Beloved, with whom I am well pleased" (Mt 3:17). Indeed creaturely desire was the echo in creation of the divine life. Through Jesus all that remains is for humanity male and female to enter this desire, his desire (Jn 17:21-26). Desire, through the Son, will be returned to its life-giving, healing direction toward the Father in the Spirit. The life of the Son will heal our desire. Jesus shows us desire's telos—its beginning, its middle in redemptive struggle with us, and its end in new life. Surrounded by us with our distorted desires, our broken relationship male and female, the Son will show us the way forward. With our eyes on him, the Son waits on the Spirit and listens to the voice of the Father.

We must not, however, run past the body of Jesus too quickly to look at the actions of the Son in the body. The destruction of worldly desire begins in the body of Jesus. Jesus will overcome worldly temptation in himself first as the context of making possible our victory. This is the work *of* Jesus before it is the work of Jesus *for us*. The triune relationship revealed in space and time is for the sake of Jesus. He needs the Spirit to rest on him so that he might resist worldly temptation. He seeks the Father so that his eyes may not be turned toward seeking self-gratification in the world. He will do only what he sees the Father doing. In Jesus, God enters into *our network* of desires. Jesus confronts the desire of the flesh, and the desire of the eyes and the pride in riches (as 1 Jn 2:16 describes this network). Yet Jesus transforms desire through the divine life. In Jesus, *the personal becomes the communal*. Jesus will tear open the body's desire and turn it toward his Father in the Spirit. The Spirit, from his baptism, will rest on the body, entering into the depths of creaturely desire in order to recreate it. He will invite others into his renewed desire as he is working it out. His daily victories to do the good will also mark those that follow him. Again and again, desire becomes new in his life and only in his life. The only *personal* struggle to reorder desire that matters is found in Jesus.

To make our personal struggle to re-order desire important is already to miss the point and to entertain religious narcissism masquerading as discipleship. The issue is never our personal struggle. The focus must be on the work of Jesus, his tearing open the body's desire and returning it to communion with God in the presence of his sisters and brothers. Jesus invites his disciples to leave all and follow him. They must walk in his desire and in so doing they are brought into the work of his body.

THE CHURCH AND THE REORDERING OF DESIRE

The community of Jesus' body (the church) is bound to the task of reordering creaturely desire. But how do we do that? This is one of the most difficult ecclesial and pastoral questions we face today. We are enmeshed in a world of idol production. This is not new news. We understand it as the result of the Fall, our turning away. Yet I am convinced that the church in this day is not prepared to challenge idol production. Today, we are constantly invited to re-imagine our bodies and our relationships. Our bodies male and female are woven into market desire. Our bodies are presented to us and their needs narrated to us. We are invited to live in those (public) bodies and bring those needs into ourselves, making them private. Thus every purchase would (if possible) create and recreate the body, and reinforce the power of (worldly) desire to interpret to us the body and its needs. We accumulate idols of the body in the process of accumulating things.

Moreover we have settled (even as Christians) into the loss of one flesh. We have allowed desire to remain isolated, individualized hunger that flows beneath the surface of our relationships such that our relationships remain trapped in use-value. Utility is the currency of our relationships. We have surrendered our imaginations to a gender separate while seeking equality. We refuse to believe that we actually need each other to know ourselves and to know how to live in desire. Both these ancient challenges are bound together. I would suggest then that there are two tasks before us.

The task of re-viewing the icon. The only way to overcome idol production is with the icon. Icons must be made and icons must be consumed, taken into us. What is the difference between icon and idol? What is the difference between icon making and idol production? The divine life revealed to us is the only difference. Dream and fantasy must be guided by the divine life because dream and fantasy are manifestations of desire's reality. Our ability to dream and fantasize witnesses our receptivity to the world as creatures created in the image of God for communion with the divine life. We must have image (and images) not merely as a matter of seeing but of consuming and of being whole. The life of Jesus is God's way of guiding our desire, forming dream and fantasy around the triune identity, coordinating images through the divine self-witness. The redemption of our seeing begins in Jesus. Jesus overturns our visions of the beautiful, the good, the true and the powerful—beginning with his birth and ending with his cross, resurrection and ascension. Thus contemplating the divine life is not optional. Without such contemplation, desire runs toward death.

The challenge today, especially for those of us who are Protestant, is to reflect afresh on the historical trajectories of image and art established by the iconoclastic controversies of the church. Such fresh reflection might allow us to reach conclusions about image and art similar to those of our Eastern Orthodox sisters and brothers. That is, the incarnation made it permissible and possible to create images using the materials of creation. Such images need not be idols. Indeed the body of God opens up to us God's willingness to work through image and art. Such divine workings may guide desire and strengthen devotion.

John de Gruchy in his text on theological aesthetics reminds us that there were two pastoral problems that lay behind the iconoclasm of the early and medieval church.[16] First was the *fear* of image and art as having inherently evil power: thus the church resisted image and art without ways to imagine its renewal. And second was the *failure to fear* the misuse of image and art: thus the church lost sight of the ways image and art must be chastened and disciplined to promote the formation of ecclesial life. With both pastoral problems the church faces the constant challenge of being overwhelmed by image and art. This means that a twofold strategy has always been needed. We must destroy idols while transforming idol production into icon making.

We need images. Such a statement may seem counterintuitive given the current proliferation of images and idol production on a scale previously unseen. What is needed, however, are *cleansing* images, holy icons that focus our attention and begin to destroy the formation of distorted desire through false and unholy images. We and our children are in desperate need of a form of spiritual life, communal and personal devotion that understands the use of

---

[16]John de Gruchy, *Christianity, Art and Transformation: Theological Aesthetics in the Struggle for Justice* (Cambridge: Cambridge University Press, 2001), pp. 11-52.

icons. What would it mean for our children to pray before icons? What would it mean for children whose minds are being strangled by the images of beauty pornography and beauty sadomasochism increasingly woven into every site of western media to pray before icons? What would it mean for us to believe that the renewal of our minds must include the use of holy images?

Admittedly, it would be the worst kind of romanticism and theological tourism to believe that those of us who are Protestants can simply start using icons. As with any ecclesial practice we would need to learn what form of church life is necessary for the use of icons. In addition to that requirement, the use of icons today still comes with the same historical pastoral problems. Indeed, as an Eastern Orthodox priest recently told me, it is a constant challenge to teach even those raised with icons that we do not worship them; rather they help facilitate our worship of God. This pastoral problem does not negate the importance of icons; rather it shows that word and image must always go together. The word of God prepares us to see rightly and seeing rightly (aided by icons) helps organize our desires.

The task of rediscovering communion. This first task coexists with the second—the rediscovery of communion, male and female. From the beginning we could not see each other. From the beginning we have wandered in search of oneness. The journey never began rightly, male and female, male with female before God. We are the image of God yet we cannot begin to sense, to feel, to understand that image without active communion with God and full communion with one another. In many ways we have given up. Our imaginations are exhausted in the face of the complexities of gender's performance.

We were created to turn toward each other before the face of God. This turning, constant turning, echoed the divine perichoresis. This turning, constant turning, directed desire through its proper channels—through the creation, through our bodies toward God, from God to the creation through our bodies back to God. Our turning toward the tree disrupted the turning toward one another. But now in Christ we have been turned again toward one another.

Such turning invites us to a mutual subordination in the most crucial and fundamental way—in how we know and see both the world and ourselves. We must resist patterns of life that offer up to men and women forms of self-definition that promote our isolation from one another. We must resist forms of life that have decided what it means to be a man or a woman without the voice of the other. The church is called to be the place where we learn what it means to be the one flesh of male and female. Only together in communion with God can we restore desire to community.

14

SPACES FOR AN
EVANGELICAL ECCLESIOLOGY

WILLIAM A. DYRNESS

As if the whole idea of evangelical ecclesiology is not difficult enough by itself, imagine my dilemma: I was asked to consider its "past and future," and in
addition to address the implications of the burgeoning non-American church
for all of this. This is a bit much even for a theologian of culture! But as I began
to reflect on it, I realized that many troubling issues are bound up with this
question and that I was glad to spend some time thinking about it, however
modest the result promised to be. Here is why I think this is a critical issue.

On the one hand we live in a period of spiritual renewal and experimenta-
tion with new ways of being the church. And as we have frequently been reminded, this growth and vitality is not limited to North American churches,
but is occurring throughout the world. As the African theologian John Pobee
commented last fall in Kenya, churches in Africa are experiencing a spiritual
"bubbling up," a loosening of old forms, and a lively search for the new.[1] Beyond this, what is the meaning of the many forms of churchless Christianity
emerging in various places—believers in Christ who identify themselves as
Hindu in India, or as Muslim in Bangladesh? Closer to home, consider the implications of the "emergent churches" in North America and Britain, congregations led by twentysomethings, who make creative use of art and media
while they scour the history of the church for resources. And what do we make
of the struggle to find relevant forms of worship that is accompanied by so
much controversy but also is characterized by the emergence of new forms of
worship as well as the renewal of classical forms (both sometimes taking place
in the same congregation)? In one way or another all these forms of renewal,

---

[1]In a personal interview at St. Paul's Theological College, Limuru, Kenya, October 24, 2003.

and others we could mention, have ties to the evangelical movement, and all of them have large implications for any possible ecclesiology.[2]

Yet on the other hand, all this bubbling up, while wonderfully invigorating to watch, with some notable exceptions, is accompanied by little theological reflection—or at least little reflection on the form this bubbling up should take. Many of these groups are earnestly engaged in the search for some stability of form, for some place to stand, but their theological beliefs do not seem to help them in this search. It is this quest for form that will interest me in this paper. I pick up here on Hannah Arendt's comment that what the institution adds to belief is the public space of appearance.[3] This visible representation has always been the challenge for evangelicals, but today this challenge is especially acute.

In a recent book about the church and its mission, George Hunsberger argues the Reformers left us with an unintended consequence, which influences how we understand the church today. That consequence is the understanding of the church as the "place where certain things happen"—preaching, sacraments, discipline, etc.[4] He obviously means this to be a negative inheritance: this focus on place, what he calls the church's spatial disease, is the hangover of Christendom and it too often impedes the church's sense of mission. However true and important his thesis might be—especially for so-called mainline churches—I would argue that evangelicals have very nearly the opposite problem. The evangelical focus on mission has all but extinguished any reflection on the place the church occupies in its community and its culture. Another way of putting this is to point out that, while much consideration is given to incarnating Christianity in our homes and communities, relatively little thought is given to the incarnation of the *church*. In reviewing evangelical books on "the church" I am struck by how frequently the exposition was really not about church at all, but about "mission," "evangelism" or even "spirituality": The church is a missional, purpose driven, or world oriented community, and so on. The "church" part of this is whatever shape or trajectory this mission or activity happens to take at a given time—bursts of Christian energy responding, often creatively, to a rapidly changing environment.

Clearly the priority of mission, even the bias for action, represents histori-

---

[2]See Eddie Gibbs, *ChurchNext* (Downers Grove, Ill.: InterVarsity Press, 2001), <www.theooze.com>, etc.

[3]Quoted in Paul Ricoeur, *Figuring the Sacred: Religion, Narrative, and Imagination*, ed. Mark I. Wallace, trans. David Pallauer (Minneapolis: Fortress, 1995), p. 88.

[4]Darrell Guder et al., *The Missional Church: A Vision for the Sending of the Church in North America* (Grand Rapids: Eerdmans, 1998), pp. 79-80.

cally the strength of the evangelical movement. For Protestant churches generally "what happens" at church is the key to understanding the nature of that church. At the Reformation the church became more of an event than a place. In fact, Gerhard Nebel in an important book on Protestant aesthetics—which he calls interestingly *The Event of the Beautiful*—goes so far as to argue that "event" plays the same role in Reformational ontology that "substance" plays in Thomistic-Aristotelian metaphysics.[5] For both Luther and Calvin it was the event of the preaching of the Word that constituted the church and called it back to its biblical roots.

For Calvin the performance of the preaching of the Word and its reception was theologically central to his understanding of the church. He saw the act of preaching as a performative utterance that was the locus of God's presence.[6] In his instructions on preaching in the 1541 *Catechism* he gives perhaps his clearest indication of the location of the true church:

> In the preaching of the word, the external minister holds forth the vocal word and it is received by the ears. The internal minister the Holy Spirit truly communicates the thing proclaimed through the word that is Christ to the souls of all who will, so that it is not necessary that Christ or for that matter his word be received through the organs of the body, but the Holy Spirit effects this union by his secret virtue, by creating faith in us by which he makes us living members of Christ.[7]

In the congregational singing, the public prayers, in the words of institution and above all in praise—all that is allied to the preaching of the Word—the body of Christ is constituted. Indeed Belden Lane has put this even more strongly, arguing that for Calvin these performances actually effect what they celebrate and honor. He writes: "The exaltation of God's glory is a performative act, extending and enhancing what it sanctifies. . . . The character of praise, then, is not simply celebrative, or even restorative, but also *constitutive* of the world maintaining its life and well being."[8]

While the focus on the event of worship gave worship a dynamic and living character, it could also give it a vaguely disembodied feel—a weakness that will serve as the subtext of what I want to say. As Calvin's quote above makes

---

[5]*Das Ereignis des Schönen* (Klett, 1953), p. 17, quoted in Hans Urs von Balthasar, *The Glory of the Lord: A Theological Aesthetics*, trans. Erasmo Leiva-Merikakis (Edinburgh: T & T Clark, 1982), p. 56. So he opposes an "analogy of event" to the more static "analogy of being."
[6]See the excellent discussion of this in Belden Lane, "Spirituality as the Performance of Desire: Calvin on the World as a Theatre of God's Glory," *Spiritus: A Journal of Christian Spirituality* 1, no. 1 (2001): 1-30, esp. pp. 18 and 19.
[7]*Theological Treatises*, ed. J. K. S. Reid (London: SCM, 1954), p. 157.
[8]"The Performance of Desire," pp. 18-19, emphasis his.

clear, no physical mediation was necessary—though the ear is clearly the privileged organ, union with Christ is accomplished inwardly by the Holy Spirit.
His reaction against the medieval practices of worship made Calvin highly
suspicious of any physical or spatial symbolism. The elements of Communion,
for example, only had meaning in the performance of the Eucharist; they had
no symbolic meaning outside of this context. Similarly, even though it was en-
joined in Scripture, the Reformers forbade pouring oil on a sick person for fear
the meaning would attach itself to the oil rather than the prayer.[9] The pulpit
and table were all that remained in Calvin's St. Pierre Church, and the table
was only set during Communion.

What then of the place in which this took place? It was the stage on which
the performance of worship was played out, and when that was finished it had
no further role to play. In what amounts to a metaphor of Protestant attitudes
toward worship space, Calvin insisted that outside of regular worship hours—
outside the event of this performance—the buildings were to be locked. This
was to be done so that "no one outside the hours may enter for superstitious
reasons. If anyone be found making any particular devotion inside or nearby,
he is to be admonished; if it appears to be a superstition which he will not
amend he is to be chastised."[10] What if one wants to enter to pray? But prayer
is unconnected to any particular space; like the ministry of the Christian it is
to permeate the whole of life.

This direct knowledge of God was the treasured fruit of the Reformation
and, as mediated by the pietist movement and the evangelical revivals, it came
to characterize the evangelical movement. This experiential Christianity was
given eloquent expression by the Puritans who came to settle New England,
and it powered the Wesleyan renewal and the Pentecostal awakenings of the
twentieth century. One comes to church to feel the touch of God—that is what
church is for. As a Pentecostal preacher put it last fall in Nairobi, the house of
God is the house of healing. The church is here to bring people into contact
with the God of power. People need this power because they are sick. So the
worship, indeed the congregation itself, is constituted by the activities, the
prayer, preaching, lively singing, even dancing, that make possible the powerful touch of the healing God.

All of this is not wrong, of course; it is biblically and theologically impor-

---

[9]See Brian Gerrish, *Grace and Gratitude: The Eucharistic Theology of John Calvin* (Minneapolis:
Augsburg/Fortress, 1993), p. 162. And Carlos Eire, *War Against Idols: The Reformation of Worship from Erasmus to Calvin* (Cambridge: Cambridge University Press, 1986), p. 223 n. 130.
[10]Calvin, *Theological Treatises*, p. 79.

tant. Yet, though necessary, I want to argue it is not sufficient for a developed ecclesiology. And what is missing, I argue, is a theological conception of the representation, the space the church occupies. For the church is not simply the gathering of believers into the body of Christ by the power of the Spirit to the glory of God, not even those theologically important activities which constitute its worship—prayer, preaching, praise, confession, ministry and performing the sacraments—it is also an historically and culturally situated institution that presents some shape to the world. Moreover, I will argue, these spheres are related in ways that are theologically significant.

Evangelicals have claimed since the Reformation that they are simply following Scripture in their understanding of the church. They have not always seen that hidden in this claim is a particular way of reading these authoritative texts. The way the church lives out its corporate life in the world and the form that life takes, constitute a hermeneutical activity—the people of God interpret Scripture by the way they shape their life together. In this sense there is no timeless or universal essence the church must express; rather, under God it constitutes itself afresh in each generation.

The church is what it does. But what is its public appearance? What space does it occupy? In this paper I will use "space" as a trope for the way the church comes to cultural and social expression—the forms it takes. What are the spaces of these forms? And what theological meaning do they have? I want to consider this aspect of space under three headings: social, historical and symbolic—as aspects of place which best counter the docetic tendency of the evangelical church.

THE SOCIAL SPACE OF THE CHURCH

Whether or not it is recognized, the church constitutes a particular social space. Though the church, theologically, is the eschatological community which is the sign and instance of God's new creation in Christ, formed by the Holy Spirit, it is at the same time people from a particular region who come together at particular times, and, using one language or another, do things together. As the Amsterdam declaration puts it: "Here in the world, the Church becomes visible in all local congregations that meet to do together the things that according to the Scripture the Church does."[11] This visible aspect of the church, moreover, has theological significance—how these people shape their lives together directly reflects the presence of Christ by his Spirit.

The personal presence of Christ is typically celebrated in evangelical

---

[11]"Amsterdam Declaration," *First Things*, January 2001, pp. 65-66.

churches. Indeed the emphasis on the gathered people of God may be the major contribution of Protestants in general and evangelicals in particular to the church universal. Protestants, Wolfhart Pannenberg has argued, are custodians of a unique heritage in this respect. "A church office did not exist for its own sake. Its purpose was to serve the gospel and thus the faith of those entrusted to its care, in order to help them come to their own relationship with God, and not leave them in a state of immaturity."[12]

While the personal presence of Christ is celebrated, Christ's corporate presence is frequently ignored. The awareness of their spiritual unity typifies evangelicals around the world—witness the meaning of *hermano/a* among Latin Americans or the deep awareness of "Christian fellowship" among African Christians. But evangelicals frequently do not value the earthen vessel in which this treasure is found. They do not appreciate that the focus on the people of God and their corporate relationship to God implies a social space takes particular cultural and political shape. I want to emphasize here the social space that correlates with the spiritual reality.

First, the social space of the church consists in the interpersonal unity of all the people of God. In his important study of the church Miroslav Volf seeks to discover the nature of "ecclesiality"—what makes the church what it is. His search leads him to the question I am raising: the church's external conditions. "If one is to speak meaningfully about ecclesiality, one must know not only what the church is, but also how a concrete church can be identified externally as a church; one must also be able to say *where* a church is."[13] Though he goes on to say that features of the church cannot be purely external, he argues that "questions about the identity and identification of the church are inseparable."[14]

Pointing to sixteenth century separatist John Smyth, he argues that this early expression of free-church ecclesiality rests on the theological importance of the visible organization of the church. Smyth's "entire ecclesiology is based of the fundamental *theological* conviction that *Christ's dominion is realized through the entire congregation.*"[15] Smyth wrote: "We say the Church or two or three faithful people Separated from the world & joyned together in a true covenant have both Christ, the covenant & promises, & the ministerial power of

---

[12]Wolfhart Pannenberg, *The Church*, trans. Keith Crim (Philadelphia: Westminster Press, 1983), p. 91.

[13]Miroslav Volf, *After Our Likeness: The Church as the Image of the Trinity* (Grand Rapids: Eerdmans, 1998), p. 129, emphasis his.

[14]Volf, *After Our Likeness*, p. 130.

[15]Ibid., p. 132, his emphasis.

Christ given to them . . . [such a] true visib[l]e church is Christs kingdome."[16]

This church then may be identified by its external representation: their corporate lives are characterized by obedience to the Scripture and, therefore, freedom from all known sin; they assemble at a specific place and time; and corporately confess their faith in Jesus Christ before and with others. This pluriform, intersubjective confession of faith, Volf argues, is the basis of free-church ecclesiality.

> That which the church *is*, namely believing and confessing human beings, is precisely that which (as a rule) also *constitutes* it. It is not that each person constitutes himself or herself into a member of the church; rather, through their common pluriform confessing all the members together are constituted into the church by the Holy Spirit.[17]

Volf later defines this pluriformity in terms of the church's "polycentric" character, which is expressed both in a Christian call to faith and in the charismata. More significantly, Volf notes, this conviction is grounded in a particular understanding of the Trinity as characterized by symmetrical relations. "This yields the ecclesial principle that the more a church is characterized by symmetrical decentralized distribution of power and freely affirmed interaction, the more will it correspond to the trinitarian communion."[18] So the unity that is envisioned, as Colin Gunton has argued, is not "an organic, so much as . . . an interpersonal unity: the personal unity of distinct but freely related persons."[19]

While Volf seeks to place Smyth's ecclesiology in a more consistent theological framework, he wants to underline the significance of this communal life together that is open to other churches and to all human beings. Theologically central to church is a particular way of being people together. This view of sociality not only makes visible the dominion of Christ in the whole congregation, but also serves as the basis for a theology of the whole church—the whole people of God. Historically this impulse had a major impact on the Wesleyan conception of small group accountability and the evangelical revivals more generally—which, in promoting these values, became arguably the most important social space in frontier America. This focus on the church as "the Pilgrim People of God" appears prominently in the documents of Vatican II, in-

---

[16]John Smyth, *The Works of John Smyth*, ed. W. T. Whitley (1915), pp. 403, 267, quoted in Volf, *After Our Likeness*, p. 132.

[17]Volf, *After Our Likeness*, pp. 151-52, his emphasis.

[18]Ibid., pp. 224-25, 236.

[19]Colin E. Gunton, "The Church on Earth: The Roots of Community," in *On Being the Church: Essays in Christian Community*, ed. Colin E. Gunton and Daniel W. Hardy (Edinburgh: T & T Clark, 1989), p. 75.

dicating perhaps the broader influence of these currents.

A second dimension of the social space of the church is the particular practices that make this people what it is. Perhaps the most pointed contribution to this aspect of the church's visible representation comes from Stanley Hauerwas. He has argued that the church as a contrast society has a particular political profile. Following his mentor John Yoder, Hauerwas believes that the cross of Christ is not simply an abstract transaction between God and the world, but implies a particular set of political arrangements that reveals the nature of the broken world. "In fact," Hauerwas argues, "the God we worship and the world God created cannot be truthfully known without the cross, which is why the knowledge of God and ecclesiology—or the politics called the church—are interdependent."[20] This politics implies a specific ethic that is consistent with the narratives of our lives as God's children and followers of Jesus Christ.[21] Hauerwas believes this politics, which defines the church, does not only derive from the gospel but is actually constitutive of it; indeed it is constitutive not only of its own redemption but of the redemption of the world.[22]

Hauerwas insists that the church's witness is correlated to the way things are in the world—its witness is appropriate and necessary because the world itself lives off the values of the gospel.[23] Hauerwas's contribution here is to focus on the concrete life of Christians—their politics—as central to the theological meaning of the church, since it grows out of and reflects the narrative of the cross. This gives concreteness to the church in much the same way as John Smyth's focus on the local congregation. Clearly this focus on the particular shape of the local congregation, what Yoder called the "hermeneutics of peoplehood," represents one the most compelling recent statements on the nature of the church. One appreciates the shift of focus away from the church universal and invisible and toward the visible community that gathers in his name. Hauerwas's contribution is to point out the theological significance of this politics as reflective of God's redemptive program revealed in the gospel. The danger is not giving this witness a theological significance but also to invest it with too much theological authority—making it, as he puts it, constitutive of redemption.

---

[20]Stanley Hauerwas, *With the Grain of the Universe: The Church's Witness and Natural Theology* (Grand Rapids: Brazos, 2001), p. 17.

[21]He spelled out the content of this narrative ethic in his earlier work, such as *A Community of Character: Toward a Constructive Social Ethic* (South Bend, Ind.: Notre Dame University Press, 1981).

[22]Hauerwas, *With the Grain of the Universe*, pp. 145, 194.

[23]Ibid., pp. 203, 223.

But what evangelicals have to learn from Hauerwas is that some authority does lie in this set of practices, for they constitute a particular construal of biblical truth, one that by the Spirit can embody the external form of the gospel. When I was growing up, I heard frequently that "being in a church does not make one a Christian any more than living in a garage makes one a car." The impulse behind this of course was to insist that the commitment to Christianity must be personal and not simply nominal. But I have come to believe this is mistaken because it denies the social space of the church. It does not recognize that in an important sense the disciplines and practices of the people of God *do* form a person into the likeness of Christ, just as they constitute the most visible witness to the gospel. As Calvin put this: "We see how God, who could in a moment perfect his own, nevertheless desires them to grow up into manhood solely under the education of the Church."[24] Perhaps the problem is that evangelicals conceive of their relationship to the church in the same way a car is related to the garage: as a place where it is parked. It is not a living, dynamic social space.

Third, a conception of the social space of the church makes it easier to understand the relation of this space to all other spaces. If the church occupies a real social location and exhibits a particular polity, as the eschatological community which anticipates God's eternal purposes it implicates all spaces. Gerhard Lohfink has argued that the church as a spiritual community within human hearts, dating from Augustine's City of God, has undermined the biblical conception of church as a "visible, tangible community."[25] Jesus, he argues, came to reconstitute Israel as a new family, a visible contrast society "precisely in order to make this people a visible sign of salvation."[26] This community is constituted by the gift of the Spirit and is characterized by its togetherness, its elimination of social barriers and renunciation of violence—all the practices that flow from the narrative of the gospel, but most of all by its orientation toward the world. Precisely in its role as contrast society, Lohfink argues, it transforms the world.[27] He notes:

> The rule of God comes not only in word, but also in deed. It grasps the whole of our existence; we never exist as individuals. The society which surrounds us is part of us. For this reason, Jesus' healing miracles cannot be seen solely as actions on behalf of individuals. They are always concerned with the people of God.

---

[24]*Institutes* 4.1.5. This persuasion gives Calvin the freedom to refer to the church as Mother.
[25]Gerhard Lohfink, *Jesus and Community*, trans. John P. Galvin (New York: Paulist, 1984), p. 5.
[26]Ibid., p. 28.
[27]Ibid., p. 66.

Many diseases are curable only if the environment of the sick person is also healed. . . . When the reign of God becomes present, its healing power must not only reach deeply into human corporeality but also extend deeply into the social dimension of human existence.[28]

The social space of the church then refers to all spaces. By the Spirit it is made to embody something of the righteousness and justice that God intends for all creation.

A focus on the particular social shape of the church therefore is important in allowing these areas of authority to be given theological "voice," and a specific social presence. I would argue that theological conversation about the multiform social shapes of the church best enables us to bring the gifts and graces of the many cultures of the world into the body of Christ (see Rev 21:24, 26). These theological and biblical warrants, however, raise the question of whether in fact one sees signs of this reality in churches today. Does the evangelical church intentionally consider its social space as a form of its ministry in the world? Which is another way of asking, in light of the social and political challenges it is facing, what impact is the church, as a social space, having on its community? What authority does this space exert?

The importance of this question is underlined by the fact that in many of the neediest places in the world, the church exists as the only functioning institution. Edgar McKnight argues this in the case of our inner cities in America.[29] In Africa where civil strife, AIDS and bad government have created widespread poverty and underdevelopment, the churches often stand as the only remaining institution with credibility. Even if, all too often, these congregations do not have a vision that incorporates the whole community, they still represent an essential resource for the development of these places.

Fortunately in many places outside the West, the very intensity of the challenges requires the church to face its role in the community. Last fall I visited a small rural village in the Coast Province of Kenya. Makobe used to be a regional center with regular bus service to Mombasa. Now poverty, AIDS and government neglect have left the main street a ghost town and emptied the surrounding farms. But the small African Inland Church has not given up and is determined to renew the village. In partnership with some American Christians they have started a home for twenty-two girls orphaned by AIDS; the pastor, who is also a local school teacher has begun to remodel the decrepit school buildings and attract new teachers to the school, which is now recog-

---

[28]Ibid., pp. 82-83.
[29]See *The Careless Society: Community and Its Counterfeits* (New York: Basic Books, 1995).

nized as the best in the area; another church member, a special education teacher, has moved back into the town from Mombasa and started schooling for mentally challenged children. Meanwhile she and her family live in an abandoned storefront and are working to revive the business area. But the center of this life is the three hour worship each Sunday when this community sings, dances, prays, recites the creed, hears the Word and brings their gifts— often the produce from their shambas (gardens) which is auctioned off and given to the children's home. This is the social space that is transforming the community, and it provides an instructive model for evangelicals.

THE HISTORICAL SPACE OF THE CHURCH

In addition to its social space, every church necessarily occupies a particular historical space. For evangelicals the focus on the church as event and on experiential Christianity has not served to highlight historical continuity. Pannenberg argues, in a way that is consistent with Calvin's point, that "the public exposition and transmission of Christianity, which nourishes the faith of individual Christians, have no other form than that of the denominations."[30]

Denominations, or the historical form that churches have taken, embody the historical traditions that, for better or worse, have made Christianity what it is. Evangelical expressions of the church have typically refused to believe that they are the product of anything except the Bible, refusing even to call their groupings of churches "denominations." (Recently those claiming to be "nondenominational" passed for the first time Presbyterians as the largest group of students at Fuller.) The event orientation reveals itself here in its most worrisome aspect, as though the body of Christ were reinventing itself from scratch week by week. Whatever the attitude of evangelicals toward denominations, it is a fact that one cannot be a Christian without being the product of one or another of the traditions of the Christian church.

At the same time, ironically, Christians of this generation are experiencing a revival of historical consciousness—or at least an awareness of the importance of history. On the popular level the emergent churches are busy exploring history for worship resources. Their websites reveal a fascination with aspects of the tradition evangelicals have rarely valued: Celtic worship, medieval spirituality, Iona, Taize and so on. This exploration shows promise, even if the attraction is not based on much thought and reflection. Lutheran pastor and researcher Karen Ward reported the experience she had as a speaker at a conference of the emergent churches. The worship leader at one

---

[30]*The Church*, p. 14.

point put the Nicene Creed on an overhead for the people to recite together. Karen noticed that many were writing down the creed and she overheard one of them say, "This is wonderful, where did this come from?"

Still it may be that an enriched repertoire of worship practices will help Christians in this generation to rediscover their historical heritage. Consistent with their experiential bias, it is true that the attraction of historical elements consists in their relevance rather than their significance. Indeed in many respects the attraction is primarily aesthetic, which is a point to which I will return. Yet this is not to say that this historical interest is unaccompanied by thoughtful teaching. Karen Ward, and others like her, have become gurus to this widespread and growing youth movement, even if most of the writings of these gurus appear on the web. Significantly this movement, and similar groups in Great Britain, focus on new shapes for being the church—new social spaces. And this church shaping has led them to a deeper awareness of the need for historical connection, however inchoate this feeling may be—even as it has led them to a deeper social involvement in the community.

There are of course thoughtful resources that these groups make use of. Most prominent among them are writings of Robert Webber, whose *Ancient-Future Faith* provides a kind of outline for those searching for historical resources, even historical roots.[31] Webber insists that the authority of Christianity and of Scripture in particular will be recovered in the postmodern era only by returning the Bible "to its rightful place in the development of the entire spectrum of Christian thought in the first six centuries of the church." Similarly who would have guessed that an evangelical publishing house would undertake one of the most ambitious publication programs of patristic commentaries? While some of us might have wished this could be matched with similarly important medieval, Reformation or Puritan commentaries, the historical interest cannot be underestimated.

Outside North America and Europe, Christian churches are experiencing a similar interest in their past. But this past is not so much the early and medieval church as their own colonial and missionary history. The wholesale disparagement of their tradition past which occurred during that period is being widely questioned and a reevaluation is in process. In his book *Theology and Identity*, for example, Ghanaian Kwame Bediako has argued that the missionary importation of western Christianity was a modern application of the New

---

[31]See Robert Webber, *Ancient-Future Faith: Rethinking Evangelicalism for a Postmodern World* (Grand Rapids: Baker, 1999). The quote that follows is from p. 31.

Testament party of the circumcision, in which Christianity was assumed to take a particular cultural form.[32]

Perhaps the most important of the movements of historical retrieval is known as Radical Orthodoxy, which invites a closer examination and reflection. According to their self-description Radical Orthodoxy "combines a sophisticated understanding of contemporary thought, modern and postmodern with a theological perspective that looks back to the origins of the church."[33] It is a radical orthodoxy in the sense that it wants to return to the roots of Christian theology, especially its patristic sources, to recover a more coherent vision of Christianity which, on their reading, was lost both in Protestant biblicism and in Post-Tridentine Catholic positivist authoritarianism.[34] This involves a careful rereading of the earlier tradition in order to discover resources with which to address the dilemma caused by the collapse of modernity.

Graham Ward has made perhaps the most explicit application of this historical method to ecclesiology in his book *Cities of God*.[35] In this book Ward combines a careful analysis of the contemporary city, which is ruled by what he calls the disordered erotics of desire, with a recovery of the wisdom of the ancient church, especially Augustine and Gregory of Nyssa. From Augustine, Ward recovers the Christian notion of desire. He argues that "desire is fundamental to our nature as human beings as God created us" and that "theology will have to show how Christian desire operates in a way that does not accord the operation of desire in secular culture, the culture of seduction." From Gregory of Nyssa, Ward develops an ontology that matches this theology of desire. Gregory helps us avoid the commodification of reality as self-grounded, which he argues is a form of over-realized eschatology. Rather, as Gregory believed, materiality is an expression of divine energy, a mode of Trinitarian *dynamis*. Corporeality then is to be read spiritually, for nature exists through the prioritization of the spiritual; this animating principle "enables nature to prosper." Since everything subsists only in God, Ward argues, the "world is a Eucharistic offering."[36] Christ in his risen and ascended reality has been displaced from his historical (and gendered) rootedness and now exists

---

[32]Kwame Bediako, *Theology and Identity* (Grand Rapids: Eerdmans, 1993); see also *Christianity in Africa: A Renewal of a Non-Western Religion* (Edinburgh: Edinburgh University Press, 1995).

[33]On the book jacket of the series of books Radical Orthodoxy edited by John Milbank, Catherine Pickstock and Graham Ward.

[34]Cf. "Introduction," in *Radical Orthodoxy: A New Theology*, ed. John Milbank, Catherine Pickstock and Graham Ward (New York: Routledge, 1999), pp. 2-3.

[35]Ward, *Cities of God* (New York: Routledge, 2000).

[36]Ibid., pp. 76, 89, 88, 91, respectively.

"transcorporeally" in the *corpus mysticum*, which does not indicate the Eucharist as it has traditionally been understood, but the displaced and extended body of Christ. The church then is the social body of Christ that signifies this sacramental body to the world.[37] Institutional churches are necessary places for the display of this *corpus mysticum*, but they are not ends in themselves. "They are constantly transgressed by a community of desire, an erotic community, a spiritual activity. . . . The body of Christ desiring its consummation opens itself to what is outside the institutional church." This view of the mystical body, Ward believes, best answers to the contemporary erotics of desire, and it best shows "what it is to be called by God as an embodied soul to participate in Christ's body."[38]

Both the retrieval of historical sources and the attention to contemporary erotics are admirable, and, in many ways, instructive. But there are two fundamental problems with this project that similarly infect the other historical soundings we reviewed. First, however interesting Gregory of Nyssa's view of the relation of God to the world, it represents a historically situated reading of theology that needs to be read and interpreted contextually—both in terms of its culture and its historical trajectory. Culturally one might argue that the Capaddocians were creatively contextualizing the gospel for the Greek worldview they inherited. Their use and transformation of that worldview is instructive and there are certainly resources here that we need to exploit. But one must also examine the ways in which this tradition developed in the medieval period, and led, fatally in the minds of the Reformers at least, to a confusion of divine and human activity. These developments may constitute, not a fall into positivism and rationalism as Ward believes,[39] but an alternative reading of the way God relates to the world, and therefore the way the church is to be conceived.

Christoph Schwöbel has argued that the catholic intention of the Reformers focused precisely on this attempt to define the relationship between the work of God and that of humans. While distinguishing God and creation, both Luther and Calvin believed "the action of God, Father, Son and Spirit makes human action possible and enables human beings to act in accordance with the will of the creator."[40] God's action in calling the church into existence, like all God's works, establishes and makes possible real relationship

---

[37]Ibid., p. 92, quoting de Certeau.
[38]Ward, *Cities of God*, pp. 180, 77.
[39]See Ward's discussion on pp. 60-66 of *Cities of God*.
[40]Schwöbel, "The Creature of the Word: Recovering the Ecclesiology of the Reformers," in *On Being the Church*, ed. Colin Gunton and Daniel Hardy (Edinburgh: T & T Clark, 1989), p. 119.

by the Spirit, and a genuine human response. It is true that this construal of the relationship between God and the world could lead to Descartes and the radical dichotomy that Ward deplores, but it did not have to do so. It could also lead to the pietist renewal, and the spirituality of a Jonathan Edwards or John Wesley.

The point is not that a Reformed reading of developments is privileged, but that theological conversation has an historical and cultural context that must be taken into account. This leads to the second problem with Ward's project. One of the most admirable aspects to his book is the attempt to address Christianity in terms that relate to contemporary worldviews. But at the same time it is precisely this project which calls his methodology into question. The dependence on a fourth century bishop, and the dismissal of the last five centuries of Christian thought, while it may provide some nuance to a purely contemporary theological reading, considered on its own, carries serious liabilities. Because Ward cannot see any possible use of Reformation developments, he has to be overly critical of contemporary products of that worldview and the rationalities it fostered—virtual reality, for example. Surely seeing theology as a developing conversation, one that responds to actual cultural situations, would better enable him to address realities that in one way or another resonate with that conversation. A living theological tradition, while it always risks being compromised by its context, also offers the best prospect of challenging that context.

But this conversation only serves to support my larger argument. Churches, like theological conversations, are in fact situated in some historical trajectory. Whether realizing it or not, every church displays its convictions about the way history works. Evangelicals have been allergic to the very idea of tradition of course, but that has not kept them from embodying a tradition that is quite easy to specify—from the Reformation through the various pietist movements and evangelical revivals. History then is constituted for them by a series of renewals, or in some circles, repristinations, and that is reflected in the need week by week to construct—often from scratch—a worship experience that is spiritually renewing. This is true of evangelical churches and students everywhere. Last fall, while I was lecturing on the value of theological traditions in Kenya, one student expressed the view of most of the class by saying "I think we would say that we want to examine all traditions and take what is good from them, but that we do not have a tradition ourselves"—which is not a bad summary of the evangelical use of history in general. I could not get him to see that he was giving very articulate expression to a particular, that is evangelical, tradition of spirituality.

The danger then in the contemporary use of history is that an eclectic ecclesiology would result that has no sense of the rootedness (and difficulties) of
the practices they adopt—represented by a kind liturgical potpourri: this
month let's do icons! History is meant to define and nourish our ecclesiastical
identity. It is not a collective attic through which we rummage for some interesting and exotic practices with which to embellish our worship experience.
Nor is the solution to modern secularization or postmodern pluralism to be
found by a leap back to a previous era. Rather we must find ourselves, by recognizing that we do stand in a living tradition—Reformed, Anabaptist, Wesleyan, Roman Catholic—which represents gifts that can be brought to the
work of our corporate maturity in Christ. Having a place to stand historically
is not a limitation, it is a grace—it makes possible a situated reading of Scripture that can mediate the special gifts of our cultural particularity.

THE CHURCH'S SYMBOLIC SPACE

These considerations of spaces lead naturally to a third notion of space, what
I will call the church's symbolic space. The church not only comprises a social
space; it not only occupies an historical space; it also embodies and displays a
symbolic space. I will argue that if this is not the most important theological
aspect of the visible church, for postmodern people, it is the most salient. And
for evangelicals it is clearly the most challenging.

With the eclipse of Enlightenment rationality, for most educated people in the
West, the quest for truth and knowledge has been replaced by a search for pleasure and beauty. Pierre Bourdieu has described the rise of what he calls symbolic
goods, and a resulting symbolic capital, which are made into objects of desire in
the contemporary economy. As Graham Ward notes, in the modern city the pleasure principle has replaced the reality principle. "For enjoyment now belongs to
the symbolic order, the symbolic exchange in which we invest all our hopes for
the fulfillment of our desires. A euphoria follows from the new lightness of being. Aesthetics, rather than ethics or even physics, provides the sole criterion for
judgment."[41] Though Ward wants to recapture a Christian notion of desire, he
has trouble seeing anything but problems with many of the products of this contemporary situation—such as virtual reality for example. While evangelicals
have eagerly made use of developments like the Internet, they have resisted the
broader implications of the aesthetic turn. But I want to argue that in this unre-
lieved pessimism about the aesthetic turn they are mistaken.

For evangelicals, I believe, the problem is not simply the tradition of suspi-

---

[41]*Cities of God*, p. 60. He refers here to the work of Jean Baudrillard.

cion toward culture, though this certainly plays a role. More critical is what might be called the symbolic illiteracy of the evangelical tradition. Depth symbols, what medieval Christians called "sacramental," were replaced by signs employed "semiologically" in the activities of Christian ministry. Evangelicals do not appreciate and thus cannot understand symbolic objects and practices. They do not understand how objects, specially inscribed spaces, or ritual acts can teach, form and nurture believers. What is worse, since symbolic sensitivities have been progressively leached out of their tradition, evangelicals view this situation as normal. This weakness has important implications for their understanding of the visible church.

The events and reflection of the Reformation are critical here of course, as we observed earlier with respect to Calvin. But to remind ourselves of the change represented by the Reformation, consider this description by Andrew Martindale of the situation of the medieval worshipper.

> It really was not possible to stand in church and look in any direction without finding some detail of architecture, some image, or indeed some ceremony which did not inform one about the church as an institution, of the means to salvation which she afforded, and of the vision of heaven beyond.[42]

Notice that Martindale refers to two kinds of symbolic entities, images that refer to particular persons and events, and ceremonies that enact meaning. The surrounding space moreover was designed to accommodate and enhance certain objects and facilitate particular actions.

We cannot develop here the aspects of medieval worship that particularly offended the Reformers,[43] but we can observe the contrast that came to characterize Protestant spaces. The Reformers explicitly denied that any particular "spaces" had symbolic significance.[44] Calvin's locked church became a metaphor for a space that was symbolically vacant. In the worship spaces that resulted, there was no particular place, or object, or ceremony, that, by itself or considered together, would inform one about the salvation or the meaning of the church. The pulpit of course had a kind of symbolic significance as the place where the Word of God was preached. But the pulpit itself had none of the symbolic or iconic significance that medieval images had, nor did preach-

---

[42]"Medieval Liturgy as Theatre," in *The Church and the Arts*, ed. Diana Wood, Studies in Church History (Oxford: Blackwell, 1992), 28:144.

[43]On this see Dyrness, *Reformed Theology and Visual Culture: The Protestant Imagination from Calvin to Edwards* (Cambridge: Cambridge University Press, 2004), chap. 2.

[44]One might argue that this was more characteristic of Reformed than Lutheran areas, but it is not hard to show that Calvinist sensitivities came to dominate even in Lutheran regions. See Carl C. Christensen, *Art and the Reformation in Germany* (Athens: Ohio University Press, 1979).

ing have the same intrinsic meaning that the liturgy had earlier. Preaching "happened" in relation to particular times, not particular spaces—indeed some of the most famous preaching in this tradition took place outdoors. The sacraments of course continued to have theological and symbolic meaning, but these had no relationship, symbolic or otherwise, to the spaces in which they took place. Their meaning related to their performance as this was controlled by the preached Word.

Now I would be the last person to suggest that this made impossible any noteworthy developments in church architecture (or in the allied arts like church music). After a fire destroyed eighty-four of the churches in central London, Sir Christopher Wren (1632-1723) was chosen as an architect for about fifty of the new churches, including the most famous St. Paul's Cathedral—the largest space for Protestant worship in the world. In their restrained beauty many of these structures are admirable, but their central purpose was not to provide a space symbolic of heaven or a throne room for Christ the king; they were designed simply as a meetinghouse for the congregation. Wren's primary concern was that "all who are present can both hear and see." He even calculated how close people had to be to hear distinctly. His auditory plan became the norm for Protestant architecture for two centuries.[45] One can certainly even speak of a "grounded aesthetic" of simplicity, silence and order that characterizes these spaces.[46] But this aesthetic is innocent of specially constructed symbolic objects or actions.

Objects and actions did come inevitably to fill Protestant spaces. Pews, pulpits and tables could even become beautiful objects, but they had no intrinsic religious significance. And the space they occupied had a strictly utilitarian function. The common attitude toward such space was captured nicely by separatist pastor Francis Johnson in seventeenth century Holland:

> Now there is not any one place holy, and peculiarly consecrate [sic] to the ministrations of the Lord's Supper, as there was of old for sacrifice only at Jerusalem. So as now therefore a place being a generall circumstance that perteyneth to all actions, commodious and necessairie for people to meet in together, and to be kept from injurie and unseasonableness of the weather.[47]

---

[45]See Frank C. Senn, *Christian Liturgy: Catholic and Evangelical* (Minneapolis: Fortress, 1997), pp. 30-31.

[46]Paul Willis refers to a "grounded aesthetic" as those aesthetic values that grow out of the life and commitments of a community (see *Common Culture* [1991]). See Dyrness, "Protestant Aesthetics," unpublished lecture given at Wheaton College, April 2004.

[47]Quoted in Arian Car Donnelly, *The New England Meeting Houses of the Seventeenth Century* (Middlebury, Conn.: Wesleyan University Press, 1968), p. 100.

There was frequently symbolic significance in the *location* of the worship structure, at least in New England. It was to be placed in the center of town as nearly equidistant as possible from the majority of the population. It was in one sense the "center" of life—but the space of that center was—theologically and symbolically—"empty."

This emptiness is the reverse side of the positive impetus to see one's Christian vocation, and the glory of God, diffused throughout all of life, as Calvin liked to say. As one hears frequently in this tradition the church is the people, not a building—which is the kind of aphorism that too often passes for theological reflection. So looking around today one is not surprised to see churches in store fronts, banquet halls of large hotels, even in night clubs. Recently a black megachurch in Los Angeles, Faithful Central Baptist Church, purchased the "Great Western Forum," previously home to the Los Angeles Lakers. In a front page article in the *Christian Science Monitor,* Bishop Kenneth Ulmer defended the church's new location in this way: "Church is how you behave in society after the sermon, how you live your life after the benediction. . . . The building is not important, except as a vehicle through which we dispatch and deploy others."[48] The emptiness then is the other side of a positive impulse to extend the impact of the gospel into the world but, I want to argue, it is by no means necessary to that positive impulse.

In fact our symbolic poverty may actually impede the imagination that is necessary to creative ministry. Both Scripture and contemporary psychology agree that embodiment is essential to our humanity. Recent studies have shown that our emotional life is dependent on our being embodied. Therefore visual objects, ritual acts and one's emotions are inextricably related.[49] Thus Calvin, insofar as he insisted on the uniqueness of the Word in mediating God's presence, was unrealistically isolating the experience of hearing from the larger context of objects and actions in which this takes place. People move about in space, see and touch their environment, in ways that are not only practical but also affective.

We are *homo symbolicus*; we do respond to the world symbolically whether we are aware of this or not.[50] Who could have imagined the implications and the symbolic import of Calvin's decision to lock the church (I had always wondered why Protestant churches in Europe, especially the Calvinist re-

---

[48]Daniel B. Woods, "Black Churches as Big Players in City Renewal," *Christian Science Monitor,* January 25, 2001, p. 4.

[49]See Antonio R. Damasio, *The Feeling of What Happens* (New York: Harcourt, Brace, 1999).

[50]See on this David Freeberg, *The Power of Images: Studies in the History and Theory of Response* (Chicago: University of Chicago Press, 1989).

gions, are always locked)? I once attended a prominent Presbyterian Church in Southern California in which the distinguished pastor liked to come down in front of the communion table to preach without notes. He would bring his Bible with him, read the text and then turn to put the Bible behind him on the communion table while he preached. I am sure neither he nor his congregation gave the act much thought, but its symbolic impact was still powerful ("now I have finished with this text")—it communicated whether he intended it to or not. A chapel at a seminary in Africa where I go to teach has a giant wooden door behind the pulpit—it is the only thing visible in the space besides a Bible verse. Every time I go into the chapel I am reminded of Psalm 24:7: "Lift up your heads, O gates! And be lifted up, O ancient doors!" But when I inquired I discovered that there was no such intent; my meaning was accidental and unintended. We look for meaning, even if the service and space are designed to frustrate this search. Standing, sitting, have no meaning—"let us all stand for the third verse." Our buildings and spaces for better or worse do express a grounded aesthetic; they just do not express a discerning symbolic sensitivity—certainly not one that is grounded on Scripture or the traditions of the church.

We do not need to remind ourselves of how many postmodern people, including many of our children, are put off by this symbolic poverty and find a home in other traditions, form alternative church structures with symbolic and aesthetic richness, or leave the church altogether.

We have come a long way from the church which Andrew Martindale described, in which every act and object has its intrinsic and theological meaning. These many sacramentals were reduced by some Reformers to the seven sacraments, by others to two, and in many respects even these have lost their sacramental depth for most modern people. I am reminded here of the important intervention by Cardinal Godfried Danneels of Belgium at the May 2001 Consistory of Cardinals in Rome. The modern person, he noted, tends to be "in love with rites and ritualization, but is allergic to the Christian sacraments." He went on to note that sacraments are no longer the center of gravity for Catholic pastoral life. He might have said this center has become empty—though it is still "filled" with words and preparation for *diakonia*. He went on to say: "The church seems to be nothing more than a place where one speaks and where one places oneself at the service of the world. The sacramental life is shifting from the center of the church to its periphery. Is it, perhaps, a matter of a slow and unconscious protestantization of the church from within?"[51]

---

[51] *America: The National Catholic Weekly*, July 30-August 6, 2001, pp. 6-7.

Visits to a variety of our contemporary evangelical worship spaces lead me to wonder if our worship spaces, filled as they are with words—preaching, announcements, even our singing—can fix and hold our faith for us? Can words ultimately, by themselves, fix our minds and hearts in a way that shapes us theologically? Like the ever-changing images on the omnipresent screen, lacking any fixed spatial reference point, do words too slip and slide around?

These questions, indeed all the challenges of the visible representation of the church I have addressed, raise the issue of "authority" in the church. I have said that the life of the visible church is an ever-renewed (and embodied) interpretation of Scripture. I would argue that these three spaces—social, historical and symbolic—are necessary for such an embodied interpretation. These spaces give us fixed points by which we orient ourselves and from which we give our situated reading. We interpret Scripture by our corporate life together, the social space that is formed by the Holy Spirit; we construe the text in ways that reflect the historical place that we find ourselves in (or that we have chosen), and which we will do our part to enlarge and elaborate; but above all we make our interpreted witness by the shapes and objects of our worship. The authority of Scripture must always take some historical shape to become visible. These spaces provide churches with the opportunity to exhibit the reality of their evangelical commitments.

In the end, it may be the case that symbolic space is the most critical one for us evangelicals at this moment in history. For corporate ritual acts and symbolic objects cement our social lives; they give us visible and public points—concrete metaphors—around which we can orient our lives. These also give important expression to the historical place that we stand in—recalling with discrimination ancient practices and images that Christians have lived with for centuries. Indeed the symbolic spaces and objects give form to the social and historical spaces; they become places where these spaces coalesce and which, by the Holy Spirit, can be used to shape us together into the body of Christ.

I believe, though, that the most important role these sharpened sensitivities can play is theological and pastoral. Understanding the sacramental, or perhaps I should say, the incarnational dimension of worship, may force us to give new attention to the forms and reminders of our baptism and of the Lord's Supper. More importantly it may force us to think with many of our Christian mothers and fathers, mystics and saints—about the implications of the fact that God became part of the human creation in Jesus Christ. We might learn to say with John of Damascus: "I salute all remaining matter with reverence, because God has filled it with his grace and power."[52] In short evangelicals may come to see that the church is not at all like a garage; it is more like a richly furnished home into which we may gladly invite our friends and neighbors.

[52]St. John of Damascus, *On the Divine Images*, trans. David Anderson (New York: St. Vladimir's Seminary Press, 2002), p. 23.

CONCLUSION

The Body of Christ, the Bread of Heaven

ELLEN T. CHARRY

Unlike us, biblical characters complain a lot. And they complain even in the midst of good things. In Exodus 16, the children of Israel have only been out of Egypt for four chapters, and have been saved from the pursuing Egyptian troops only one chapter, when they start to complain about food. God, of course, listens to their complaining sympathetically, and feeds them right away. But as usual, God is one step ahead of them. He feeds them and teaches them at the same time. That is, God recognizes a teachable moment when he sees one, and doesn't miss a beat. Their hunger has gotten their attention.

God sends down the magic food and tells them that they are to gather as much as they can eat. When they took stock of their harvest, the stronger ones had gathered more and the weaker less. "But, when they measured it with an omer, he that gathered much had nothing over, and he that gathered little had no lack; each gathered according to what he could eat." From each according to his ability to each according to his need. God removed both the temptation to boast and the fear of being outclassed. The struggle of the strong against the weak just won't work here.

Now why had God added this Marxist touch? Well, it seems to me that God made an acute psychological analysis of the situation. Things were tense out there in the desert. People were understandably afraid that they might starve to death, that they might be deprived of what they needed most. God also realized that greed is the other side of fear. And when greed sets in, jealousy is not far behind. So God made sure that the power dynamic of the strong against the weak would not be grounds for the people's self-destruction. And greed and jealousy are the pathway to death in the desert, not to speak of the faculty, the shop floor, or the church.

Through Moses, God next told them that after eating they might keep no leftovers. No hoarding. Of course, the people didn't take this seriously and tried to see if they could get away with hoarding, but God foiled them by rotting or melting the food. Does God know us, or what? This story has a powerful leveling effect. When it comes to being nourished by God, all get the same. God is no respecter of persons. Whatever they take to be their advantage over others—one can gather more, or one is cleverer at finding a way to save up more for tomorrow—is of no avail. No tricks work here, where God intends to teach the people of their equality of status before him.

So, this story is about both grace and discipline. Indeed, God is really smart. He knows that grace and discipline belong together, for without the hope that comes with grace, the chastisement would not work, but only alienate his charges from him, and so they would languish in their greed and jealousy. He also knows that without chastisement, grace could easily feed an attitude of entitlement that would eventually corrupt the wellbeing of the community. So he brings the food in a manner that catches their attention. God looks mighty clever in this story: no lecture, no moralizing, no threats. Just food in the right proportion as long as they needed it. God willing, those who read this story will take in food for the soul as well as the body. It takes both nourishment of the body and the calming of the spirit to get Israel through the desert years and into the land of promise. We may infer from this that hardship alone is not sufficient to hone the Israelites into the people of God. They need to be both fed and taught new habits of mind and heart that better fit them for the life that they must construct together, once the shackles of Egypt are removed.

Now let us turn to another twist on the bread from heaven. When I read John 6 it is hard not to take the side of the scoffers in the story. Jesus does sound pretty crazy here. After all, it is a big jump from recalling that God sent food in the desert to having Jesus say that he *is* the food from heaven, and that the people are to eat him and thereby live forever! Even though it is clear that the same God provides both types of food, the second version is strange to the point of sounding bizarre to normal people. It is cannibalistic or magical to eat a person, no less a god, and psychotic to believe that we avoid death thereby. It is little wonder that the synagogue goers who heard this speech concluded, "This is a hard saying; who can listen to it?" I doubt that I would have been as generous.

One way I have found to hear these hard words of Jesus is through a later passage in this Gospel, John 14. There, Jesus explains what he is doing. His work on earth is to take people to the Father, or rather, to bring the Father to them so that he will live in them. The Son, who is one with the Father, enables this to happen when Jesus takes up permanent residence in the hearts of his friends, and they come to understand that in their devotion, radical obedience to, and adoration of him, God, Father and Son, make their home in them.

Now for many this is still a hard saying, scarcely able to exonerate the earlier passage. What is all this intimate indwelling? The Eucharistic dimension of John 6 is about eating Jesus?

Precisely. Eating is the most concrete way in which we are indwelt. We understand eating. God always stoops to our level, speaking in language we understand. We become what we eat, as the middle-aged know only too well. Later sacramental theology, including Luther's, argued that that is precisely what happens to us in ingesting the body and blood of Christ. His flesh and blood are so powerful that they overtake our own. As Luther put it, it is as if a wolf devoured a lamb and the lamb was so powerful that it turned the wolf into itself. The sixteenth century debacle over Eucharistic theology may have missed the point entirely, and so deprived the heirs of the Reformation of the spiritual power of Eucharistic eating.

Feeding expresses love, as the Exodus narrative makes clear. John takes the link between food and love further. In feeding us with himself, Christ shows us that the Father's love takes up residence in our bodies, empowering them with that love. It is not difficult to love those who feed us. In John 14, the cruder image of eating Christ softens into the equally intimate image of being indwelt with, even overwhelmed by the gentle power of divine love, so that we melt in God's hands. Physical eating puts this spiritual reality in our face.

Note well, if we can be indwelt by divine love we can also be indwelt by less worthy powers, by demons, in fact. Parents, or a culture that does not feed its children the nourishing food of love, but the food of wrath, jealousy, anger and suspicion, feed their children demons. Such traumas take years to overcome later on. Whether we wish to or not, we internalize how we are treated. When we internalize true nourishment it is the food of angels. To put it in technical theological jargon, in the Eucharist, by the power of the Holy Spirit, the Father and the Son take up residence in our bodies and our souls, beating back the destructive demons of anger, fear, injustice and oppression that may also indwell us. This is the bread of heaven in a concrete, but not crude way. It is the way to heaven, that is, to true happiness.

What we see in the Eucharist is the cosmic struggle between good and evil, between happiness and misery, between God and the devil being played out through eating.

What happens then, when you feed people with the Lord's body and blood? It is a great honor to watch people in such an intimate act. When people come forward, leave their seats and walk up the aisle, they come despite their pretensions. Some will overdress, trying to display their wealth. Some will underdress, trying to play down their need for this heavenly food. Some will be in various states of undress, crudely sexualizing the proceeding as if trying to destroy its power. Despite their transparent anxieties at partaking of God, they are coming to take God into themselves, even if they cannot say why. The reason is, all pretension aside, they sense they need him, even if they are too proud to admit it. Even if the words sound bizarre or repugnant, they want God to dwell in their bodies. God is good for them.

We are living in a spiritually starving nation in which many flail about, not knowing what they seek, beyond expunging the demons that have traumatized them. Those of us who crave to be and claim to be indwelt by God, believe that we have something to offer the spiritually starving, but sometimes it is hard for us to articulate what it is and how to get it.

Let us rely then on our Scripture passages. Both passages are about the power of feeding, and the depth of our hunger, our fear that we will be left out in the desert to die. American capitalism sometimes feels like that desert. We want bread from heaven, but the market feeds us plastic. It all ends up in the trash. We cannot give one another heavenly food, but we can help one another gently break through those dysfunctional defenses, through the pride that prevents us from recognizing our neediness, which may be hidden under the bravado of intellectualism, commercial power, moral indignation, socialized victimization, sloppy or seductive dress, or whatever we have access to to cover our naked need. Only when we can recognize what we truly need, can we see how thoroughly manipulated we are when we say to the fast food server, "I need a burger and a biggie fries," knowing all the while that we need no such thing, but God's body instead. Learning to distinguish what we truly need from what we think we want, that may be polluting our bodies and souls, or may be damaging to others, is true illumination. It is an experience of emergence into Christian freedom.

Ironically, in the process of feeding us, both texts point to God's stripping us at the same time. I, for one, take strength from the stripping power of these two passages and from the Eucharist as we now celebrate it. By stripping power, I mean the power of needing to be fed by God to strip us of our pretense at autonomy. Nothing makes one step back from self-assurance more than not being able to feed oneself, as is the case in both the Exodus and the John passages. I remember when my father was dying of cancer in the hospital, and was already too weak to feed himself. At one meal, just before I arrived at his bedside, the food was put before him, but no one came to help him eat it. As he lay there watching the hot food get cold and the ice cream melt, in a burst of humiliated anger, he shoved the whole tray onto the floor. They punished him, further humiliating him by serving him on paper plates and plasticware thereafter until he died. The story of the manna and Johannine Eucharistic theology state boldly that we cannot feed ourselves this special food. It must be fed to us. This itself is purgative for a culture like ours that believes that everything is possible. Discovering what truly satisfies and what is not possible for us are Christian steps on the path to happiness. Fortunately, the church is authorized to feed the bread of heaven to those who cannot feed themselves.

There is another illumination that I think these stories about being fed by God's grace offer our spiritually starving culture. And that is that we are not alone. Our culture is now crazed with the need to be in constant communication, in instantaneous touch with everyone in our life. The other day I saw two people having lunch together in a restaurant, each on their cell phones talking to someone else. Now that, I suggest, expresses a fear of self, as if our identities would melt away if others were not validating our existence. It suggests dissatisfaction with being where one is or with one's present company. It exemplifies the frazzled style we are all forced to adopt, with its haunting "to do" lists and never enough time to the point of exhaustion. This culture now indwells us so thoroughly that we think that being overextended is normal.

Those in whom God dwells have no such anxieties. The emptiness that the frenetic activity tries to still is not there. There is nowhere better to be than where one is, for God is there too. There is no one better to be with than one's present company, because where two or three are gathered in his name, he shall be in their midst. And the one who bears God's redeeming power in herself always brings God along, no matter what the gathering.

Not only are those fed of God not alone, but in being fed of the same food at the same table, the communicants experience this oneness as the mystical body of Christ. Christians are made members of Christ's body by the Holy Spirit in baptism. This solidarity is fully evident at the Lord's Table. Here, considerations of age, race, power, authority, sex, what have you, are utterly powerless. Here we stand shoulder to shoulder with our enemies as well as our friends, united as the one mystical body of Christ. In this unity all enmity is dissolved.

In speaking of the spiritual effects of the bread and cup, St. Augustine cited Acts 4:32: "they were of one soul and one heart towards God." And he goes on, "Remember my brothers, how wine is made. There are many grapes hanging on the vine, but the juice of the grapes is mixed up together in unity. In this the Lord Christ was giving us a picture of ourselves. He wanted us to belong to him; at his table he consecrated the mystery of our peace and of our unity. He who receives the mysteries of unity but does not keep the bond of peace, receives not a mystery that will profit him, but a testimony that will witness against him" (Sermon 272). The sacrament of the table is the moment of truth that stands in judgment on our worldly ways.

Those who know themselves to be indwelt by God, on the other hand, can find contentment in being who they are, being with themselves, because to be with oneself is to be with God. This by no means suggests that Christians become reclusive. But it does take the edge off the frenetic pace of life that is increasingly difficult to bear.

So from these Scripture passages we draw the completeness of the Christian spiritual life: purgation, illumination and union with God—final happiness. That life calls us to be purged of our defenses against God and our pretentiousness toward others, to acknowledge our emotional fragility, to come to the stark realization of our need for God in our mouths as well as in our minds, and to have God make his dwelling in us. This threefold path ennobles, uplifts and feeds us with himself. This is the path to abundant life. It awaits us at this table. Thanks be to God.

CONTRIBUTORS

William J. Abraham is Albert Cook Outler Professor of Wesley Studies and University Distinguished Teaching Professor at the Perkins School of Theology, Southern Methodist University. He has written numerous books, including *The Logic of Evangelism*, *Canon and Criterion in Christian Theology* and recently *The Logic of Renewal*.

Gary D. Badcock is Associate Professor of Systematic Theology at Huron University College, University of Western Ontario, after having taught previously at New College, University of Edinburgh. His books include *Light of Truth and Fire of Love: A Theology of the Holy Spirit*, *The Way of Life: A Theology of Christian Vocation* and a forthcoming work on ecclesiology.

Craig A. Carter is Associate Professor of Religious Studies at Tyndale University College, where he served until recently as vice president and academic dean. In addition to various papers and articles, he has written *The Politics of the Cross: The Theology and Social Ethics of John Howard Yoder*.

Ellen T. Charry is Margaret W. Harmon Associate Professor of Systematic Theology at Princeton Theological Seminary, and the editor of the journal *Theology Today*. Among other projects, she has edited *Inquiring After God: Classic and Contemporary Readings* and written the widely regarded *By the Renewing of Your Minds: The Pastoral Function of Christian Doctrine*.

William A. Dyrness is Professor of Theology and Culture and Dean Emeritus in the School of Theology at Fuller Theological Seminary. His most recent books are *Visual Faith: Art, Theology and Worship in Dialogue* (2001) and *Reformed Theology and Visual Culture: The Protestant Imagination from Calvin to Edwards* (2004).

Darrell L. Guder is Henry Winters Luce Professor of Missional and Ecumenical Theology at Princeton Theological Seminary. In addition to translating numerous German works into English, he has written such books as *Be My Witnesses*, *Missional Church* and *The Continuing Conversion of the Church*.

D. G. Hart is Director of Academic Projects and Faculty Development at the Intercollegiate Studies Institute. Previously he held faculty and administrative posts at Westminster Theological Seminary. He has written several books, including *The Lost Soul of American Protestantism*, *The University Gets Religion*, *Recovering Mother Kirk* and *Deconstructing Evangelicalism*.

Willie James Jennings is Senior Associate Dean for Academic Programs and Assistant Research Professor of Theology and Black Church Studies at Duke Divinity School. He is the author of numerous essays, including two previously tied to conferences at Wheaton College: "Wandering in the Wilderness" (in *The Gospel in Black and White*) and "Baptizing a Social Reading" (in *Disciplining Hermeneutics*).

Dennis L. Okholm is Professor of Theology at Azusa Pacific University. Previously he taught at Wheaton College, cofounding its Theology Conference and coediting several books resulting from it, most recently *Evangelicals and Scripture: Tradition, Authority and Hermeneutics*.

James K. A. Smith is Associate Professor of Philosophy and Director of the Seminars in Christian Scholarship Program at Calvin College. His books include *The Fall of Interpretation*, *Speech and Theology* and *Introducing Radical Orthodoxy*.

Allen Verhey is moving to Duke Divinity School after many years of teaching at Hope College. He is a widely regarded author on ethical and bioethical issues. Among his recent works are *Remembering Jesus: Christian Community, Scripture, and the Moral Life* and *Reading the Bible in the Strange World of Medicine*.

John Webster is Professor of Systematic Theology at the University of Aberdeen. He taught previously at the University of Toronto, and for seven years as the Lady Margaret Professor of Divinity at Oxford. Largely responsible for introducing the English-speaking world to the thought of Eberhard Jüngel, he has also cofounded the *International Journal of Systematic Theology*. His own constructive works include *Word and Church, Holiness* and *Holy Scripture: A Dogmatic Sketch.*

Jonathan R. Wilson is Professor of Theology and Ethics at Acadia Divinity College, after many years serving as Professor and Department Chair of Religious Studies at Westmont. In addition to numerous essays, he has written several books, including *Gospel Virtues* and *God So Loved the World.*

Names Index

Subject Index